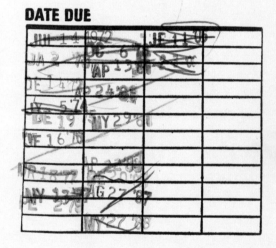

Retirement in
American Society

IMPACT AND PROCESS

Retirement in
American Society

IMPACT AND PROCESS

*by Gordon F. Streib and
Clement J. Schneider, S.J.*

Cornell University Press | ITHACA AND LONDON

First published 1971 by Cornell University Press.
Published in the United Kingdom by Cornell University
Press Ltd., 2–4 Brook Street, London W1Y 1AA.

International Standard Book Number 0-8014-0669-2
Library of Congress Catalog Card Number 71-162539

PRINTED IN THE UNITED STATES OF AMERICA
BY VAIL-BALLOU PRESS, INC.

Preface

Retirement is both an individual problem and a social pattern of modern industrialized nations. It is the result of a complicated set of factors which have emerged primarily in Western industrialized societies. While earlier social systems and less developed contemporary ones have faced the situation and the consequences of *aging*, the process of *retirement* is a unique and modern phenomenon.

For retirement to become a major institutionalized pattern in any society, certain conditions must be present: First, a number of people must live long enough to retire in later life. Second, the economy must be sufficiently productive for older workers to be transferred from full-time work to part-time work or no work in old age. Third, some forms of social insurance, pension plans, and health insurance schemes must offer at least minimum support for those older persons who do retire.

When the Cornell Study of Occupational Retirement was initiated, very few empirical studies of retirement had been conducted; thus it was something of a pioneering venture. There were very few expectations and norms of how millions of older persons would adjust to this emerging social pattern. Our task was to study a large segment of a fairly representative population of regularly employed Americans before and after their retirement. Some of the participants in the study did not retire during the period of observation, about seven years, so they constitute a very important group which is used as a base line for comparison with those who did retire at various points in the research.

We have analyzed the data in terms of statistical aggregates; that is, we are concerned with clusters of persons who have specified characteristics or report certain attitudes. It is important to make clear the aggregate nature of the analysis because some readers may wonder what happened to the individual person—the man or woman who retired and had problems of coping with poor health and declining income, and also the person who was happy in the new role of retiree. Since statistics cannot present a complete picture of the individual's personal reaction to retirement, we have included case materials obtained by personal interviews with about one hundred of our respondents. These persons were systematically sampled from the list of participants in several metropolitan areas.

Retirement is a multifaceted subject that can be approached in several ways—by studying the problems of the labor force, personnel administration, productivity, pension schemes, or the social adjustment of the individual. In this book, retirement is viewed from the perspective of sociology and social psychology. The broad analysis involves determining the effects of retirement upon the individual's health, his objective economic condition and the way he views it (which we have termed his subjective economic condition), and his social-psychological attitudes, particularly with regard to his satisfaction in life, adjustment to retirement, feelings of usefulness, and age identity.

The longitudinal nature of the study design enables the investigator to study "cause" and "effect" with somewhat more confidence than in a traditional cross-sectional study at one point in time, in which older persons usually are asked to recollect attitudes, feelings, and behavior which may have occurred some time in the past.

During the course of this study more than twenty-five reports and presentations of the study findings were made at regional, national, and international sociological and gerontological meetings by the staff of the project. More than thirty papers, journal articles, and chapters in books, and six Ph.D. dissertations at Cornell University have made available to the scholarly and scientific community many of the research results. This book brings together in a longitudinal synthesis some aspects of the earlier reports and new data.

The situation of the aged in American society has altered dramatically in recent years. A number of factors have changed: for example, there is a trend toward earlier retirement, there are more retirement communities, and there have been improvements in pensions and Social Security benefits. There are now more senior citizens' centers, and opportunities for meaningful and enriching activities among the aged have increased. The most important change is the introduction of Medicare and Medicaid and other health insurance programs for the aged. All these developments have improved the factual socioeconomic situation of the aged in American society. Of course it has been argued that the United States has been slow in effecting many of these changes, compared to other industrialized nations, and that the benefits are niggardly and inadequate when one considers the unmet needs. Whatever the merits of these arguments, however, the general economic, social, and psychological situation that retirees face today is similar to that of a decade ago, particularly from the standpoint of social psychology—that is, the adaptations that must be made in coping with the cessation of employment, the decline in health, and the reduction of income have not altered greatly in the course of ten years.

In the final chapters of the book we have attempted to relate the findings of this study and its orientation to recent theoretical and conceptual developments in the study of aging. One of the major issues has revolved around activity theory versus disengagement theory; we have proposed another conceptual-

ization which we have called "differential disengagement."
We did not attempt in this study to write a handbook on how to
retire successfully or how to age happily. Our immediate interest was not to answer specific questions on how to manage a
retirement program, or how to solve policy and programmatic
problems. We hope that some of our efforts will prove useful
and even instructive for persons concerned with the practical
implications of retirement at the group and individual level.
Certainly some of the findings of the study do refute some of the
stereotyped ideas in the field of applied social gerontology. But
clearing the way of misconceptions is one of the fundamental
steps in building a sound knowledge base in a new field. It is
our hope that this book may also serve to assist those involved
in decision-making and policy formation about retired persons.

A research project of this magnitude obviously has involved
many people. The first director of the Cornell Study of Occupational Retirement was Milton L. Barron, one of the early
pioneers in social gerontology and now Professor in the City
University of New York. It was his imagination and perception
of the research needs and knowledge of the nascent field of the
sociology of aging that resulted in the initial grant which
launched the study. The late Edward A. Suchman, who was last
affiliated with the University of Pittsburgh, played a very significant part in helping to formulate the research problems, the
methodological issues, and the day-to-day organization and
management of the project. His leadership, interest, and involvement were extremely important in the early days in providing the spark and the momentum which kept the project on
course and in motion.

A very crucial role for a number of years was played by
Wayne Thompson, who participated in many phases of the
study. He conducted a considerable amount of the basic field
work, and he shared in many administrative phases. Moreover,
his ideas were extremely important at a number of crucial junc-
tures, and he co-authored a number of the publications which

have resulted from the Cornell Study of Occupational Retirement.

At various times throughout the research a number of graduate students at Cornell University took part in a variety of aspects of the study: Aaron Cicourel, now of the University of California, Santa Barbara; William Knox, University of North Carolina, Greensboro; Martin U. Martel, Brown University.

Among the many other persons who have contributed importantly to the project are John Kosa, Janice Hopper, Margaret Anagnost, Jessie Cohen, Eleanor Litwak, Judith Aronson, Suzanne Guimarez, Hinda Neufeld, Mary O'Neill, Ruth S. Thompson, Nona Glazer, and Billa Zamir.

The initial research received generous financial support from the Lilly Endowment, Inc., of Indianapolis, Indiana. Subsequent financial support was received from the National Institute of Health (Grant M-1196) and the Social Security Administration (Grant No. 034).

The authors also wish to express their appreciation to the thousands of older Americans who cooperated in supplying us with detailed information without which this book could never have been written.

G. F. S.
C. J. S., S.J.

Contents

Retirement in

American Society

IMPACT AND PROCESS

CHAPTER 1

Introduction

Demography and Retirement

The interest in the study of retirement and other aspects of the latter part of the life cycle has accelerated in recent decades. In order to have a basic understanding of the aged one must recognize the importance of demographic facts and trends. The age structure in a society at a particular point in time is the result of past demographic patterns as they relate to the three demographic factors: fertility, mortality, and migration. Whether the society is pastoral, agricultural, or industrialized is also an important basis for understanding gerontological phenomena. For example, agricultural societies —particularly those marked by low levels of productivity— have higher mortality rates than industrialized societies. Moreover as agrarian societies become industrialized, there is a tendency for mortality rates to decline. Finally, as industrialized societies mature, they have a lower mortality rate than in earlier periods of their economic development.

The death rate is probably the demographic factor which is most obviously related to the age structure of a particular demographic area, but fertility also plays an important part in shaping the age structure of a society or community. For example, France and Sweden in modern times have a larger proportion of aged than in former years, not only because of improved mortality rates but also because of the low fertility rates.

The demographic revolution of the nineteenth and twentieth centuries as it relates to the aged is a byproduct of a complicated set of technological, cultural, and scientific factors. This revolution involves a shift from high birth rates and high death rates to a demographic condition where both birth and death rates are relatively low. This combination results in a general aging of the population.

Retirement as described and analyzed here is a concomitant of the emergence of modern industrial nation-states. In earlier societies—even in the first industrial societies—there was no retirement role. The development of this role is the result of the great productive capacities of industrialized societies. Large amounts of food, goods, and services are produced, and this has resulted in a higher standard of living for many. Along with the fundamental demographic changes and the emergence of high-energy, productive economies, the gradual development of social and institutional structures has also made it possible for persons to be supported outside the traditional family. Modern retirement implies the possibility of maintenance by national insurance and pension schemes in which one has a right to support and benefits even though he no longer has a role in the wage system. These interlocking and interdependent factors are also associated with the fact that greater numbers of people retire every year.

Since 1950, there has been a steady decline in the percentage of men over 65 who work sometime during the year. Even when employment is more restrictively defined as full-time, year-round work, a similar decline is evident: in 1950, 26 per cent of all men over 65 were so employed, but by 1962 this figure had dropped to 15 per cent.[1] It is clear that each year more older workers face retirement from the labor force.

[1] Epstein and Murray, 1967, p. 342.

The Sociology and Social Psychology of Retirement

⁄Retirement has produced what Michelon has called a "new leisure class," and its members must face not only a decline in income but also "a new set of personal values and new kinds of activity for the lifelong job of earning a living, raising a family, and overcoming the day-to-day obstacles that affect one's income, status, and career." [2] ⁄

The sociologist who studies retirement may employ several approaches. First, he may consider retirement in relation to the values which are pivotal in the society, such as progress, humanitarianism, work, or achievement. Second, retirement may be considered in terms of the membership and reference groups which are significant for work and retirement, namely cliques at work, unions, or families. Third, the sociologist may study retirement by examining the roles and role sets which are interwoven with the experiences and conditions of working and not working.

The empirical data that constitute the major part of this volume were gathered and will be reported in terms of role theory.[3] There are at least two major traditions in sociology that employ role concepts as central to their theoretical orientations: the structural and the social-psychological.[4] The structural tradition was stimulated and formulated by the writings of Ralph Linton, Robert Merton, William J. Goode, Neal Gross, Frederick Bates, and others. The social-psychological tradition in-

[2] Michelon, 1954, p. 371.

[3] For a thorough review of the nature and history of role theory and an analysis of basic conceptual problems see Biddle and Thomas, 1966, esp. chs. i–iv. Another thorough review of role theory with a detailed bibliography and an analysis of the complexity of the subject may be found in Sarbin and Allen, 1968.

[4] Among the most lucid discussions of the two points of view, albeit with primary attention to the family, are Hill and Hansen, 1960, and Heiss, 1968. See also A. M. Rose, 1962.

cludes a long list of important writers going back to the early days of sociology and social psychology: George Herbert Mead, W. I. Thomas, Charles Horton Cooley, William James, and others; more recently this school of role theory includes Ernest Burgess, Leonard S. Cottrell, Jr., Herbert Blumer, Arnold Rose, Anselm Strauss, and Ruth Cavan, among others.

The structural orientation is concerned mainly with the content, organization, and consequences of roles, and their relationships to groups and institutions. The social-psychological view emphasizes processes—interactional and learning. There are many similarities in conceptualization, in problem formulation, and in the approach to research. Arnold Rose has said: "This emphasis on process distinguishes the thought and researches of the interactionists from those of most followers of 'functional' theory in sociology (although in practically every other respect the two are very similar or identical)." [5]

Both the structural and the interaction points of view shaped the design of this study of retirement and the formulation of the research questions. Borrowing from the structural orientation, we conceived role as an independent variable, and we were concerned with the consequences of role change. Concepts of interaction were used, for example, when we employed age identity as an index of self-image. Finally, our basic approach to role stability and role change was in processual terms over a period of from five to seven years, with repeated contacts during that period. This approach is somewhat different from that of the traditional interactionist, who tends to be concerned with immediate primary relationships during a limited time period.

Our approach to role theory may be described as follows: Through a system of mores or social norms, society requires that a person enact roles in accordance with his position in the social system. Roles are defined by the social norms of the society, by subgroups in which the person may hold a membership or which he employs as a reference group, by significant other

[5] A. M. Rose, 1962, p. ix.

persons with whom he associates, and also by the person himself. These factors are balanced and weighed by the individual; and thus roles are defined and enacted in behavior as a result of a highly complex process of interaction and interdependence between social, situational, and personal factors. Not all roles are accepted with equal ease, and some may put a strain upon the actor because of the incongruity of situational factors and personal expectations. Moreover, persons often must enact several roles at one time and the integration of the multiple, and sometimes conflicting, roles is not always an easy matter.[6] A person may discard a role, however, or redefine it in ways that are more congenial to him.

In this study of retirement, we wanted to find out what happens when a major role is dropped or disrupted or altered. In the gerontological literature, the dropping of the worker role generally has been viewed as deleterious from the standpoint of the social psychology of the individual. Some have argued that there are not only severe social and psychological effects but also devastating physiological repercussions.

There are obviously other disruptions which occur at both the earlier and the later parts of the life cycle—such as children leaving home, changes in occupational status, illness and death of friends and relatives and medical emergencies. These disruptions can result in strategic role changes in the later part of the life cycle. Our study focuses its attention on the work-retirement disruption. We employ this as the basic, independent variable. Other variables such as health and income are viewed in relation to this basic change in status and role.

The Cornell Study was initiated with the broad hypothesis that retirement is a major disruption of an adult's role and would tend to have deleterious consequences for the individual. We wished to examine the effects of role disruption in three main areas:

[6] Merton (1957b, pp. 368 ff.) has pointed out the difference between role sets and multiple roles. For another reformulation see Bates, 1956.

1. Health
2. Economic situation: objective and subjective
3. Social psychological dimensions:
    a. Self-image, age identity, and usefulness
    b. Satisfaction with life
    c. Adjustment to retirement

The following propositions are among those that emerged from the theoretical perspective which guided the design, planning, and execution of the study.[7] They may be considered "educated guesses" based upon our knowledge of the subject at the time.

1. Retirement, by reducing income and disrupting the interaction pattern which accompanies gainful employment, tends to isolate the retiree.

2. Mental illness as a consequence of retirement is greater in the lower economic strata than in the upper strata.

3. Some old people are reluctant to retire because economic inactivity to them signifies a decline in status.

4. Other persons are reluctant to continue in gainful employment because of status considerations. For these people, retirement "saves face" and permits withdrawal from an area of competition and thereby adjustment is facilitated.

5. Retirement is a difficult experience to accept, for it represents a sharp cleavage in life continuity inasmuch as a gainfully employed person in the course of time usually comes to identify himself with his occupation.

6. By disrupting the daily life pattern of the individual, retirement may disturb his physiology sufficiently to induce organic illness and premature death.

Thus we have used role theory because we consider working and retirement as forms of real-life behavior for which this sociological approach has particular utility. Many facets of

[7] A more complete list of these propositions and the first published description of the then planned research appears in Barron, Streib, and Suchman, 1952.

real human behavior can be included in studies involving concepts of role theory.

One of the basic assumptions underlying our research is a modified form of social determinism. We plan to describe and analyze real-life behavior in relation to the three areas: the division of labor in society—for example, between men and women; role specialization—for example, by occupational categories; and social position—for example, being a worker or a retiree. We are aware that individual differences are very much part of the real-life behavior which constitutes the role phenomena upon which our research data are based. We are also aware of the danger of neglecting the individual in the kind of aggregate analysis which is presented here. An oversocialized conception of man does have its conceptual and practical shortcomings.[8] However, one must take a point of view which has both intellectual and practical advantages. Thus, although we are aware of individual variations, we highlight social factors and determinants. We think it appropriate to state that individual differences themselves may be the result of social determinants of varying kinds, qualities, and amounts.

It is clear that causal statements which take the form that "A causes B" are oversimplifications. Social and psychological determinants operate in a highly complex and often interdependent relationship to one another. Relationships between two factors or variables are often conditioned by many others. Attempts to sort out the major causal factors usually end up with a residual which seems to account for much of the variance. When we look at a particular individual or the roles he enacts we see very concretely how any role behavior or any personal event is the result of many factors which are interwoven and which can be understood only if one takes account of the multiplicity of variables and their interaction.

The subject of retirement is certainly a clear example of this phenomenon. Retirement may be viewed as a single event, but

8 Wrong, 1961.

more realistically it is the culmination of social processes. Even retirement considered as a single event may have a varying impact upon the personal and social adjustment of an individual. There are a number of contingent variables, some of which may be incidental to the event of retirement. In complicated and diverse ways the consequences of these single variables may be operative. Out of the constellation of situational influences modified by the retiree's own attitudes, values, and definitions of the situation, the "effect" of retirement on a particular individual will emerge. To study such a complicated sociological and social-psychological process and the causal network of variables is a most intriguing, and sometimes frustrating, task, especially when we consider the limitations of our methods and concepts.

It has been suggested by writers like C. Wright Mills that if an investigator accepts the principle of multiple causation, he denies the possibility of radical change in the social structure. We think the position of Hirschi and Selvin is more tenable when they state: "Our analysis suggests that rejecting the principle of multiple causation implies denying the possibility of *any* change in the social structure—since, in this view, nothing causes anything." [9]

[9] Hirschi and Selvin, 1966, p. 268.

CHAPTER 2

Research Design and
Methods of Research

The Significance of the Longitudinal Design

In many fields of study, and particularly in those related to the life cycle, it is almost a cliché to state the importance of and need for longitudinal research—studies conducted at two or more points in time. Nevertheless, surprisingly few longitudinal studies in social gerontology have been published. There are several studies under way and one or two being planned which should add substantially to the stock of knowledge.

A longitudinal study differs fundamentally from a cross-sectional study in that the investigator obtains information by interviews, questionnaires, or observations from the same group of people on two or more occasions.[1] The longitudinal design is useful for studying changes in behavior and attitudes because one does not have to rely only on retrospective accounts of feelings, thoughts, or actions. In this study, contacting the same individuals before and after retirement—indeed five times, with the group of participants who remained in the work force as a kind of control group—has permitted a description of change and process which is essential to an understanding of the dynamics of retirement. Such a description is almost impossible in studies that are cross-sectional in design, and it

[1] For a discussion of some problems in longitudinal research see Streib, 1963.

is in this important respect that the Cornell Study of Occupational Retirement differs from most other studies which have been completed in the field of social gerontology.[2] In brief, a longitudinal study is a way of approximating some of the rigor of the before-after design of the experiment except for two major differences: a longitudinal study does not use matched groups, and the investigator does not have control over the independent variable.

Longitudinal studies in general vary in three important characteristics: the nature of the external stimulus, the criterion or effect variables, and the time interval between contacts. In the Cornell Study of Retirement the major stimulus variable is occupational status—whether a man is working or has retired. It is difficult to classify this independent variable as specific or diffuse, for it has some characteristics of each: it is specific in the sense that it applies to a person as an individual, it is a relatively clear-cut status change, and it can be pinpointed in terms of time and location; it is diffuse because one's occupational status ramifies into many spheres of activity and feeling beyond the work situation itself.

In longitudinal research the criterion or effect variables may be broadly classified as specific or diffuse. In this study our effect variables fall into four broad categories: health, age identification, satisfaction with life and retirement, and feelings of economic deprivation. However, it should be made clear that although the areas under study involve a broad spectrum of human exeprience, the specific measures or indicators employed tend to be rather restricted because of the type of research instruments used, the nature of the contacts with our respondents, the cost of gathering data, and so forth.

Some longitudinal or panel studies of relatively short duraation involve contact with the participants every few weeks, such as in studies of elections or voting. However, in social

[2] See Stokes and Maddox, 1967.

gerontological studies of the type reported here, the nature of the observations, the kind of phenomena studied, the kind of observational methods and their sensitivity to change strongly suggest a relatively long interval of time between research contacts. In this study, the interval varied from about twelve to eighteen months, and the total period of data gathering was between six and seven years.

Selection of Organizations and Participants

Starting with the assumption that arbitrary retirement at a fixed age is characteristic of an urban, industrialized society, we decided to concentrate our attention upon urban, industrial and business organizations.[3]

The investigators were aware of the difficulty, if not the impossibility, of obtaining a probability sample of companies and persons who would cooperate in a seven-year study. However, we did wish to insure as broad a selection of organizations as possible and we wished to include the major types of industrial and business organizations, and also government agencies. Secondly, we wished to include a wide geographical coverage of the United States, and we eventually included persons who resided in the forty-eight states which at the time made up the country. Finally, we wished to make site visits to organizations that employed a substantial number of older workers in order to make the time and cost of a visit as productive as possible. At first we planned to contact only those that employed 500 or more workers in a single location. However, we soon discovered that only in organizations with one thousand or more employees at one site would we find a sufficient number of participants meeting our age criterion to warrant the time and expense of a site visit. Nevertheless, there are a substantial number of

[3] The Cornell studies of research on aging and retirement included a study of rural residents, which was reported in Taietz, Streib, and Barron, 1956.

smaller firms in our study which were contacted and decided to take part before we reached our final decision on the size of the company.

The organizations to be contacted were selected from the census classification of the major businesses and industries. Names of companies were selected by utilizing published industrial and business directories, information supplied by private and governmental organizations, and correspondence with persons having specialized knowledge of various retirement programs. We then wrote to the appropriate official in each selected organization to solicit his cooperation and the participation of the organization in our research. This involved considerable negotiation in some instances, and personal visits were made to a number of organizations to explain the nature and purpose of the study.

In those organizations which were unionized, we also secured the cooperation of the trade unions. In one or two large firms this involved contacting as many as twenty-five unions. Needless to say, these aspects of the research consumed considerable time, effort, and research funds. However, we felt it was essential to try to include companies which involved difficulties and complications as well as those in which it was easy to secure cooperaton.

In order to have a substantial number of white-collar and professional participants, we solicited the cooperation of a number of state and civil service systems. Two federal agencies, twelve states, and numerous cities and counties agreed to participate. The response from these organizations was exceptionally high, accounting for the substantial proportion of our participants who fall in this category. In the more populous states, the governmental agency selected a random sample of those in the selected age group; in other states all the members of the system in that age group were invited to participate. These participants cover a broad spectrum of occupations, from liquor store operators, highway department employees, and mental hospital attendants, to physicians and other higher level civil servants. Inasmuch as many of them were scattered over a wide geographical region, site visits were not practicable; the initial contact with these participants, as well as the follow-ups, were by mail.

We also solicited and secured the cooperation of public school systems, private colleges and universities, several ministerial pension organizations, and a sample of older doctors in New

Table 1. Original participants and participating organizations by type of industry

Category	Organizations	Participants
Machinery, except electrical	17	297
Transportation equipment	15	304
Metal industries	21	386
Electrical machinery	15	126
Lumber and its products, except furniture	6	107
Rubber and its products	2	93
Food and kindred, including tobacco	26	266
Textile	6	79
Apparel	7	110
Printing and publishing	7	62
Chemical and allied industries	17	111
Stone, clay, and glass products; petroleum and coal	10	121
Transportation and communication	10	238
Other public utilities	8	157
Wholesale and retail trade	6	67
Finance, insurance, and real estate	11	66
Federal public administration	8	106
State public administration	12	689
Local public administration	3	90
Manufacturing of professional photographic equipment, watches	5	55
Educational services	25	253
Other professional services	8	156
All other organizations	14	93
Total	259	4,032

York State. All of the persons in these diverse organizations were contacted by mail, both initially and in the follow-up phases of the research.

The initial distribution of the original participants according to type of industry is shown in Table 1. Most major types of industries are represented, according to the census. However, it was particularly difficult to obtain participants from some of the industrial types. For example, we were able to secure the cooperation of one of the world's largest construction firms, but due to the high degree of mobility of their hourly employees, this organization found it possible to include only a small number of what might be called permanent office, engineering, and supervisory personnel. Mining as an industry may also be somewhat underrepresented, again because of the nature of the industry and the kind of work involved. Persons employed in mining and construction face some unique problems in terms of retirement, and it is hoped that other investigators will undertake the task of studying them.[4]

Administration of Questionnaires

Securing the cooperation of employers and the unions was only the first step in obtaining the participation of the people themselves. This was handled in almost all business and industrial organizations by requesting the appropriate company official to write a letter of invitation to employees of the selected age cohort inviting them to a meeting at which a representative of Cornell University would explain the reasons for the study and what participation in it would involve. Of those employees who came to these meetings, almost all cooperated in the first wave of the study. In the typical situation, the employees filled in the questionnaires at the time of the meeting, which was held during work hours and for which they were given paid time-off by their employers. The participants were assured at this time of the confidentiality of

[4] Harlan, 1954, is a valuable paper on coal miners and retirement.

the information given to us. Management and union personnel were not present during the sessions.

In some organizations personnel officials screened out employees whom they thought would not want to participate in the study. In some cases, the judgment of personnel officials was probably correct. However, there were a number of cases in which, contrary to the expectations of the company officials, employees who met with the Cornell representative were interested in the project and were willing to cooperate. In any event, the selection of the participants ultimately rested upon the willingness of each individual to take part in the study. Thus, both from the standpoint of cooperating organizations and of cooperating participants, the keynote of "sample" selection was voluntary participation, and in this respect the study population clearly departs from a representative probability sample.

One obstacle to employing a self-administered questionnaire was the fact that in some organizations persons with limited reading skills wished to take part in the study. This special problem was solved at the time of the initial administration by reading the questions to such participants and thus turning the situation into an interview. The participants were interested and seemed eager to take part. The difficulty arose in the follow-up phases (described below) in which the persons with limited reading ability tended to drop out of the study at higher rates than participants with higher educational attainments. At the time the study was initiated it would have been undesirable to exclude the functionally illiterate because it would probably have created rapport and morale problems with them and perhaps with other participants. On the other hand, it was time-consuming during the first wave of the study to conduct the interviews, and it was also expensive to follow them up. The ultimate result was that persons of low educational attainments did not continue to take part. We recall one plaintive letter from an illiterate participant who had some one else write a letter for him and asked us not to send him another question-naire. He was foreign-born and his command of English was limited. The letter said please don't send any more question-naires as he could not afford to hire some one to translate them and fill them out for him. Such are the real problems which one must face regularly in conducting a large-scale, longitudinal field study.

Follow-up Procedures

The first follow-up was made from a year to eighteen months after the first contact, at which time some participants had retired. This contact and subsequent follow-ups were made by mail, with the exception of approximately one hundred respondents who were interviewed personally in their homes, most of them after the fourth mail contact.

It may be useful to outline the details of a follow-up oper-ation, using the third survey as an illustration. Follow-up letters of invitation and explanation were mailed to the 3,021 par-ticipants who were on the mailing list at the time. We included a return postal card which would confirm or correct the participant's address and would tell the research staff whether the participant was still employed, whether he had retired, or, if he had previously retired, whether he had returned to gain-ful employment. To obtain meaningful information from the respondents, we found it necessary to use three different forms of the questionnaire corresponding to the three employment categories; we labeled them questionnaires for the "working," the "retired," and the "retired-working."

More than 2,300 cards were returned to Cornell University within a month after they were mailed out. To those who did not respond we sent a first and, if necessary, a second follow-up letter and postal card. About six weeks later we were able to mail out approximately 2,700 questionnaires; and within a period of about a month approximately 2,000 of these question-naires were completed and returned to us in the postage-free envelopes provided. For this wave of the study, approximately 2,500 of the questionnaires which were sent out were completed and sent back to us, or a return of about 92 per cent. We were able to maintain a high level of response and thus have a fairly substantial number of respondents to include in the analysis.

Perhaps it is useful to mention that in the follow-up just described there were about 150 persons who did not respond to the most persuasive letters we were able to compose, or the United States Post Office was not able to deliver their mail to them. Rather than drop them immediately from the study panel, we wrote to their former employers, enclosing a special information form, in an attempt to find out, at the very least, whether the respondent was alive, and if possible, his most recent correct mailing address. The former employers of our participants returned about 80 per cent of these "terminal" forms. Finally, by one means or another, we learned that for this wave 110 participants had died since the previous contact with them.

The original research population of the Cornell Study of Occupational Retirement consisted of a group of 3,793 men and women. About eighteen months after the initial questionnaires were completed, the second contact was made, and completed questionnaires were received from 2,857 people, or 75 per cent of the initial participants. In the third wave of the study, approximately two years later, 2,465 persons returned questionnaires, and thus an additional 10 per cent of the original participants dropped out. Four hundred and ninety-six persons dropped out of the study in the fourth and fifth waves (13 per cent of the original number), and this left a population employed in this analysis of 1,969 persons (1,486 men and 483 women).

A Comparison of the Participants and the Drop-outs

What is the nature of those persons who continued to participate in comparison to those who dropped out? In any study involving human populations this is an important question, and it is particularly important in longitudinal research where the goal is to maintain as large a subject pool as possible. We wished to determine whether the loss of participants tended to distort the nature of the study population and the findings based upon the information obtained from these persons. In this analysis we shall present data for three groups at three points in time: (1) those persons who dropped out after the initial contact in 1952; (2) those persons who dropped out between the second contact in 1954 and the third contact in 1956; and (3) those persons who remained in the study until its conclusion in 1958.[5]

How did these groups differ in terms of three basic characteristics: nativity, socioeconomic status, and attitude toward retirement? The analysis of the data show that, in general, native-born persons were more likely than the foreign-born to continue to participate in a longitudinal study and women more likely than men. Moreover, there seems to be a slight cumulative relationship in that native-born females were the most likely to continue to participate and foreign-born males were least likely.

The following data for males are based on native-born males only, for they constituted the largest segment of the original male study population, numbering over 2,000 persons. The foreign-born males will be discussed later. The data are combined for the native-born and foreign-born females, for of the 800 original female study population, only a very small percentage were foreign-born.

Between the first and second contacts, approximately 24 per cent of the males and 18 per cent of the females dropped out of the study; between the second and third contacts, approximately 10 per cent of the men and 7 per cent of the women stopped participating. Therefore, at the end of four years, about two-thirds of both the original male and female

[5] A more detailed analysis of these materials is found in Streib, 1966.

groups were still involved in the research project. This is a remarkably high degree of participation, especially when we consider several factors: The respondents were of an older age category—a group which has a true mortality rate higher than most groups in the general population. Moreover, the questionnaires used in the study were usually twenty or more pages long, and the follow-up contacts were all made by mail; it is generally known that the rate of response to mail questionnaires—and especially to long questionnaires—is lower than that for interview studies. Finally, the research was carried on over a period of years, not merely weeks or months, and the considerable degree of residential mobility in the older population—although it is not as great as among younger age categories—might have been expected to decrease the number of continuing participants.

A common finding in questionnaire and interview studies is the tendency for persons of lower socioeconomic status not to participate in the research. Therefore, we were interested in knowing whether participants tended to be persons of higher socioeconomic status than drop-outs—that is, persons of middle-class identification and of higher income and educational levels. Five indices of socioeconomic status were employed in this study: occupation, education, income, class identification, and union membership. On all of these measures the distinct tendency was for persons who continued to participate to be of a higher socioeconomic level than those who dropped out of the study. A larger proportion of both male and female professionals participated than dropped out. Furthermore, both male and female participants had more education and higher incomes, were more apt to identify with the middle rather than the working class, and were less often union members than the drop-outs. The largest differences were those pertaining to educational level and union membership.

It is interesting to note, however, that on several other important demographic characteristics there were very small or practically no differences between the participants and the two categories of drop-outs. On characteristics such as race, religion, and marital status, the participants and the two drop-out categories were very similar. Female drop-outs were slightly more likely than female participants to be Catholic than Protestant, and to be married and living with their spouses rather than never married, although the differences are small.

An examination of attitudinal variables reveals the following pattern: Anticipatory items like attitudes toward retirement and expected resources in retirement show that the persons in the participant category were slightly more optimistic in their attitudes than those who dropped out. Both male and female participants were more favorably disposed toward the idea of retirement than drop-outs, although the differences were very slight for the women. We also found that those who continued in the study had a higher income when they were working than the drop-outs. Hence, we predicted that their expected retirement income would be higher than those persons who dropped out of the study, and this prediction was substantiated.

In regard to adjustment measures, the findings generally reveal only minor differences between the participants and the drop-outs. On only one of seven measures of adjustment, namely, "hopelessness," was there a substantial difference between the two categories. The drop-outs were more pessimistic and tended to be classified as "hopeless" compared with those who participated. On items which index "satisfaction with life," economic deprivation, religiosity, ability to get used to change, and self-image, there was very slight, if any, difference between the two categories. Among the females, "hopelessness" did not appear to be a differentiating item. However, female participants less often classified themselves as dejected, were slightly more likely to view their present income as adequate, and more often stated that they found it comparatively easy to adjust to change. On indices of religiosity and self-image, there was little difference between female participants and drop-outs.

The Cornell Study relied primarily upon self-evaluation indices of health. One of these measures was a general five-step rating. A comparison of both male and female participants and drop-outs shows that those who previously reported a better state of health were more apt to remain in the study.

It is important in a study of retirement to ascertain the degree to which participants emphasize the importance of work, for work-centeredness is correlated with other significant variables. Our study found a slight tendency for both the male and female drop-outs to be more attached to their work than those who continued in the study.

In another comparison of the participants and the drop-outs, respondents were asked: "Which of these things gives you the most satisfaction and comfort in life today?" The respondents were then asked to choose from a list of twelve items and activities. The list included, for example, "just being with my family at home," "working around the house, garden or yard," "my religion or church work," etc. In general the response pattern was quite similar for male participants and drop-outs. "Being with the family at home" was the number one item for the three groups and "my job" was second. Among the women, however, work ranked first with the drop-outs and second with the participants. The major deviation from the general rank order pattern is found on the item "reading," which was ranked third by male participants and fifth and sixth by the two male drop-out groups. The women participants, on the other hand, ranked reading first, and the two drop-out groups ranked it fifth and second. These differences are understandable in view of the higher educational level of those who continued in the study.

It was stated previously that the percentage of drop-outs among the foreign-born was higher than that among the native-born. Between the initial contact and the first follow-up, approximately one-third of the foreign-born respondents dropped out of the study and between the second and third contacts another 14 per cent stopped participating. Thus, at the time of the third contact the research mortality was almost 50 per cent for the foreign-born males. Foreign-born females followed a similar pattern, with the mortality at the close of the study reaching 57 per cent.

Among foreign-born males, the following findings were observed concerning socioeconomic status: Those who continued in the study were slightly more likely to be of a higher socioeconomic status than those who dropped out. The participants were also more likely to hold jobs associated with higher skill and prestige, to have received more education, to have greater incomes, to identify with the middle class, and not to have been union members. In general, the differences between the drop-outs and the participants on socioeconomic indices were not as great among the foreign-born as was reported for the native-born category.

On work attachment, however, no difference was found between the foreign-born participants and drop-outs; on anticipatory items, very small differences between the two categories were observed. Once again the largest difference was found on the question pertaining to expected resources in retirement. The foreign-born drop-outs, compared with the foreign-born participants, were much more likely to say that they did not know what their income would be.

On the seven adjustment measures the same general pattern was noted as was reported for the native-born; the participants and the drop-outs did not differ substantially. On five items almost no difference was found between the two groups; on one (self-image) a small difference was observed, and on another ("breaks in life") a rather large difference was found. There were very slight differences in the health rating of the categories; the percentage of persons who reported themselves in "good" or "excellent" health was 66 per cent for the drop-outs and 69 per cent for the participants.

Finally, a consideration of the question which measures satisfactions and comforts in life reveals that the general rank order for all subgroups was approximately the same for the foreign-born and the native-born.

A comparison of the findings in this study with those reported in the literature on drop-outs shows agreement on some points: continued participation is related to interest, social class, and education. Furthermore, this study showed that foreign-born persons were more likely to drop out of the study than native-born respondents, and that women were more likely to remain participants than men.

Unfortunately it was not possible to obtain systematic information to explain the relatively high degree of continued participation (49 per cent of the men initially contacted and 63 per cent for the women). However, a subgroup of approximately 100 participants interviewed personally in their homes after the fourth mail contact may help to explain this phenomenon. The two interviewers were greeted very cordially by nearly all the participants who were contacted. These participants seemed pleased to be part of an ongoing research project conducted by a leading university. In many cases the respondents were so eager to talk about themselves and their situation that the interviews had to be terminated because of the shortage of time. These respondents had evidently acquired some feeling of identification with the research, even though it involved only transitory impersonal contacts with them. Most of these 100 persons had retired, and this fact may have increased their sense of involvement in the project. The completion of questionnaires about retirement may have been a meaningful, personally gratifying activity for them as retirees and perhaps also a research activity of some social benefit to other retirees.

Qualitative data from these 100 personal follow-ups suggest that the initial personal contacts by the senior investigators, which were made at the place of work, were extremely persuasive and increased the amount of continued participation in the study.

Another possible explanation for the high degree of continued cooperation is the fact that the overwhelming majority of the initial participants were volunteers and were interested in the study and its purposes. It seems likely that "captive respondents" will drop out of a longitudinal study if they have been coerced in the initial phases of the research. In fact, although systematic data are not available, it is assumed that the high degree of participation would have been even higher if, in the initial contacts, foreign-born persons and other persons with a low level of literacy had not been included in the study.

Content of the Questionnaires and Focus of the Analysis

Included as an appendix to this report are six of the thirteen questionnaires employed in the study. It was necessary to employ three different forms in each of the four follow-up surveys: one for those still working, one for those who retired, and one for those who retired and then returned to work. The initial questionnaire is included, plus selected follow-up forms for the working, retired, and retired-working groups.

The items in the questionnaires can be classified according to content: work, retirement, health, economic factors, general items pertaining to adjustment, specific attitudes and adjustment toward retirement, age identification, leisure activities, stereotypes regarding aging, and demographic characteristics. In this analysis we are dealing with a limited domain of information. Because of their importance we have focused upon the following topics: health, general satisfaction with life, age identification, feelings of usefulness, income and economic de-

privation, and the retirement situation, particularly as it compared with the former work situation.

Limitations of the Study

The study has scientific and methodological limitations, for,
although the number of participants is large, and is probably
larger than in any published longitudinal study in social gerontology, the persons who took part do not constitute a representative sample of America's older population. The most important limiting factor is that participation was voluntary. The
organizations that agreed to participate tended to be relatively
large or relatively affluent. In some cases, the personnel de-
partments of the participating organizations "weeded out" those
who they believed would not be interested in participating or
who would not be able to do so. Attendance at meetings with
a representative of Cornell University was voluntary, as was
initial and continuing participation in all aspects of the study.
These facts necessarily restrict the generalizability of the results and also place limitations upon the kinds of statistical
tools and tests which may be utilized.

We have, of course, no systematic data concerning the individuals who did not volunteer. We assume on the basis of
other studies [6] and the experience of the interviewers that
the least well adjusted declined to participate in the study.

The basic source of information was a series of self-administered questionnaires which included mainly structured
questions and which the respondents completed by means of
checks or brief written answers. Respondents were encouraged
in all phases of the study to offer more detailed information or
qualifications of their responses when a particular set of answers
did not describe their situation, their attitudes, or their behavior. A number did so, and some respondents even included
letters and commentaries which were valuable for the investi-

[6] For example, Havighurst, 1960; Scott, 1957.

gator, if somewhat difficult to summarize in quantitative form.

This type of information-gathering is open to several lines of criticism. A fundamental criticism of *all* questionnaires is that they impose a cognitive and attitudinal structure upon the persons responding. The respondents may, of course, not perceive this structure—indeed in some instances the researcher may not wish them to do so. There is little question that structured methods in sociology and social psychology are not able to take account of all the varied life experiences of the people answering the questions. Another objection is that structured methods usually assumed a type of invariant language structure which may not correspond to that of the respondents. Simple and straightforward questions were used to index complicated concepts like age identity. Here again, however, one must keep in mind that the questionnaires were designed to be easily understood by persons with about seven or eight years of primary education and therefore the nuances of expression and the use of complex words which may be employed with respondents with higher levels of education were not possible. We tried to minimize the possibility of anxiety and so used words, phrases, and forms which were not too formidable. Most researchers who employ structured instruments are aware of these and other limitations.

It has been made explicit that the basic sources of information were self-evaluating reports, and that such information may depart from "objective" conditions. In the case of health information, we have compared these reports to the observations made by examining physicians. Although there are differences in reported health conditions, there are aspects of subjective health for which the self-reports are better sources of data.[7]

Several other issues concerning the validity and reliability of the data must be raised and at least some preliminary answers offered. In social science research on attitudes, values, and similar social-psychological phenomena, it is very difficult to

[7] See Suchman, Phillips, and Streib, 1958.

determine the validity of the items which are used to index the concepts. Our approach was to assume a form of face validity for the items employed. The questionnaires were developed after field interviewing and observation and after a careful pre-testing on several populations. However, face validation is essentially a subjective process. Even the use of more sophisticated techniques involving criterion-validation or construct-validation results in considerable ambiguity. Moreover, sophisticated techniques can be quite expensive and time-consuming, with little gain in validity. We tend to agree with Bernard S. Phillips when he wrote: "The investigator never possesses a perfectly valid measure of any given concept." [8]

The problem of item validity is more complicated in a longitudinal study because one usually assumes that the initial attitudes, feelings, or behavior were correct and may safely be used as the base line. Thus, when a change is reported, the investigator is faced with the interesting dilemma of trying to decide whether there has been instability of the measuring instrument or whether a genuine change has taken place. Further, one cannot be certain whether the earlier interviews or the experiences in answering a questionnaire have influenced responses in subsequent phases of the gathering of the data.

In the hope of increasing the credibility of the results, multiple items were clustered into scores or combined into crude scales. Scales and scores also increase in some degree the precision of this type of research. We have employed multiple items, for example, in our indices of subjective health, attitudes toward satisfaction with life, and attitudes toward retirement. Because of restrictions imposed by time, space, and the nature of the study population, we were not able to employ multiple item measures for a number of concepts.

Finally, it should be placed on the record that the original data analyzed here were gathered before the more efficient, high-speed computing equipment of the present generation of

[8] Phillips, 1966, p. 162.

social scientists was available. The counter-sorter and then the IBM 101 counter-sorter were the basic computational equipment by which the data were processed. It would require a tremendous outlay of money and time to reprocess the original data on contemporary equipment, and then to carry out the kind of fine-grained analysis which may be suggested by the data.

CHAPTER 3

Characteristics of
the Participants

Although the demands of a large-scale longitudinal study and other practical requirements made it difficult to meet rigorous statistical sampling criteria, we did obtain a large number of cooperative participants, and many hundreds of them filled out successive forms of the questionnaires sent to them. What were the respondents like? What kinds of occupational categories did they represent? In what kinds of industries did they work? How much education did they have? What was their marital status? This chapter will present a statistical summary of the basic characteristics of the participants in the Cornell Study of Occupational Retirement. We do not claim that the participants in the study constitute a sample necessarily representative of the population of older employed men and women. That some judgment might be made of how much and in what direction the participants differ from the general population of working men and women, we shall present the reader with some background characteristics of the participants and comparable information about the total population.

We wished to contact persons one year before the common retirement age of 65. Hence, we used the year of birth for the basic selection process. The participating individuals were first contacted in 1952 or early in 1953, at which time they were

all gainfully employed. Subsequent contacts were made by
mail in 1954, 1956, 1957, and 1958.[1]

At the time they were first contacted, about three out of four
of the participants were 64 years old, about one in four was 63,
and the few remaining were already 65 years old (Table 2).
The participants, therefore, belong to a very specific age cohort.

Table 2. Year of birth of participants
(in per cent)

Year	Women (483)	Men (1,486)
1887	4	4
1888	75	70
1889	21	26

This is predominantly a study of the urban aged. Of the 231
participating organizations, 72 per cent were located in cities

Table 3. Participating organizations by size
of city of location

Size of city	% of participating organizations (231)
Over 1,000,000	40
500,000 to 1,000,000	16
100,000 to 500,000	16
10,000 to 100,000	12
2,500 to 10,000	7
No single location *	9

* Includes state employees from various states,
ministerial alliances, transportation companies,
and the like.

[1] These dates do not mean that the questionnaires were filled out exactly
one or two years apart. They are approximate indicators of time lapse.
Some respondents, for example, completed their forms in 1959.

with a population of 100,000 or more, while only 7 per cent were located in communities with a population of less than 10,000 (Table 3). But apart from age and urban background, the participants are in most aspects markedly heterogeneous. Although they do not constitute a representative sample, they are from all parts of the country, from many walks of life, and from a wide range of backgrounds; and they express a considerable variety of attitudes and points of view.

Marital Status and Race

Most of the male participants were married. In fact, relatively more married men were to be found among the participants than within the urban male population aged 60–64 taken as a whole. Compared with their relative participation in the work force, single women who had never married were overrepresented, while married women living with their spouses were underrepresented among the participants in the study (Table 4).

With regard to race the male participants (96 per cent white,

Table 4. Marital status of participants when first contacted, as compared with more general segments of the population (in per cent)

Status	Men	Total urban males aged 60–64	Women	White, urban women over 50 in labor force
Single	3	8	31	23
Married, living with spouse	85	75	21	33
Widowed, divorced, or separated	12	17	48	44

Sources: Men: U.S. Bureau of the Census, *Census of Population, 1950* (Washington, D.C.: Government Printing Office, 1953), vol. II, pt. 1, Table 104, p. 1-184. Women: *ibid.*, Table 121, p. 1-255.

4 per cent nonwhite) do not differ significantly from the total urban male population aged 60–64 (94 per cent white, 6 per cent nonwhite). Only 1 per cent of the women in the study were nonwhite, as compared to 6 per cent of all women aged 60–64.[2]

Industrial Classification

In soliciting cooperation in the study, small business organizations and self-employed individuals were excluded, with the

Table 5. Distribution of participants by industrial types, as compared with more general distribution of employed population (in per cent)

Type of industry	Men	All employed males aged 60–64	Women	All employed female civilians
Construction	1	12	0	0
Manufacturing	44	39	16	23
Transportation, communication, and public utilities	14	14	3	4
Wholesale and retail trade	1	20	4	22
Finance, insurance, and real estate	2	5	2	5
Business and repair services, personal services, entertainment and recreation services, professional and related service, public administration	36	8	75	38
Other and not ascertained	2	2	0	8

Sources: Men: U.S. Bureau of the Census, *Census of Population, 1950* (Washington, D.C.: Government Printing Office, 1953), vol. II, pt. 1, Table 132, p. 1-286. Women: U.S. Bureau of the Census, *Current Population Reports: Population Characteristics,* Series P-20, no. 60 (Washington, D.C.: Government Printing Office, 1955), Table 1, p. 3; data are for Sept. 1954.

[2] United States Bureau of the Census, 1953b, Table 97, p. 1-173.

exception of a sample of medical doctors. An effort was made to obtain the proper proportion of individuals from the industrial categories which were included, but it is clear that the participants do not, in fact, reflect the distribution of all employed persons in these industries (Table 5). Manufacturing and professional services alone account for the bulk of the participants, and disproportionately fewer participants are employed in construction, wholesale and retail trade, finance, and allied categories.

Occupational Categories

Categorizing the participants by industrial background is less meaningful than categorizing them by occupation. While important differences among various kinds of industry cannot be denied, it could be argued that there is a greater community of interests and attitudes among persons in a given occupation than there is within any given industrial type. For example, in their behavior and attitudes, file clerks employed in a manufacturing concern hypothetically would less closely resemble

Table 6. Distribution of participants by occupations as compared with distribution of employed persons aged 60–64 (in per cent)

Occupation	Men	Total employed males	Women	Total employed females
Professionals	19	8	34	14
Managers, officials, white-collar, skilled workers	50	53	42	32
Unskilled, semiskilled service workers	30	38	21	51
Unascertained	1	1	3	3

Source: U.S. Bureau of the Census, *Census of Population, 1950* (Washington, D.C.: Government Printing Office, 1953), vol. II, pt. 1, Table 127, pp. 1-273–1-275.

punch press operators employed in the same industry than they would other file clerks employed in construction companies, retail firms, insurance agencies, and government bureaus.

As shown in Table 6, the distribution of male participants by occupational categories roughly approximated the distribution of the total employed male population aged 60–64, excepting the disproportionately large number of professionals. The occupations of the female participants were generally higher on the status ladder than the general population of working women of similar age.

Socioeconomic Status

One of the most useful tools in studying behavior and attitudes is the concept of socioeconomic status. Because people in different positions in the stratification system have differential access to society's resources, socioeconomic status is of particular relevance in the context of aging and retirement, a time when resources generally become scarce. In many respects the different strata of society form types of subcultures, each with its own values, standards, and attitudes. Because socioeconomic status is such a significant variable, it seems important to determine the degree to which the participants, in this respect, mirror the structure of the total urban population.

Survey researchers employ several methods to determine a person's position in the social stratification system. The most direct method offers a set of three or four class categories and asks the subject to which class he thinks he belongs. The four categories employed in our questionnaires were: upper, middle, working, and lower class. We found that most of the participants consider themselves members of the middle class; relatively few consider themselves members of either the upper or the lower class (Table 7). In this respect, the distribution of male participants is remarkably similar to the pattern reported by Centers in his study of white males. The women, however,

Table 7. Self-assigned social class position of participants, as compared to Centers' findings (in per cent)

Class	Men (1,486)	Women (483)	Centers' study of white males (1,097) *
Upper	4	9	3
Middle	45	51	43
Working	50	39	51
Lower	0	0	1
No answer, don't know, don't believe in classes	1	1	2

* Richard Centers, *The Psychology of Social Classes* (Princeton, N.J.: Princeton University Press, 1949), p. 77.

were more likely to consider themselves members of the middle class.

Class position can also be delineated through the use of objective criteria which symbolize or constitute differences in social prestige or resources. One criterion which has been used

Table 8. Distribution of participants by education as compared with distribution of more general segments of the population (in per cent)

Education completed	Men	Total urban males aged 60–64	Women	Total white females aged 60–64
Grade school or less	40	63	21	59
At least some high school or business college	30	22	36	28
At least some college	29	11	42	10
Not ascertained	1	4	1	3

Source: U.S. Bureau of the Census, *Census of Population, 1950* (Washington, D.C.: Government Printing Office, 1953), vol. II, pt. 1, Table 115, p. 1-240.

for this purpose is occupation. As noted in Table 6, a disproportionately large number of the participants would be considered in the "upper" levels of the social structure, since professionals are regarded as "higher" than nonprofessionals.

That lower socioeconomic status levels are underrepresented among the participants is shown by further comparisons with

Table 9. Distribution of participants by income, as compared with distributions of segments of the population (in per cent)

Men			
Yearly income *	Participants	Yearly income †	Non-farm males aged 55–64
Less than $1,500	0 ‡	Less than $1,500	17
$1,500–$3,380	22	$1,500–$3,499	39
$3,381 and over	77	$3,500 and over	54
Not reported	1		

Women			
Yearly income *	Participants	Yearly income †	Employed civilians 14 and over
Less than $1,500	0 ‡	Less than $1,500	40
$1,500–$3,380	55	$1,500–$3,499	51
$3,381 and over	44	$3,500 and over	9
Not reported	1		

Source: U.S. Bureau of the Census, *Current Population Reports: Consumer Income* (Washington, D.C.: Government Printing Office, 1953) Series P-60, no. 14, Table 4, pp. 16–17 (data are for April 1953).

* The categories in the Cornell study represent data reported by weekly income; $3,380 a year corresponds to $65 a week.

† The categories are Census categories as nearly approximating our categories as possible.

‡ For comparison purposes, we have assumed that none of our participants was making less than $30 a week or $1,500 a year at a full-time job.

the population at large using other criteria of social position. For example, a considerably larger proportion of the participants were better educated than the general comparable population (Table 8).

Our participants were also disproportionately from the upper income brackets (Table 9).

Summary

The Cornell Study of Occupational Retirement is based on responses to questionnaires administered in 1952–53, 1954, 1956, 1957, and 1958–59. The participants—1,486 urban males and 483 urban females born in 1887, 1888, 1889—were all gainfully employed when first contacted. The respondents constituted neither a probability sample nor a representative sample in the statistical sense, but they were from widely divergent backgrounds and from all parts of the country.

A disproportionate number of the participants were in manufacturing and professional industrial categories. Disproportionately fewer of the participants were employed in construction, wholesale and retail organizations, finance, and allied categories.

When measured both by subjective and objective measures, the participants tended to be of higher socioeconomic status than the population as a whole. This is a consideration of particular importance in terms of which our analysis must be qualified, for retirement clearly presents serious economic problems for many segments of the population.[3] And it is also important because the various social strata tend to have different standards and attitudes, some of which may enter into the problem of retirement in many important ways.

Other investigators have noted the problems and biases in carrying out longitudinal studies of older people.[4] In a longitudinal study of the employees of a large insurance company, the investigator reported that when a comparison was made of those

[3] See, for example, President's Council on Aging, 1963, pp. 7–11.
[4] For example, C. L. Rose, 1965.

who volunteered and those employees from whom the study population was obtained, it was found that the higher socio-economic levels and the occupationally stable tend to volunteer.

The Cornell Study has the important advantage of being longitudinal in design and analysis and this means that we are able to gather and to report information from the *same* people over a period of approximately seven years. Hence, unlike most other studies in social gerontology, we are able to analyze problems related to process and change.

CHAPTER 4

How and Why
People Retire

To understand the impact of retirement and how people adjust to it, we need to know why people stop working. What retirement means for the individual is affected by the circumstances surrounding retirement. His past experience foreshadows the readjustment the retiree must face and in part determines the way he deals with retirement problems.

The Meaning of Work

One highly significant factor is the cutural myth that work is the most meaningfnl experience in a person's life. The United States has been frequently described as a work-oriented culture. What does this observation mean in terms of the older individual as he approaches retirement and when he becomes a retiree? In answering this question, four major elements must be considered: the structural, the social-psychological, the ideological, and the behavioral.

1. The structural context includes two subdivisions: (a) the macro-social or macro-institutional framework, that is the roles and norms related to economic and political structures, and (b) the micro-environment or the immediate work situation.[1] The macro-institutional framework includes the highly differenti-

---

[1] The distinction between the macro-social and the micro-social in relation to work and occupations is made in Berger, 1964, pp. 227 ff.

ated and complex nature of work as illustrated by the *Dictionary of Occupational Titles,* which lists about 20,000 different titles, reflecting the complexity of the work situation in an industrialized society. Work has many characteristics for thousands of different occupations, ranging from work that is dirty, dull, and repetitive to that which is challenging, creative, and highly interesting. Jobs range from janitor or subway track walker to brain surgeon or president of large industrial corporations. Also involved in the structural aspect is remuneration, which is a reflection of how society values the individual's occupation and also how an employer values the individual.

The micro-environment includes the more immediate aspects of work, particularly in social terms: Does the person work in a small group with congenial colleagues? Or does he work alone in a factory watching dials?

2. The social psychological situation involves the subject's attitudes toward his work, and also involves processes such as socialization into the work role that are more closely related to the functioning individual. How do people perceive their objective work situation? Some may have intrinsically interesting work and disagreeable associates or supervisors; others who do uninteresting work may find psychological gratification in sociable and pleasant surroundings.

3. The ideological considerations are the rationalizations a person or group uses to explain, justify, and integrate the work situation.

4. When the three preceding components are integrated in the individual's experience, they affect both how he adapts, reacts, or copes with the realities of his job and also his readiness to relinquish the work role. Some people adapt easily, no matter what their circumstances, and follow an "orderly career." Of these, some may have a higher involvement in their careers and find retirement upsetting. Other workers experience intermittent or persistent difficulties, and change

jobs often; in short, they have "disorderly careers." [2] They may not have as much invested in their careers, and they also have considerable experience in adapting to new situations, and thus may adjust quickly to the role of retiree.

To speak of a society as being work-oriented is to over-simplify a complex sociological situation. In this study of thousands of older people, it would be difficult to refine the the aggregate data and probe for the specific meaning of each profession or occupation, particularly with a self-administered mail questionnaire. The meaning of his work—in all its variations—is a significant factor in shaping the older person's attitude toward retirement. In this study we realized the importance of this dimension of work—its meaning—as an antecedent variable and at several points in the study, limited information was gathered on this component.

In addition to the meaning of work, a number of other factors influence the diverse views people hold of retirement. For example, the person who retires because of poor health may regard retirement as a welcome release from a demanding, painful work situation. On the other hand, the person in good health who enjoys his work, yet must retire because of company regulations may feel restless, angry, and frustrated. Then there are people who find their work meaningful, yet view retirement positively because they regard it as a "well-deserved rest" with leisure to pursue their special interests.

Retiree Cohorts

The longitudinal nature of this study makes it essential to differentiate the cohorts in the study according to their work or retirement status. Throughout this report the letter R stands for retirement and W stands for gainful employment. All persons in the study were employed (W) at the first contact.

[2] The distinction between orderly and disorderly careers was made in Wilensky, 1961, and has been employed in Simpson et al., 1966, pp. 55–74.

We have grouped the respondents in the following six categories, according to the year they retired:

R'54: those who retired in 1954 and remained retired throughout the rest of the study.

R'56: those who retired after the second contact and before the third, and remained retired.

R'57: those who retired between the third and fourth contact and remained retired.

R'58: those who retired between the fourth and fifth contact and remained retired.

WW'58: those who remained working throughout the study.

RW: those who retired, then went back to work and either stayed working or retired again.

Let us first turn our attention to the retirement patterns of men and women throughout the seven years of the study. The over-all pattern for men and women is remarkably similar. In Table 10 we note that between the first and second contact, about 25 per cent of the men and a slightly smaller percentage of the women retired and remained retired. During each period between the next three contacts, from 10 to 18 per cent of the men and women retired. Thus, at the time of the fifth contact, 61 per cent of the men and 63 per cent of the women had re-

Table 10. Distribution of respondents by sex and retirement category

Sex	R'54	R'56	R'57	R'58	WW'58	RW
Men						
Percentage	25	15	10	11	19	20
Number ($N = 1,486$)	373	216	153	166	282	296
Women						
Percentage	21	14	10	18	19	18
Number ($N = 483$)	103	67	48	87	94	84

$X^2 = 16.83$ / $p < .01$

tired and remained in that status. On the other hand, the same percentage of both men and women (19 per cent) continued working. About a fifth of the men and women did not act in any consistent fashion: they retired and then went back to work, and sometimes retired again.

The data from the study suggest that there was a slight tendency for men to retire at an earlier age than women. This seems to indicate that women who work into the later part of the life cycle—age 60 and beyond—may not differ markedly from men in their work-retirement patterns.

There is substantiating evidence from a study by Palmore, based upon a representative sample of Social Security beneficiaries, which shows that women who have been working for some time by age 65 do not differ in their retirement patterns from men. As Palmore says, "Although women in general have higher retirement rates than men, this particular group of women has a total rate almost as low as men (56 and 54 per cent, respectively). This is probably because they represent those relatively few women who continue to work full time until age 60 or beyond." [3]

Retirement at Age 65

For fifty years the normal retirement age in the United States has been considered to be 65 years. Many pension plans and the Old Age and Survivors' Insurance program have been organized in terms of this arbitrary age. However, many people continue to work past age 65. In this study in which we contacted people one year before "normal" retirement, we found that at age 65 only 41 per cent retired. A more detailed analysis showed that most of these had been employed by private businesses and industrial concerns. Persons who were employed in public service, education, and the professions tended to work beyond 65. The data shown in Table 11 indicate the basis for this generalization. Of the 1,083 men in private industry, 55 per

[3] Palmore, 1965, p. 5.

cent retired at age 65. Two thirds of these were retired because of employer decision and one third because of personal decision.

The tendency of people in private concerns to retire at age 65 is a result of the retirement programs of their employers, which often differ from those in other work contexts. The self-employed professional, for example, has a flexible retirement pattern and often tapers off gradually. People in civil services and public education tend to retire at 70 because their pension plans are geared to that age. Therefore, when we speak of arbitrary retirement at age 65, we are primarily concerned with people working for private business firms.

Voluntary or Administrative Retirement and Attitudes toward Retirement

Two factors are of primary importance concerning why people retire: the company policy, that is, whether or not retirement is mandatory; and the pre-retiree's personal attitude toward retirement.

Many workers have no choice at age 65 as to whether or not they will retire, for their employer specifies 65 as a "com-

Table 11. Men who retired at age 65 and who did not retire, by employment background and retirement decision (in per cent)

Status	Employees in private industry (1,083)	Self-employed physicians (62)	Ministers (83)	Public service employees (333)	Educators (64)
Retired					
Personal decision	18	5	6	12	12
Employer decision	37		2	3	5
Not retired	45	95	92	85	83

Note: The total *N* here varies from that in other tables in the report for some of these men subsequently dropped out of the study.

pulsory" retirement age. These are the people in this study who said that the company, not themselves, said they should stop working. Persons who are subject to formal retirement policies for a given age must retire regardless of their own attitudes, and thus may be retired against their will. However, not *all* persons subject to retirement at a certain chronological age are reluctant to retire; some welcome the step.[4] This fact is often overlooked in discussions of retirement—probably because of the value-laden word "compulsory." In order to avoid the negative overtone of the more common expression, we prefer to call such forms of retirement "administrative retirement." [5]

Not all older people are involved in administrative retirement plans and thus may have some degree of choice as to whether they will stop working. What they actually do is, of course, closely related to their pre-retirement attitude, modified by personal circumstances—economic, health, familial—and the importance of these should not be minimized. Of 896 men in the study, 46 per cent retired voluntarily, and the remainder retired because of administrative decisions. The data show that there is a slight tendency for women to retire because of voluntary action (55 per cent of 305 women in the study) rather than administrative decision.

Table 12 shows the distribution of voluntary and adminis-

[4] George Katona reported in 1965 that a majority of a sample of heads of households aged 35 to 64 looked forward to retirement and only a minority expressed a dread of it (cited by Riley, Foner, *et al.*, 1968, p. 444). In a nationwide poll in the United States conducted by Louis Harris it was found that the younger age categories desired to retire earlier than older persons and the older people were more likely to report that they never desired to retire (*ibid.*, p. 443).

[5] Slavick has made a very careful analysis of the diversity of pension plans and policies. The dichotomy flexible-compulsory is a very simplistic classification. Company size is an important factor to take account of. For example, the larger the company the greater the likelihood of some kind of compulsion in the retirement plan (Slavick, 1966, esp. pp. 35–39).

trative retirees over the five contact periods. The largest proportion of administrative retirees among the men (47 per cent) occurs at age 65, as we would expect, and the next largest number at age 70. In contrast, among the women, the greatest percentage of administrative retirees is found at age 70.

Table 12. Distribution of voluntary and administrative retirees by sex and retirement category (in per cent)

Sex and decision	R'54	R'56	R'57	R'58
Men				
Administrative ($N = 481$)	47	19	13	20
Voluntary ($N = 415$)	34	29	21	15
Women				
Administrative ($N = 138$)	35	16	10	39
Voluntary ($N = 167$)	33	27	20	20

Men: $X^2 = 30.26$ / $p < .001$.
Women: $X^2 = 18.64$ / $p < .001$.

Pre-retirement Attitude

Almost every adult in an industrialized society has some preconceptions of and perhaps prejudices toward retirement. Studies have shown that younger persons tend to be more favorable in their attitudes to retirement than older people. That negative attitudes toward retirement increase with age is probably related to the fact that with increasing age, retirement becomes more personalized, and a positive or negative attitude begins to relate to one's own prospects and expectations.

In this study we devised a measure of attitudes toward retirement which employed a scaling technique.[6] Our measure of pre-retirement willingness or reluctance to retire combines answers to the following questionnaire items:

1. "Some people say that retirement is good for a person, some people say it is bad. In general, what do you think?"

[6] Scaling is discussed in Guttman, 1949.

2. "Do you mostly look forward to the time when you will stop working and retire, or in general, do you dislike the idea?"

3. "If it were up to you alone, would you continue working for your present employer?"

An individual was defined as "willing to retire" if he said he thought retirement was mostly good for a person and was looking forward to it, whether or not he said he would stop working. An individual was defined as "reluctant to retire" if he said he would not stop working and did not look forward to it, whether or not he said retirement was mostly good or mostly bad for a person. This method of dichotomization makes the more specific attitude of looking forward to retirement the crucial indicator.

Table 13. Distribution of 1952 pre-retirement attitude-toward-retirement scores by sex and retirement category (in per cent)

Sex and attitude	R'54	R'56	R'57	R'58	WW'58	RW
Men						
Willing ($N = 544$)	40	17	8	8	8	19
Reluctant ($N = 942$)	17	13	12	13	25	20
Women						
Willing ($N = 139$)	43	14	5	9	6	22
Reluctant ($N = 344$)	13	14	12	21	25	16

Men: $X^2 = 142.86$ / $p < .001$.   Women: $X^2 = 75.42$ / $p < .001$.

In short, the prospective retiree holds certain expectations about retirement which he evaluates in a particular way and this evaluation is the basis for his desire to follow one of several alternative courses of action. Persons who are favorably disposed toward retirement view it as a positive goal and those who are negative regard it as a course of action to be avoided.

We had anticipated that men would be less willing to retire than women, since, traditionally, work for wages is a more integral part of their life role. We found, surprisingly, that a larger percentage of male respondents (37 per cent of 1,486 men) were willing to retire than were the women in the study (29 per cent of 483 women).

Now let us turn our attention to the patterns of retirement of our respondents at various phases of the study in relation to their pre-retirement attitude. Turning to Table 13, we find that about equal proportions of men and women (40 and 43 per cent) who were willing to retire actually retired at age 65 and stayed retired for the duration of the study. Conversely, a much smaller percentage of reluctant retirees actually retired at age 65 and remained retired (17 and 13 per cent).

At the three other points in which our respondents retired, there are smaller differences between those who were willing to retire and those who were reluctant to retire. Note, for example, that among the men who retired in 1956, 17 per cent in the willing category retired in comparison to 13 per cent of reluctant retirees and among the men who retired in 1957 and 1958, there was a slightly larger percentage of reluctant retirees than willing retirees. A similar pattern prevails for the women. The most striking difference is observed among those persons, both men and women, who worked throughout the entire seven years of the study (WW′58). Here again we note the importance of attitude toward retirement when it comes to actual retirement. For example, among the men, 25 per cent of the reluctants were still working, while only 8 per cent of the willing retirees were, and an even larger percentage difference is found among the women.

The complexity of the relationship between pre-retirement attitude and actual behavior (retirement) is shown by the way in which pre-retirement attitude is associated with whether one went back to work after retirement. Table 13 shows that similar proportions of both willing and reluctant retirees returned to work at some time during the six years after the initial contact. In summary, the reluctant retirees were more likely to retire later, or to keep working.

The Retiree Typology

In order to clarify the complex way in which a cohort of 65-year-old workers may be sorted into a variety of types as a consequence of their attitudes, their situational alternatives, and their behavior, we have prepared a flow chart (Figure 1). At the bottom of the chart is a classification of six retiree types at age 66.

In the following analysis we shall consider the retirees in terms of the two variables: whether the person or his organization determined retirement and whether his attitude was willing or reluctant. Therefore we have four types: willing-voluntary, willing-administrative, reluctant-voluntary, and reluctant-administrative. Table 14 shows the typology for the 1,194 men and women retirees in the study.

Table 14. Distribution of the four retiree types by sex

	Willing				Reluctant			
	Voluntary		Administrative		Voluntary		Administrative	
Sex	%	No.	%	No.	%	No.	%	No.
Men (N = 896)	29	261	22	193	17	154	32	288
Women (N = 298)	30	89	13	40	25	74	32	95

$X^2 = 5.07 \ / \ p < .05$

Comparing the men and the women, we find that equal proportions are found in the two largest categories of our typology—the willing-voluntary and the reluctant-administrative. The difference between the sexes appears in the other two types: in the willing-administrative we find a larger proportion of men, and in the reluctant-voluntary women are the larger proportion. Looking at men and women in regard to attitude to retirement, we find that women are more reluctant to retire

Figure 1. Prospects and behavior at age 65 with regard to work and retirement

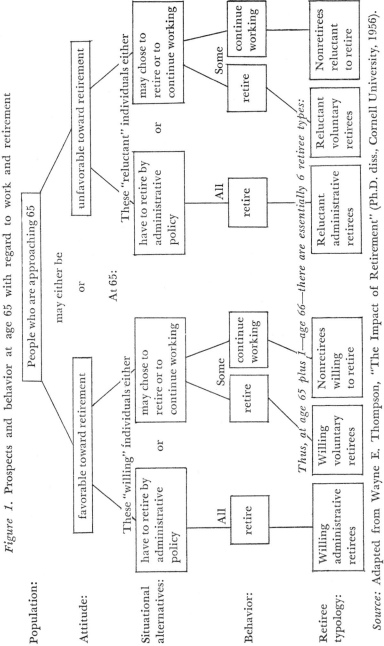

Source: Adapted from Wayne E. Thompson, "The Impact of Retirement" (Ph.D. diss., Cornell University, 1956).

than men. Among all the women retirees, 57 per cent were reluctant retirees compared to 49 per cent of the men.

These findings are contrary to what we would have predicted; we anticipated that a larger percentage of men than women would have been reluctant voluntary retirees. We assumed that, in American society, men are more devoted to the work role and women, having a homemaker role as an alternate possibility, would be more willing to retire. The fact that these predictions are not borne out leads to two speculations. First, perhaps many men are not as devoted to work per se as we had anticipated and perhaps the importance of the work role has been exaggerated for those with tedious jobs. Second, perhaps the women who are still in the labor force at age 65 are those who have consciously chosen the work role, for those who did not desire to work could have found ways to remain in the homemaker role.

In Table 15 we see the result of cross-tabulations for both men and women who retired at the four research contact points. Among the men, the willing retirees are almost equally divided between voluntary and administrative categories at age 65 (R'54) and age 70 (R'58). In the interim years, more than twice as many of the willing retirees retired voluntarily than administratively. For the women, however, among the persons who were willing to retire, from two to three times as many retired voluntarily as administratively during all phases of the study.

Another pattern which can only be observed with longitudinal data of this kind is that persons who hold unfavorable attitudes to retirement are increasingly apt to retire voluntarily as time passes. We infer from our general knowledge of the aging process that these reluctant retirees are probably declining in health and this may force them to retire in spite of their hostile attitudes.

The pattern of reluctant voluntary retirement among the women is somewhat different from that of the men. We find the

Table 15. Relationship of situational alternative and attitude,
by sex and retirement category

Category and attitude	Men			Women		
	Volun. (%)	Admin. (%)	Total (No.)	Volun. (%)	Admin. (%)	Total (No.)
R'54 willing	49	51	216	67	33	60
R'54 reluctant	24	76	153	28	72	39
R'56 willing	71	29	108	76	24	25
R'56 reluctant	43	57	106	63	37	41
R'57 willing	69	31	83	74	26	19
R'57 reluctant	45	55	68	69	31	29
R'58 willing	53	47	47	64	36	25
R'58 reluctant	38	62	115	28	72	60
Total willing	57	43	454	69	31	129
Total reluctant	35	65	442	44	56	169

Total men: $X^2 = 45.29$ / $p < .001$.
Total women: $X^2 = 17.75$ / $p < .001$.

initial percentage of female reluctant voluntary retirees is approximately equal to that of the men, but in the third and fourth contact (R'56 and R'57) the percentage of voluntary reluctant retirees among the women more than doubles. In the fifth and final contact point, it drops back to the original proportion. Among the men the percentage increases, but not quite as much as for the women.

Marital Status of Women and Retirement

Table 16 presents the distribution of women by marital status and retirement categories. We would have expected that married women living with their spouses would be the group most likely to withdraw from the labor force. However, we note that the group that retired in 1954 at age 65 contains an even larger percentage of single women. In fact, twice as many single women retired as widows. We can conclude that the exigencies of widowhood resulted in economic pressure to continue working that the single woman who has worked throughout her life has not faced. Furthermore, the single woman, who may have planned throughout her life for her retirement, faces a different prospect upon retirement than the widow, who has been supported by a husband throughout most of her life. This situation is described by our data for those women who continued to work and those who re-entered the labor force. Looking at the right side of Table 16, we note that a larger percentage of widows and divorced women continued to work throughout the study or returned to the labor force after retirement than was the case for the single and married women.

Table 16. Distribution of women respondents by marital status and retirement category (in per cent)

Status	R'54	R'56	R'57	R'58	WW'58	RW
Married ($N = 101$)	26	19	11	14	16	14
Widowed ($N = 176$)	14	15	10	16	24	21
Divorced or separated ($N = 52$)	19	6	4	27	25	27
Single ($N = 149$)	28	13	11	21	15	11

$X^2 = 30.93 \; / \; p < .01$

The early and continued retirement of married and single women cannot be explained by saying that they are more likely to be subject to administrative retirement at some fixed time, for Table 17 shows that both married and single women are more likely to retire voluntarily than are widowed or divorced women. The differences between the categories are not large but are suggestive. The complexities of the interrelationships between objective circumstances (economic conditions, marital status, etc.) and the subjective definition people may place on these circumstances is again pointed out by the data in Table 18 in which the pre-retirement attitude of the marital status categories are indicated. We find that the single women are the most willing to retire (43 per cent) and that the married and widowed women are the least willing to retire (24 per cent and 20 per cent).

Table 17. Distribution of voluntary and administrative women retirees by marital status (in per cent)

Status	Voluntary	Administrative
Married ($N = 71$)	61	39
Widowed ($N = 97$)	53	47
Divorced or separated ($N = 27$)	55	45
Single ($N = 109$)	58	42

Table 18. Distribution of women's pre-retirement attitude scores by marital status (in per cent)

Status	Willing	Reluctant
Married ($N = 101$)	24	76
Widowed ($N = 176$)	20	80
Divorced or separated ($N = 52$)	29	71
Single ($N = 149$)	43	57

Why do single women want to retire? We can only conjecture by way of explanation. Many have been working all their lives. Not all of their jobs have been interesting. Probably many have made new economic and household arrangement plans; in contrast, the married women are more likely to have continuity of domestic arrangements. The single women have probably had a lifetime desire to stop work eventually, or they may have experienced a decline in health which made disengagement from work seem desirable. Also, retirement may provide a final chance to engage in domesticity and leisure pursuits which the married woman has engaged in all her life and taken for granted. We cannot assume that work is the central life focus of the single woman. Given a choice, some would prefer the married, nonworking status to the single, career status.

A comparative analysis was made of 141 matched pairs of willing and reluctant female retirees in the Cornell Retirement Study.[7] The respondents were matched on five characteristics: marital status, number of children, subjective health, income, and outside sources of income. The reluctant women retirees are more likely to say they want to continue working because they enjoy their work. The willing retirees, on the other hand, are five times as likely to say they plan to stop work to enjoy more leisure time and to say they have made plans for retirement. Willingness or reluctance to retire among women is also related to health conditions, and we find that our index of self-reported health shows that the willing retirees are not as healthy as are the reluctant retirees.

These attitudes toward work and retirement are probably related in complex and interdependent ways with one's physical condition. Again, the detailed analysis of 141 matched pairs of women in the Cornell Study shows the willing retirees are more than twice as apt to report they tire easily than are the reluctant retirees. Similarly, the willing are more likely to report they were able to work better at age 50 than the reluctant. These self-reports must be interpreted in the context of other information; for example, the willing retiree is more likely to report (48 per cent) that physical strength is not important on her job than the reluctant retiree (41 per cent).

Occupational Status

We next turn to an analysis of the relationship between occupational status and retirement patterns. Our work was directed by the commonly accepted sociological proposition that differences in occupational status are correlated with varying attitudes and behavior. Upper white-collar and professional

[7] Schneider, 1964, pp. 66, 134–139.

workers are generally more committed to their work and derive more satisfaction from it than do blue-collar workers. Thus, we would anticipate that those who have higher status occupations would be more reluctant to retire because of the importance of the role attached to the position. The "cost" of retiring would be too great. As Table 19 indicates, it is clearly the professional type who remains working, at least among the men. While 42 per cent of the professional men remained working throughout the study and another fourth of them retired at some time but went back to work, 40 per cent of the managers and officials and about half of all other workers retired during the first two time periods and stayed retired. Among the women there is a tendency for the professional types and the managers and officials to remain working longer or to return to work in greater proportions than among other occupations. But the

Table 19. Distribution of respondents by occupational type, sex, and retirement category (in per cent)

Sex and occupational type	R'54	R'56	R'57	R'58	WW'58	RW
Men *						
Professionals (N = 276) †	7	5	6	14	42	26
Managers, officials (N = 190)	29	11	8	11	20	21
White-collar, skilled, and kindred workers (N = 546)	30	17	10	10	16	17
Unskilled, semiskilled, and service workers (N = 451)	28	19	13	11	10	19
Women						
Professionals (N = 166) ‡	21	8	9	22	18	22
Managers, officials (N = 28)	14	10	4	18	36	18
White-collar, skilled, and kindred workers (N = 176)	18	17	13	14	25	14
Unskilled, semiskilled, and service workers (N = 100)	29	18	10	17	10	16

* Total: $X^2 = 186.89$ / $p < .001$.
† Professional vs. all other: $X^2 = 167.24$ / $p. < .001$.
‡ Professional vs. all other: $X^2 = 12.73$ / $p < .05$.

pattern is not as clear as for the men. We note that a higher proportion of professional women retire than do professional men. Women in white-collar jobs retire in the same proportions as the corresponding groups of the men, but women leave the labor force later, as we have seen.

Conversely, we would expect that men in the lower occupations would be more likely to express a willingness to retire than persons in higher occupational categories. Turning to Table 20 we observe, however, that the white-collar males are the "most willing" to retire, followed by the skilled workers and the managers, and finally the unskilled workers. The professionals, are the least willing to retire, as we would expect. Among the women, however, the professional and managerial workers were the most likely to be scored willing to retire, with the others more or less equally unlikely to be so scored.

Table 20. Distribution of those classed as "willing to retire" in 1952, by sex and selected occupation (in per cent)

Sex	Professional	Managerial	Other white-collar	Skilled	Unskilled
Men	27	39	45	40	35
Women	37	39	24	19	26

$X^2 = 209.96$ / $p < .001$

Income

Let us now examine retirement patterns according to income level. Table 21 shows two categories of wage earners: those with pre-retirement incomes of $65 a week and more, and those with incomes of less than that amount. The data in the table indicate little relation between the year of retirement and income level. Among the males there is a slight tendency for those with a lower income level to retire later. Among the women, there is a differential in the reverse direction with the lower income women more apt to retire early.

Table 21. Income distribution of respondents by sex and
retirement category (in per cent)

Sex and income	R'54	R'56	R'57	R'58	WW'58	RW
Men						
$65/week or more (N = 1,160)	26	15	10	10	20	20
Less than $65/week (N = 322)	20	14	13	16	18	19
Women						
$65/week or more (N = 215)	20	9	10	22	19	20
Less than $65/week (N = 268)	23	17	10	15	20	15

Men: $X^2 = 14.68$ / $p < .02$.   Women: $X^2 = 13.22$ / $p < .05$.

We were also interested in the relationship between subjective income and retirement patterns. We asked the respondents whether they thought their pre-retirement income was
sufficient to meet their needs. In Table 22, data are presented
for men and women by subjective income classification and
retirement cohort. It is interesting to note that in the total
group of respondents—both male and female—79 per cent
stated that their income was adequate. The data in Table 22
show a slight tendency for persons to retire at age 65 if they
considered their income to be enough. The small differences
in each cohort between those who judged their income as adequate and those who did not shows that subjective income is a
minor factor in the decision to retire or to continue working.

Table 22. Distribution of subjective income by sex and
retirement category (in per cent)

Sex and income	R'54	R'56	R'57	R'58	WW'58	RW
Men						
Income is enough (N = 1,171)	26	15	9	11	19	20
Income is not enough (N = 315)	22	13	14	12	19	18
Women						
Income is enough (N = 382)	23	14	9	17	20	17
Income is not enough (N = 101)	15	14	14	21	17	20

Men: $X^2 = 9.55$ / $p < .10$.   Women: $X^2 = 6.17$ / $p < .30$.

More important are such factors as health or retirement because of administrative procedures.

Education

If we assume that individuals with a higher level of education are more likely to be psychologically involved in their occupations, then we hypothesize that employees with a higher education level would tend to continue working longer or go back to work if they were retired. The information in Table 23 indicates that the more highly educated respondents do remain at work longer than those with less education. Some professionals may work longer because they are in a better position to control their work situation. For example, physicians, lawyers, and professors can often transfer their skills to a new setting. The trend to continue working is particularly strong among men. More than half of those who had some college education worked during practically all of the study period (33 per cent did not stop working and 27 per cent returned to work after retiring). These tendencies are not as noticeable among the women.

Assuming that a higher level of education tends to be as-

Table 23. Distribution of respondents by educational level, sex, and retirement category (in per cent)

Sex and education	R'54	R'56	R'57	R'58	WW'58	RW
Men						
Grade school or less (N = 601)	34	18	12	10	10	15
At least some high school or						
business college (N = 442)	25	15	10	12	18	19
At least some college (N = 430)	12	9	7	12	33	27
Women						
Grade school or less (N = 101)	27	21	11	11	16	14
At least some high school or						
business college (N = 176)	19	18	7	17	25	15
At least some college (N = 206)	20	7	12	23	17	21

Men: $X^2 = 158.21$ / $p < .001$.   Women: $X^2 = 29.82$ / $p < .001$.

sociated with a more rewarding occupation, there is support for our broad hypothesis. However, this role analysis—linking education, job involvement, and the wish to work—does not apply to the older women in this study. We interpret our data as suggesting that women in higher level occupations tend to work for governmental and educational organizations whose retirement policies permit later retirement. Moreover, as pointed out earlier, those women who continue to work, or who return to a job after retirement, are predominantly widowed or divorced, and the complicating experience of widowhood or divorce result in a different orientation to the work role and the trajectory concerning working or retiring.

Summary

It might be helpful to summarize some of the situational and attitudinal factors which we have considered in relation to time patterns of working or retiring. There is some indication that the men retire earlier than the women, especially if they are retired by their companies. There seem to be two retirement foci: at age 65 and age 70 for both men and women voluntary retirees and for women administrative retirees, and at age 65 for male administrative retirees.

There is a tendency for both men and women with higher incomes, more education, and higher status occupations to continue working longer during the period under study. Among the women, single women and married women living with their spouses tend to retire earlier than widows and those who are either divorced or separated from their husbands. As we might expect, those respondents who tell us they are "willing to retire" actually tend to retire early, whereas those who say they are "reluctant to retire" tend to continue working or to retire later.

We saw in Table 10 that the work pattern for the men was similar to that of the women. Yet there are some interesting differences between the two groups even at this stage of analysis.

Among the women, the proportion of professionals is almost twice the proportion of men who are professionals. A higher proportion of women than men have at least some college education. The women earn less money from their jobs, but they are as satisfied with the amount they make as the men are. Nine per cent more women than men say they are "voluntary" retirees, yet 8 per cent fewer of the women are "willing to retire."

Table 24. Selected comparisons between men and women (in per cent)

Characteristics	Men (1,486)	Women (483)
Retirement characteristics		
Retired during the study	61	63
Were "willing to retire"	37	29
Retired "voluntarily"	46	55
Socioeconomic factors		
Had at least some college	29	43
Received over $65/week	78	44
Reported "enough" income	79	79

In Table 24, comparisons of men and women for retirement characteristics and socioeconomic status are presented.

In this chapter we have offered some descriptive information about our major independent variables and have shown the influence of some of these variables upon the length of work life. We shall now look at these variables as they change over time and see how they are influenced by change in work status.

CHAPTER 5

The Influence of Retirement on Physical Health

While health and illness are topics of major interest to persons at all stages of the life cycle, these subjects may take on even greater meaning for the aged. Indeed, the most character-istic universal feature of old age is the striking changes which take place in the structure and function of the body. There is usually a decline in strength, a reduction in speed and agility in motor activities, impairment of the senses of sight and hearing, and lowered resistance to disease. The illusory search for the fountain of youth by those of earlier days is matched today by the tremendous interest of the young and old in the gradual conquest by scientific means of the conditions and diseases which affect the middle-aged and old.

It is popularly assumed that retirement leads to a decline in physical well-being, for everyone knows of at least one person whose health deteriorated or who died suspiciously soon after retiring. The notion of this kind of relationship between re-tirement and health has gained credence among some profes-sional students of gerontology. The organism becomes adapted to certain behavior patterns—so the argument runs—and the loss of such sustaining patterns through retirement leads to, or at least precipitates, physiological collapse. The abrupt change of activities and pace at retirement, it is contended, contributes to a physiological disruption of major importance. This point of view is particularly stressed in the "activity" approaches to successful aging.[1]

Frequently cited in support of this hypothesis are cross-sectional studies which find a disproportionate incidence of poor health among retirees as compared with the gainfully employed. However, more analytical re-examination of these mortality and morbidity tables by some writers suggests the possibility that the causal sequence may be the reverse. McMahan and Ford, after their analysis, write: "it cannot be concluded that the 'impact of retirement' shortened the life expectancy of the population." [2] And Myers concludes that people in poor health retire and that is why retirees die.[3] In other words, mortality and morbidity statistics among the recently retired population may contain a disproportionate percentage of people who chose to retire or were retired *because* of their poor health. Clearly, a comparison of the incidence of poor health and mortality among the retired and the working is not sufficient to establish the reasons for any differences which might be found.

Indicators of Health

In an analysis of behavior, the principal focus of interest typically is the actor, and correct understanding must involve considering as a foremost datum his orientation to the context of his action—his own evaluation of the situation in which he finds himself. A discussion of the relationship of health and retirement, then, must take the retiree's own evaluation of his health as a prime datum. Our measure of health is based on the respondent's evaluation of the state of his own health. It is therefore perhaps not restricted to actual physiological health. The same measure was used in each phase of the study. It is a combined measure made up of three items which relate in a Guttman scaler pattern yielding a four-point score:

[1] See Hamlin, 1967, and Havighurst, 1961.
[2] McMahan and Ford, 1965, p. 215.   [3] Myers, 1954.

1. "How would you rate your health at the present time?" (Positive response: good, excellent.)

2. "Do you have any particular physical or health problems at present?" (Positive response: no.)

3. "Have you been seen by a doctor during the past year?" (Positive response: no.) [4]

The items are arranged in order from item one, which received the largest number of "good health" responses (i.e., "good" or "excellent"), to item three, which received the fewest ("no"). We consider the measure to include, first, a general subjective evaluation of one's health; second, a more specific reporting of the facts of one's health; and third, something of a specific behavioral expression about the state of one's health. It is clearly, however, a subjective self-evaluation measure.

We divided the respondents' scores into two categories: (a) "good health," that is, those who not only said their health was "good" or "excellent" but also reported having no physical or health problems, whether or not they said they saw a doctor;

---

[4] The third item leaves us with some ambiguity. We do not know whether having been seen by a doctor is an indication of a real illness or simply a routine check-up. For this reason we chose to use the scale in a form which would utilize the negative response to item three. *Not* having been seen by a doctor most probably means for our respondents that they have no health problems worth troubling a doctor about. Reproducibility and error ratios were computed at the following times and for the following groups:

Women:	1952	WW'58, R'56, R'57, R'58	R: .97	ER: .46
	1952	R'54	R: .97	ER: .42
	1954	WW'58, R'56, R'57, R'58	R: .97	ER: .38
	1954	R'54	R: .97	ER: .33
Men:	1952	All groups	R: .95	ER: .54
	1954	All groups	R: .96	ER: .57
	1956	All groups	R: .96	ER: .47

At the time the coefficients were computed for the men the scale included an additional item at one extreme. The exclusion of this item in later years did not affect the scalability of the other three items. For a discussion of scaling see Guttman, 1949.

and (b) "poor health," that is, those who not only said they had a physical or health problem, but also reported having been seen by a doctor, whether or not they said their health was "good" or "poor." This makes the crucial item the one concerned with a specific health problem.[5]

We have said that other studies show that poor health itself may *lead* to retirement; our data tend to confirm this in Table 25. If we compare the 1952 health scores of the respondents in the various retirement categories, we see some

Table 25. Distribution of 1952 subjective health scores by sex and retirement category (in per cent)

Sex and health	R'54	R'56	R'57	R'58	WW'58	RW
Men						
Good ($N = 961$)	24	14	11	12	20 *	20
Poor ($N = 525$)	28	15	10	10	16	20
Women						
Good ($N = 355$)	20	15	8	19	22 *	16
Poor ($N = 128$)	26	10	16	14	13	20

Men: $X^2 = 6.25$ / $p < .30$.   Women: $X^2 = 15.39$ / $p < .01$.
* Significant at $p = .05$ difference between good and poor health in WW'58.

indication that those persons in good health tend in slightly higher proportions than those in poor health to work all the way through the study without retiring.

[5] Schematically the dichotomization looks like this ($+$ means the "good health" response to the item; $-$ means the "poor health" response to the item):

	item		
	1	2	3
"good health"	+	+	+
	+	+	−
"poor health"	+	−	−
	−	−	−

The Impact of Retirement on Health

Now we are in a position to ask: Does retirement lead to poor health? Longitudinal data can offer us a more convincing picture than a cross-sectional study. The hypothesis we seek to test here is that, in general, *retirement leads to a decline in health.* Our test of this hypothesis will be comparisons not merely of the incidence of poor health among the retired and the working, but more specifically of changes in the incidence of poor health among men and women who retire in contrast to men and women of the same age who continue in gainful employment. In other words, given a certain condition of health among people of the same age group who are gainfully em-

Table 26. The over-all effect of retirement on subjective health scores by sex and retirement category (in per cent scored in "good health")

Sex and year	R'54	R'56	R'57	R'58	WW'58	Total
Men	(373)	(216)	(153)	(166)	(282)	(1,190)
1952	**60**	62	67	68	69	65
1954	**58**	**59**	65	62	66	62
1956	56	**49**	**52**	**55**	63	56
1958	55	52	**52**	**54**	65	57
Women	(103)	(67)	(48)	(87)	(94)	(399)
1952	**68**	81	56	79	82	74
1954	**69**	**67**	54	72	75	69
1956	65	**52**	**50**	**63**	69	61
1958	68	48	**52**	**68**	64	61

Note: Crucial before and after comparisons, showing percentages before retirement and in the year of retirement, appear in boldface.

ployed, is a decline in health more likely among those who retire than among those who continue working? [6]

Using the self-evaluative measure of health which we have just described and comparing the different categories of our respondents, we find that, for the most part, a majority of both men and women say they are in good health both at the beginning of the study and at its end (Table 26). First, looking at the broad health picture at two-year intervals, we find that among both the men and the women there is a moderate decline over time in self-evaluation of health. At the first contact in 1952 approximately two-thirds of the men and almost three-fourths of the women were classified as being in good health. At the end of this period, the men reporting good health had declined to 57 per cent and the women declined to 61 per cent. Thus, the picture of self-evaluated health at ages 64 and 70 on an aggregate basis does not seem to be one of general disability.[7]

The data do show that those people who worked throughout the study have the largest percentage of self-reported good health of any group in the study. We also noticed that in the initial year of contact, before retirement, there was a slight tendency for those groups who later retired at 70 or were still at work at 70 to have a larger proportion of persons in good

[6] For the purpose of the analysis that follows, we have decided not to use the respondents who retired and went back to work. The numbers in each category become quite small and the data are hard to interpret. An analysis of retirees who return to work is found in Chapter 11.

[7] We have used as a measure of change the net result of changes. It should be clear to the reader that there are internal changes in the groups. We are saying, for example, that more individuals in R'57 changed from good to poor health than changed from poor to good health between the years 1954 and 1956, with the result that in 1956 the proportion of those · scored in good health is lower than it was in 1954. We did not analyze the changers and compare them with the nonchangers, for the number of cases in some cells was too small for meaningful analysis.

health. However, at the last contact we observed that the percentage of persons in good health is approximately the same for all retirement categories. Indeed, the first cohort of retirees (R'54) have the highest percentage of self-reported good health in 1956 and in 1958.

Turning to the women in the study, we find the trends concerning health scores over time are quite variable. For example, the 1954 retirees have exactly the same proportion of persons in good health in 1952 and, six years later, in 1958. On the other hand, other cohorts show substantial changes over time. Among the 1956 retirees, for example, 81 per cent reported good health at the time of the initial contact in 1952, but only 48 per cent reported good health in 1958—a decline of 33 per cent. In contrast, in the next cohort 56 per cent reported themselves in good health in 1952 and 52 per cent reported it in 1958—a decline of only 4 per cent. It is also interesting to note that among the women who worked throughout the study, there is a steady decline in the proportion who report themselves in good health—from 82 per cent in 1952 to 64 per cent in 1958. The kinds of information which we have available do not permit us to interpret these differences, although some analysts might emphasize the smaller number of cases in the female categories.

If our data are any indication of a general trend, then we might say that there is a comparative stabilization of health in the vicinity of 69 or 70 years of age. We see also that, although slightly more women than men are scored in good health at all time periods, the women show more change and variability than the men.

We have seen that age itself seems to carry with it some decline in health. However, we are interested specifically in net changes in the proportion of those in good health occurring between the time just before retirement and the time just after. These figures are shown in boldface in Table 26. Thus, for R'54 in Table 26, the crucial comparison is between 1952 and 1954; for R'56, the crucial comparison is between 1954 and 1956, and so forth. If we compare the net change in the retirement categories at the crucial before-after periods with the net changes that occur in the WW'58 category or in the retirement categories at the noncrucial times, we find that the *act of retiring* from the work force seems to make no *distinctive difference* in the proportion of those who report themselves in good health. For example, as Table 26 shows, while R'56 males show a net decline of 10 per cent in the proportion of those who say they are in good health between 1954 when they were working and 1956 when they were retired, R'57 males show a 13 per cent decline between 1954 and 1956 even though they were working at both times.

These data show that those persons who are working at any two points in the study report as much or more health change as do those who were working at one point and retired at the next point. The common notion that retirement has a depressing effect on health may surely be questioned.[8] This observation holds not only regarding the immediate effect of retirement but also for the later stages of retirement, as a comparison of the health scores of the R'54 in 1956 and 1958 shows.

Health Appraisal—Before and after Retirement

We would like at this time to examine how our respondents themselves view the effect of retirement upon their health. Do they come to the same conclusion that we do? We saw that although there was a decrease in the proportion of those who gave a favorable evaluation of their physical health as time went on,

[8] A very carefully conducted study in England (Martin and Doran, 1966) reported similar findings. In fact, the investigators concluded that "retirement is associated with a substantial lowering in the incidence of serious illness."

this could not be attributed to retirement itself. How do our respondents evaluate the impact of retirement on their health condition?

We asked those respondents who retired the direct question: "Do you think stopping work has made your health better or worse?" We find that the majority of respondents, both men and women, say that stopping work made no change in their health. (Table 27). Moreover, very few (never more than 6 per cent) say that retirement has made their health *worse*. Surprisingly enough, in view of the fact that the net result of aging indicated a decline in health through the years, fully 20 to 40 per cent say that stopping work has made their health better. Whatever else this means, it seems clear that our subjects themselves do not attribute a decline in health to retirement.

Table 27. Subjective evaluation of the effect of retirement upon health (in per cent responding to the question "Do you think stopping work has made your health better or worse?")

Year and evaluation	Men				Women			
	R'54 (373)	R'56 (216)	R'57 (153)	R'58 (166)	R'54 (103)	R'56 (67)	R'57 (48)	R'58 (87)
1954								
Better	32				40			
Worse	3				2			
No change	65				57			
Total	100				99			
1956								
Better	38	33			39	33		
Worse	5	5			3	4		
No change	57	62			58	60		
Total	100	100			100	97		
1958								
Better	33	33	27	22	30	35	29	22
Worse	4	5	6	3	1	3	0	1
No change	63	62	65	73	68	60	69	75
Total	100	100	98	98	99	98	98	98

Because we have the same respondents both before and after retirement, we can ask them before retirement what they think the effect of retirement will be and compare this to what they say after retirement. At one of the study periods, 1956, we asked a series of questions about the probable effects of retirement. We asked those respondents who were still working in 1956 (that is, R'57, R'58, and WW'58) what they thought stopping work would do to their health. Their responses are shown in Table 28. A majority of those who do commit themselves say it will make no difference. A number of them (from 7 to 27 per cent) think it will make their health better, and

Table 28. Pre-retirement evaluation of the effect of retirement upon health (in per cent responding to the question "Do you think stopping work would make your health better or worse?")

	Men			Women		
1956 evaluation	R'57 (153)	R'58 (166)	WW'58 (282)	R'57 (48)	R'58 (87)	WW'58 (94)
Better	27	11	9	21	14	7
Worse	9	18	26	6	7	7
No difference	39	45	41	48	61	64
I don't know	25	26	24	25	18	22
Total	100	100	100	100	100	100

Men: $X^2 = 40.10$ / $p < .001$.   Women: $X^2 = 7.43$ / $p < .30$.

about the same over-all proportions think it will make their health worse. From 18 to 26 per cent say they do not know. However, there is quite clearly a relationship between a negative view of the effects of retirement and length of work life. Those who foresee negative effects stay at work longer. Twenty-six per cent of the men in WW'58 say that retirement will make their health worse, while only 9 per cent of R'57 and 18 per cent of R'58 do so. The women are generally more optimistic since no more than 7 per cent of any group say retirement will make their health worse.

We can now compare pre-retirement and post-retirement evaluations of the effect of retirement upon health for groups R'57 and R'58 (Table 29). A large majority seem to have had a fairly accurate idea of what retirement would do to their health. We note that about a quarter of the respondents were unwilling to make any prediction about the influence of retirement on their health. These persons probably had a variety of motivations. Perhaps they did not want to "tempt fate" by asserting an optimistic view of their future health. We note that in the follow-up survey, most of these people said retirement had made no change in their health.

It seems equally clear that a sizable number of the respondents overestimated the adverse effects of retirement, and very few underestimated these effects. For example: 18 per cent of the men in R'58 had said in 1956 before retirement that they thought retirement would make their health worse, and only

Table 29. A comparison of pre- and post-retirement evaluations of the effect of retirement upon health (in per cent responding to the statements)

Pre-retirement (1956): Stopping work *would* make my health			Post-retirement (1958): Stopping work *has* made my health		
Response	R'57	R'58	Response	R'57	R'58
Men	(153)	(166)	Men	(153)	(166)
Better	27	11	Better	27	22
Worse	9	18	Worse	6	3
No difference	39	45	No change	65	73
I don't know	25	26	No answer	2	2
Total	100	100	Total	100	100
Women	(48)	(87)	Women	(48)	(87)
Better	21	14	Better	29	22
Worse	6	7	Worse	0	1
No difference	48	61	No change	69	75
I don't know	25	18	No answer	2	2
Total	100	100	Total	100	100

3 per cent said in 1958 after retirement that it *did* make their health worse. In the same way, 11 per cent of R'58 predicted that retirement would improve their health, and twice as many reported in 1958 that it did improve their health. The pattern for the women is very similar to that of the men.

Retiree Reports

Statistical generalizations cannot give the reader the nuances of meaning and feeling which quotations and life-history material can offer. Therefore we shall employ data gathered in a follow-up field study in which the senior author interviewed a random sample of fifty participants, some of whom had been retired five years or more. The field study, in addition to giving us illustrative materials, also enabled us to validate on a small scale some of the findings resulting from the analysis of the questionnaire data. The over-all optimistic view of post-retirement health which had been obtained from the survey made us question whether there might have been bias toward a response set or unwillingness to admit difficulty in adjusting to retirement. Were the retirees really more depressed, sick, and lonely than they indicated.

The field follow-up revealed that the questionnaire materials were indeed reflecting quite accurately the condition of the respondents. In the fifty interviews, not one retiree indicated that his health had deteriorated since retirement. Several cases had been forced to retire abruptly because of heart attacks and other serious medical conditions, but all of them reported that they "felt better." Several even considered seeking work again. Quotes from four respondents in poor health illustrate their feelings. One man said:

I can't say I'm crazy about retirement. I would not have retired if I was well—I would work. While I can do just what I like now, I'd rather be well and working. I think Reuther is wrong about the four-day week. Even though work is not pleasant, it is the most enjoyable thing that I know. When I first retired, I'd just lie around

—that's all I could do. Now I watch a lot of TV. Then I do some housework and cooking. But I'd rather be working.

Another stated:

Retirement is all right if you have got your health. Mine is not too good—I had a coronary and I have arthritis. I have to take it easy. I can't mow the lawn or shovel snow. I have a garden and work in it some. Then I watch the ball games and take a nap every afternoon. I read more and wash the car—only now my wife helps. I do little repair jobs with my tools sometimes. I get up later in the morning—that's nice, especially in the winter.

Another respondent was more positive:

I just retired. I went to the hospital May 19 and when I got out and went back to the plant, they told me since I was 68, it was time to retire. I think this is fine—I am ready to retire. It means taking it easy. Getting up when I want. Eating breakfast when I want. I like it. A man can't work all the time.

And finally, a man who had just recovered from a stroke, stated:

I have the Lord and nice people on my side. What more could I want? I don't have any difficulty keeping busy. I do some painting and plumbing. I'll tackle anything. You can't just sit around. I'll look up my insurance contacts from when I used to sell a little insurance and see if I can make a little money on that. My wife is only 56. She may have to go to work. I will do the housework and learn how to cook. My problem is that I'll have to learn to slow down.

In two of these cases, retirement was viewed with some distaste, but it should be emphasized that it occurred suddenly with no chance for preparation and was inextricably bound up with a health crisis. In the last two cases, the respondents were "counting their blessings" and feeling fortunate to be alive rather than railing against retirement.

Health and Occupational Status

It has been contended that occupational status may be a crucial factor in the health of older workers and retirees. Therefore, it will be interesting to examine the changes in health over time for the various male retirement cohorts holding occupation constant. In Table 30 the data are presented for six occupational categories—from the top, middle, and bottom of the prestige ladder.

First, comparing the six occupational categories, we find that in every instance a larger proportion of people who would be continuing to work for the next six years reported themselves in good health in 1952 than those who actually retired in 1954. The percentage difference between the retired (R'54) and the working category ranged from 2–15 per cent. There was no consistent pattern of difference between blue-collar and white-collar workers. When we look at the data for the final year of the study, we find that, again, in every occupational category, the percentage of persons who reported themselves in good health was larger in the working category than those retired in 1954.

The subdivision of the data into occupational categories also enables us to analyze the internal patterns *within each occupation*. In order to simplify the analysis, we shall only compare the percentage of persons who reported themselves in good health at the beginning and at the end of the study in each occupation. Among the professionals, it was found that in every retirement cohort, there was a decline in the proportion of persons reporting themselves in good health. There was a considerable range—from 3 per cent (R'54) to 37 per cent (R'57)—but the general trend of reported health was downward, as we would expect. The same pattern prevailed in all of the other occupational categories except the unskilled retirees. In this occupational grouping there were two cohorts which reported a slight improvement over time and one cohort reported the same proportion in good health both at the beginning and end of the study. This suggests that retirement among unskilled workers may be a positive factor in improving health conditions of persons who were engaged in heavy physical work. There is some evidence for this pattern in the other two blue-collar

Table 30. Self-reported health of men by occupational categories for various time periods (in per cent reporting "good health")

Category and year	R′54	R′56	R′57	R′58	WW′58
Professional	(19)	(15)	(16)	(39)	(115)
1952	58	47	81	67	66
1954	58	33	69	64	63
1956	47	27	63	56	56
1958	55	40	44	59	63
Managerial	(55)	(21)	(16)	(21)	(38)
1952	62	76	63	57	76
1954	60	62	75	52	71
1956	56	62	37	48	61
1958	60	67	44	43	66
Clerical	(32)	(22)	(16)	(16)	(28)
1952	66	68	69	75	68
1954	56	59	56	50	64
1956	56	41	50	56	68
1958	50	54	44	63	75
Skilled	(132)	(69)	(44)	(37)	(57)
1952	65	58	73	65	74
1954	65	59	59	57	74
1956	59	51	57	43	68
1958	58	61	45	51	72
Semiskilled	(59)	(49)	(31)	(26)	(57)
1952	59	67	61	73	74
1954	44	57	68	81	74
1956	56	41	48	85	68
1958	47	47	61	58	72
Unskilled	(69)	(35)	(27)	(23)	(27)
1952	55	54	63	74	67
1954	59	66	67	61	59
1956	55	63	52	43	59
1958	55	57	67	52	56

categories; however, this is not evident among the three white-collar occupations.

When we compare the white-collar and blue-collar occupation categories for those who continued to work throughout the study, we find that the pattern is irregular. The start-to-finish pattern, comparing the first and last years of the study, shows that the largest decline in health is reported by the managerial and unskilled categories (10 per cent and 11 per cent, respectively). The professionals and the skilled and semiskilled workers show a very small downward change, and the clerical category report an improvement of 7 per cent. On the basis of this evidence it appears unwarranted to make any generalization about occupational differences over time among older men who continue to work.

The aggregate analysis of the data has shown that in the impact year—the year after retirement—there is little evidence to suggest that health declines at retirement. Is this pattern found for the impact year among the various occupational categories? Do we find that the immediate year after retirement affects persons differentially according to their occupational level? The data in Table 30 enable us to investigate these questions. If we divide the population into two broad occupational categories—blue-collar and white-collar—there is a very slight tendency for white-collar occupations to have a decline in reported health in the impact year compared to those in blue-collar occupations. In the blue-collar occupations there were three instances of a reported improvement out of nine possible comparisons; in two cases the percentage was the same before and after retirement and in five instances there was a percentage decline in reported health. Among the white-collar occupations, there were six cohorts which exhibited a decline in the reporting of good health, two remained the same, and one increased in the percentage who reported good health. It is interesting to note that two of the three instances where a reported increase is observed are found among the unskilled workers. If we assume that persons in this category are more likely to have engaged in more demanding or more onerous physical activity at work, then retirement may be viewed as a possible respite and hence an improvement in health may be the result of stopping work. The generalization does not hold, however, for persons in semiskilled occupations.

Let us now compare the cohort of retirees who retired in 1954 with those who retired in 1958, according to occupational categories. The proportion who report themselves in good health initially is larger in four categories for the late retiree cohort as compared to the early retirees. Among the skilled workers, the same percentage (65 per cent) of both early and late retirees report themselves to be in good health, and among the managers, a slightly larger percentage of early retirees (62 per cent) report themselves in good health compared to the late retirees (57 per cent). Turning to the comparisons of early and late retirees at the end of the study, we find that in three occupational groups (the professionals, the clerks, and the semiskilled) the late retirees report a larger percentage in good health. In the other three categories—the managers, the skilled workers, and the unskilled—the reverse prevails: a larger percentage of early retirees report themselves in better health than late retirees. Since these data do not show any consistent trend for the blue-collar and white-collar categories, it appears that occupational level may not be a discriminating variable.

Summary

The data show that the proportion of those "scored" in good health declines moderately through the years 65 to 70. This does not seem to be attributable to retirement itself because those who do not retire show the same decline. Moreover, the respondents themselves do not attribute a decline in health to retirement. It is clear that while the majority do not expect retirement to cause any changes in their health, more of our respondents overestimate than underestimate the adverse effects of retirement upon their health.

When we examine the data by the six occupational categories (professional, managerial, clerical, skilled, semiskilled, and unskilled), we find that in five categories, those who retired declined in health slightly more than those who remained working, particularly in the clerical and semiskilled categories. However, among the unskilled who retire, three of the four cohorts showed a slight improvement in health from the start of the study in 1952 to the end in 1958.

CHAPTER 6

The Economics of Retirement:
Objective and Subjective Aspects

The social gerontological literature recognizes the drastic effects of retirement on the retiree's economic situation. A reduction of income in retirement is practically universal; it is the rare retiree whose income in retirement equals or exceeds his previous income from gainful employment. For example, in this study the median income before retirement was about $360 a month. After retirement, the average was $157 a month, or a decrease of 56 per cent.[1] This precipitous drop in income is not atypical, for a careful nationwide probability survey of approximately 2,500 older persons in the United States found that retired couples have an income which is about one-half that of persons who are employed full-time.[2] It is clear that the objective economic factor almost invariably changes in a dramatic fashion at retirement.

It is a folk observation that "money isn't everything." Yet money is a central concern of many people, for it is the means for the realization of a range of important values in American

[1] These data are based on 1,260 volunteer respondents employed by private organizations, of whom 477 had retired (Thompson and Streib, 1958, pp. 19, 25).

[2] Shanas et al., 1968, p. 403. Similar results were also reported for large national probability samples in Great Britain and Denmark.

culture. The significance of money to the older person becomes particularly acute as retirement approaches, for he faces the inevitable prospect of a contraction of income upon retirement and the resultant necessity to reduce desires for the goods and services that money can buy. This outlook is markedly in contrast with that of the young, whose horizon includes the expectation of an expanding income. Furthermore, the almost universal decline in physical health may necessitate increased expenditures for medical care.[3]

The impact of retirement on the monetary income of the respondents is shown in Table 31, where data are presented for

Table 31. Impact of retirement on actual income by sex and retirement category (in per cent receiving more than $65 a week or $250 a month)

Sex and year	R'54	R'56	R'57	R'58	WW'58
Men	(373)	(216)	(153)	(166)	(282)
1952	82	79	73	68	80
1954	28	73	70	77	78
1956	34	27	84	86	88
1958	37	34	36	47	91
Women	(103)	(67)	(48)	(87)	(94)
1952	41	30	46	55	42
1954	25	34	48	52	53
1956	29	13	56	69	62
1958	31	15	23	45	79

[3] The data in this study were obtained prior to the institution of Medicare. This national program of health care for the aged meets many of the medical expenses of the retirees. Furthermore, many retirees are now entitled to the benefits of supplementary medical care programs related to income in states like New York.

the weekly earned income for all respondents.[4] In the category of persons who continued to work throughout the study period, the percentage who received more than $65 a week remains relatively stable or increases. In contrast, in the retiree categories, the proportion generally declines. The decline is sharpest in the first year of retirement, and then the data suggest that the percentage who report this amount rises slightly. The pattern for men and women is very similar except that the percentage of women earning $65 a week was about half that of the men.

Subjective Aspects of Income Decline

We assumed that a decrease in income would create a problem for retirees only if it were not accompanied by a corresponding reduction in wants. The amount of income is the objective fact; but the *adequacy* of the income varies with the desires of the people who receive it. Thus a given amount of income might be considered plentiful by one retiree while the same amount would represent dire poverty to another. The amount of income an individual receives may not be as important as whether he thinks it is "enough." Therefore, one of the questions we asked was: "Do you consider your present income enough to meet your living expenses?"

The data show that while the proportion of respondents who report actual income of more than $65 a week drops drastically upon retirement, the proportion of those respondents who say they "have enough" does not decline so precipitously (Table 32). Moreover, the proportion of men and women (with one exception) who say they have enough increases slightly after the impact year as they adjust to their changed circumstances.

[4] In 1954 the retired persons were asked their income from all sources and then categories were set up in monthly units. The change from a weekly to a monthly basis was made because most of the respondents were weekly wage earners who upon retirement received OASI benefits and private pensions by monthly check. In 1956–1958 questions requested information in monthly amounts.

Respondents who continue to work, however, continue to say that their income is sufficient in ever increasing proportions as time goes on. In general, the same proportion of men and women evaluate their income as sufficient, and both sexes indicate that they feel the impact of retirement to about the same degree. For example, among the men who retired in 1954, 82 per cent had said they had a preretirement income of $65 a week and over; only 28 per cent said they had this income upon retirement—a drop of 54 per cent. Among this same group of men, 81 per cent said their income was sufficient before retirement and 56 per cent said it was sufficient afterwards—a decline of 25

Table 32. Impact of retirement on subjective income evaluation by sex and retirement category (in per cent saying their "income is enough")

Sex and year	R'54	R'56	R'57	R'58	WW'58
Men	(373)	(216)	(153)	(166)	(282)
1952	81	80	71	77	79
1954	56	85	77	87	87
1956	65	54	78	82	87
1958	60	65	68	70	88
Women	(103)	(67)	(48)	(87)	(94)
1952	85	79	71	76	82
1954	69	82	81	87	86
1956	71	75	79	86	88
1958	64	55	67	78	90

per cent. In other words, the group reporting an actual cut in income was more than twice as large as the group who reported an inadequacy of income after retirement.

Our data show that the subjective evaluation of retirement income is a significant fact in the retirement situation of the participants in this study. In the retirement literature there is a tendency to focus attention upon the objective economic circumstances. We do not mean to maintain that economic security is not a very important factor in retirement. Indeed, the level of income can shape the way in which the retiree views retirement in prospect. Our main point here is that an important component of the retirement situation is the way in which the retiree perceives and interprets subjectively his economic circumstances.

In studies of the meaning of work, sociologists and social psychologists have placed emphasis on the differential meanings which persons have given to their objective conditions of employment. These meanings of work constitute the basis for concern about the implications of work in terms of the employee's feelings of alienation, self-worth, estrangement, etc. Similarly, in the retirement situation there are subjective meanings—definitions of the situation—which affect the retiree's evaluation of his circumstances and must be taken into account by the analyst who wishes to understand the dynamic variability of retirement for the persons involved.

The data in Table 31 and 32 once again illustrate the advantages of longitudinal over cross-sectional and retrospective data, for in these materials we can examine at successive points in time the way the same categories of people reacted to the real drop in income, and also their perception of it.

In order to extend further our understanding of the respondents' evaluation of the impact of retirement, we asked whether their standard of living "is better today," "was better during most of my lifetime," or "has not changed" (Table 33).[5]

The over-all pattern of the responses indicates that a majority of the men, while they were working, said their standard of

---

[5] This question was not included in 1952 and so we cannot show precisely the impact of retirement on those who left the labor force in 1954. However, by comparing the 1954 retirees with those who continued to work, we can infer the same effect between 1952 and 1954 as we find for the other cohorts in the impact years.

living was better than during most of their lifetime. Women, in general, tend to have a somewhat more negative evaluation of their present economic situation than the men.

What is the effect of retirement upon evaluation of changes in the standard of living? In those cohorts for which we have pre- and post-retirement answers, we again observe that there is a sharp drop in the percentage of persons who offer a positive evaluation of their standard of living as compared to earlier periods. Among the men in the 1956 cohort, for example, there

Table 33. Impact of retirement upon evaluation of changes in standard of living, by sex and retirement category (in per cent saying "My standard of living is better today")

Sex and year	R'54	R'56	R'57	R'58	WW'58
Men	(373)	(216)	(153)	(166)	(282)
1954	21	57	61	62	56
1956	17	24	75	66	64
1958	25	31	41	39	61
Women	(103)	(67)	(48)	(87)	(94)
1954	30	60	44	45	42
1956	18	33	62	59	62
1958	27	37	35	38	48

Note: There are no clear indications in the data that there is a differential response according to occupational categories.

is a drop of 33 per cent, from 57 per cent to 24 per cent, and among the 1957 cohort the drop is 34 per cent upon retirement. In general, there are fifty per cent fewer persons who upon retirement offer a positive evaluation of their standard of living compared to earlier periods. Again, it appears significant that, despite the sharp drop in real income reported earlier, a quarter to a third of the retirees still state that their retirement standard of living is better than during most of their lifetime.

Needless to say, we do not have data on what constituted the standard of living during this earlier period, but it seems likely that some of our respondents were economically deprived when compared to their retirement economic situation. One possible interpretation of these findings is that the persons who participated in this study were in middle age and raising families during the Great Depression of the 1930's. It seems reasonable that when they look back at a lifetime, they conclude that their present situation in old age is comparatively better than during earlier periods of greater economic insecurity. These judgments of the standard of living by a minority of our respondents indicate again the great amount of flexibility displayed by retirees in adjusting to the changing circumstances of retirement. Our data do not enable us to determine whether this adaptation is realistic or whether it entails economic hardship and a tendency to accept adversity without complaint.

Anxiety about Money Matters

The equanimity with which older respondents viewed the realities of their economic position was a continual surprise to our investigators. We asked, "How often do you worry about money matters?" We might expect that if money is the motivation which keeps workers at their jobs, then those who stay at work longer would be those who are more concerned with money matters. Actually, this is not true. Table 34 shows that the proportion of people who say they worry about money is essentially the same before and after retirement for each cohort of retirees. Indeed, upon retirement there is a slight decline in the percentage of people who say they worry often or sometimes about money matters. These data for both men and women suggest that worry about money matters before retirement may be greater than during retirement itself. Moreover, about the same proportion of those who continued to work throughout the period under study reported they worry about money matters as those who retired. The impact of retirement per se, then, does not seem to have a traumatic effect on money worries in this study population.[6]

The relatively constant percentage of older persons—working or retired—who say they worry about money matters suggests the usefulness of comparing our findings with those of other

Table 34. Worry about money matters by sex and retirement category (in per cent who say they "often" or "sometimes" worry about money matters)

Sex and year	R'54	R'56	R'57	R'58	WW'58	Total
Men	(373)	(216)	(153)	(166)	(282)	(1,190)
1952	42	45	54	57	40	45
1954	35	41	43	39	34	37
1956	38	35	38	42	39	38
1958	36	38	36	35	35	35
Women	(103)	(67)	(48)	(87)	(94)	(399)
1952	47	55	52	59	40	49
1954	31	61	54	45	36	43
1956	36	40	50	44	39	40
1958	40	51	46	34	34	39

research conducted on different populations. At the time of our 1957 follow-up a nationwide survey of mental health was carried out by the Survey Research Center of the University of Michigan in which a representative cross-section of adults 21

[6] The relative economic stability of the persons who continued to participate in this study is shown by the fact that the proportion of persons who owned their homes did not decline in the period from 1954 to 1958, either among those who continued working or among those who retired. Approximately three-fourths of all cohorts reported they owned their homes at both points of contact.

years and older (2,460 cases) were interviewed on the average
for about two hours. The Michigan researchers reported that 18
per cent of the older persons in the survey (55 and over) stated
they *never worried,* compared to 6 per cent in the youngest
category (21–34 years). A steady increment in the proportion
who said they never worried is evident as one ascends the age
scale.[7] The Michigan researchers specifically singled out the fact
that in the economic area the older people appear to worry less
than the younger persons in the study. There are interesting
problems of interpretation in relation to the Michigan study
which we cannot pursue here. Two interpretations which seem
appropriate are that problems of old age tend to involve more
apathy than anxiety because the period of aspiration and
achievement are about over, and that, considering the population as a whole, economic insecurity does not appear to be such
a conscious problem for the older segments of the population.
Gurin, Veroff, and Feld summarize the situation aptly in these
words:

Although old age is a period of lower aspiration, it has also been
considered a time of great insecurity, especially economic insecurity,
and in these terms we might have expected the older people to have
evidenced a higher level of worrying. In this connection, the fact
that older people worry less than younger people about economic
and material things is rather striking: 41 per cent of the youngest
age group (21 to 34 years of age) give economic and material concerns as the first mentioned source of worry, as contrasted with only
18 per cent of the people over fifty-five years of age.[8]

Perhaps a broad conclusion to be drawn from the reported
lack of worry among older persons in our study is that many
apparently are not anxious about the economic situation of
their old age. James Morgan and his associates, who conducted
a nationwide economic survey, reported that there is general
optimism among persons in spending units who had less than
$500 in the bank for the years preceding the interview.[9] These

[7] Gurin, Veroff, and Feld, 1960, p. 43.   [8] *Ibid.,* pp. 44–45.
[9] Morgan, David, Cohen, and Brazer, 1962, pp. 440–444.

persons expect that they will get along financially during the retirement years. To what extent this optimism is realistic or unrealistic is hard to ascertain. However, the evidence from carefully drawn probability surveys conducted by the economists and others at the University of Michigan shows that most Americans have only a vague notion of whether or not retirement will present financial difficulties. These Michigan survey researchers also report that more than 40 per cent of the households with heads older than 55 years of age could not estimate their income requirements during retirement.

In summary, the aggregate data show a fairly stable pattern regarding concern about money matters throughout the period of investigation. Clearly, retirement has little adverse effect on whether or not an individual worries about money. Even increasing age seems to make little difference. This could be considered another indication that the impact of retirement is not as devastating as the stereotype would have it.

In further examining the data in Table 34, we see that a slight but consistent difference emerges between men and women in regard to worry about money matters. A larger proportion of women report that they worry about money in every time period, as shown in the "Total" column. When the men and women cohorts are compared year by year, it can be observed that this general pattern tends to prevail, although there are a few exceptions. In several of the female cohorts there are sharp fluctuations from year to year.[10] But in twenty possible cell by cell comparisons of men and women, the women "worry more" in thirteen comparisons, the same amount in two, and slightly less than men in five.

The data in Table 34 thus suggest that there is a sex difference among older persons in regard to anxiety about money. However, we must keep in mind that almost all of these men are married and their wives probably do most of the spending

10 These are aggregate data for any single cohort for a given time period. An analysis has not been made of the turnover in the 20 cells over time.

for consumer goods. Although these men report a sharp reduction in income, we speculate that the spending patterns in American society tend to create a greater awareness on the part of the women as to the adequacy or inadequacy of income. Indeed, some men may feel it is the responsibility of the wife to make the income "stretch"; hence, they are not as apt to worry. The women in the study are more apt to be single, widowed, or divorced, and thus the expenditure of funds is a nontransferable activity which is solely their responsibility and concern.

Composite Pattern of Responses about Economics

So far in this analysis we have looked at each economic questionnaire item separately. Table 35 considers all four items having to do with money for two cohorts of male respondents in the impact years, before and after retirement. The patterns for these groups are similar to those of other cohorts: there is a sharp reported drop in money income upon retirement and a substantial decline in the proportion who say their income is enough. Yet a much larger proportion attest to income adequacy as report a post-retirement income of $65 per week. After retirement the number of respondents who said that their post-retirement standard of living is lower than during most of their lifetime, increased by only a third, and very few persons assert that they worry more about money matters than they did prior to retirement. The general pattern of these data suggest a surprising adaptability on the part of these older persons in meeting the economic exigencies of retirement.

It must be stressed that survey data can be analyzed from the "positive" or "negative" point of view. Some analysts might focus on the negative side of the picture, for example, and stress that 35 per cent of the retirees in R'56 do worry "often" or "sometimes" about money matters in the year after retirement. But evidence for other research suggests that a positive interpretation of these data is tenable. A more recent study of a small random sample of retirees in New Orleans reports a

Table 35. Responses of two retirement categories
to questions about the economics of retirement
(in per cent)

Economic characteristic	R'56	R'57
Earn $65/week or more		
Before retirement	73	84
After retirement	27	36
Percentage change	46	48
Say income is enough		
Before retirement	85	78
After retirement	54	68
Percentage change	31	10
Say standard of living now better		
Before retirement	57	75
After retirement	24	41
Percentage change	33	34
Worry about money matters		
Before retirement	41	38
After retirement	35	36
Percentage change	6	2

rather optimistic picture of the income situation of the pensioners who were mainly skilled artisans and lower-paid professionals: "Very few American pensioners referred to the inadequacy of their incomes except in relation to medical bills." [11]

Retiree Reports

Results from the qualitative personal interviews in the special follow-up study illustrate also that most people were remarkably resourceful and adapted to their reduced income—regretfully but quite pragmatically. The following quotations are from four different respondents.

The honest truth is that I like retirement, but I sure miss that check. My wife has been sick for nine years. We've really got to sacrifice to make ends meet. But you do the best you can—no crying. I don't

[11] Bracey, 1966, p. 244.

worry, I just stay busy. It's kind of a treat for a man to stop working. You have to give the younger men a chance—you can't do everything. But I don't have change in my pocket any more.

Income problems? No, thank God. My wife here is the reason. I always brought home all my checks. She did the buying. We get along.

I haven't had any trouble with my income so far. I got to keep on a budget. But then I always have. All my life, I never spent too much. I worked hard. But you have to live right.

What I don't like about retirement is staying home on your vacation. You see, the pension plan is not adequate. It is unfortunate—my wife is 50 and I'm 70 so it's tough. It takes time to get used to less money when you retire. The pension is just not adequate.

Thus, these qualitative data also indicate that economic deprivation is not as traumatic in retirement as some people have maintained. Some readers might argue that death is a more common cause of worry and concern to the aged than their economic situation, but other research does not support this contention. It shows that the aged generally confront death calmly as an inexorable part of life. According to Riley, for example, very few older persons show a marked apprehension of death. Instead they talk about it freely and often express the view that death is more tragic for the survivors than for the deceased.[12]

Summary

The information on the economics of retirement presented in this chapter indicate that the average retiree's income declined 56 per cent after retirement. However the proportion who have a negative definition of the decline in income is not as marked as we had anticipated, for a surprisingly large proportion say their income is enough to meet their needs.

In conclusion, the Cornell findings seem to contradict the

[12] Riley, Foner, *et al.*, 1968, pp. 332–333.

commonly held notions concerning the extreme economic deprivation of the aged, particularly after their decline in income upon retirement. It is necessary to reiterate that these respondents have been retired from twelve months to five years and they are thus in the early phase of retirement, when health and income may be better than in later periods. Epstein and Murray point out that for persons receiving Social Security benefits there is a trend toward economic deterioration as one becomes older. They say, "Regardless of higher social security benefits, the effectiveness of the benefit diminishes for those already on the rolls since benefit increases do not keep pace with earnings and price changes." [13]

[13] Epstein and Murray, 1967, p. 85.

CHAPTER 7

The Social Psychology of Retirement: Age Identification in Longitudinal Perspective

In studies of the social psychology of adjustment and mental health, one of the basic areas of interest is attitude toward the self. More specifically, in research on aging and the aged, investigators have been interested in how the elderly view themselves in terms of age. Before reporting our data, let us examine the work of other investigators on two questions of age identification: At what age do people consider themselves to be old? Is retirement associated with a sudden change in one's age identification?

There is considerable evidence in the gerontological literature that older people *do not* acknowledge that they are old. Many think of themselves as midle-aged or even "young." Bernard Baruch is reported to have said: "To me, old age is always fifteen years older than I am." The reluctance of older people to relinquish a self-conception of youth or middle age is undoubtedly a consequence of living in a culture that stresses youth and values the characteristics of the young, such as speed and vigor. To shift one's self-conception from young to old is considered by most people to be a negative step, and one to be delayed until objective health factors make it inevitable.

But what is the definition of the word "old"? It has been customary to assume that old age begins somewhere in the seventh decade of life. This may be partly a reflection of the Biblical description of the life span as "threescore years and ten." Furthermore, many research and action programs tend to focus on age 65 since it is a common retirement age. Thus, there seems to be a general feeling that when a person is around 65 to 70, he should admit to being "old." In fact, some observers feel that to deny being old is an avoidance of reality and a form of self-deception.

The arbitrary use of chronological ages for defining the stages of later life is fraught with difficulties and ambiguities, despite its possible utility and ease of application in formal retirement and social insurance programs. In order to understand more completely the processes of aging and retirement, it is essential that a more analytical approach be developed, similar to that used to describe the first twenty years of life. These are demarcated into a number of clearly defined stages and periods by psychologists, psychiatrists, and students of social development. The richness of classification is undoubtedly due to the fact that many theorists have tended to concentrate their attention on the early phases of the life cycle.

Robert Peck is one social scientist who has attempted to conceptualize the social psychological development of the second half of the life cycle.[1] He views psychological development as a series of stages between middle age and old age in which specific social-psychological characteristics of the two periods are specified, and in which developmental criteria rather than age criteria are used. Another approach is that of Clark Tibbitts, who has created a typological analysis in which he divided advanced adulthood into three stages—middle age, later maturity, and old age.[2] Several studies suggest that Tibbitts' typology of advanced adulthood has an empirical basis.

For example, Tuckman and Lorge's study of over a thousand persons from under 20 to over 80 illustrates that persons do classify themselves into categories which are roughly congruent

[1] Peck, 1956.   [2] Tibbitts, 1960.

with those described by Tibbitts.[3] All respondents under 30 classified themselves as young, and between 30 and 60 an increasing proportion classified themselves as middle-aged. At age 60, only a small proportion described themselves by the word "old," and at age 80, slightly over half called themselves old but a small percentage persisted in describing themselves as young. As Tibbitts says: "The final period of life is old age, though it does not come to all." [4]

Another study indicates that advanced adulthood is demarcated by the old themselves into subcategories. In a study of 1,700 elderly citizens in Minnesota, Taves and Hansen asked the respondents at what age they first considered themselves old.[5] The chronological age range was from the middle sixties to the nineties and almost half of the people were in their seventies. Almost a third did not answer the question or did not have a definite opinion. Among those who did respond, about one in six said they first thought of themselves as old between the ages of 54 and 69; about a third said between the ages of 70 and 79; and forty per cent said age 80 or older. About one person in seven said they never thought of themselves as old. Although society tends to consider that a person is old when he is no longer gainfully employed, it is interesting to note that only five per cent of the Minnesota older citizens thought of themselves as old at 65.

Another study was carried out in a group of 219 members of the Age Center of New England (mean age 68 years) by Irving Zola in which he reported that only about one person in five considered themselves elderly, and there was a fifteen-year mean discrepancy between "chronological" and "felt age." [6]

[3] Tuckman and Lorge, 1954.   [4] Tibbitts, 1960, p. 10.
[5] Taves and Hansen, 1963.

[6] The complexities of the subject of age identity and felt age are pointed up by Zola's research. He concludes that for a significant portion of his sample the variable which seemed to have the greatest effect on the perception of being old was having considered one's father as "elderly" (Zola, 1962).

Zena Blau, employing data gathered in a Cornell cross-sectional study, reported that retirement and not the death of a spouse hastens the onset of old age. Her inferential evidence suggested "that the cultural evaluation implied by retirement, but not by widowhood, tends to force the person to recognize that he is socially defined as old." [7] Our study did not examine the impact of widowhood, but we have considerable information on the impact of retirement or continued employment upon age identification.

What does age identification tell us? "Age identification is conceived as a relatively high-order generalization from various social roles as well as from relatively subtle ongoing physiological and psychological processes." [8] It has been used as a correlate of morale particularly when the respondent is asked whether he thinks of himself as older or younger than his peers. [9]

Self-evaluation of Age

The respondents in the Cornell study were asked to check whether they considered themselves middle-aged, late middle-aged, old, or elderly. [10] Those who checked the first category were designated "younger" and those who checked the other three categories were considered "older." We speculated that if retirees do think of themelves as older, perhaps it is because

[7] Blau, 1956, p. 203.   [8] Phillips, 1957, p. 214.

[9] See, for example, Kutner et al., 1956, ch. vi, "Morale and the Social Self," esp. pp. 98–100. Raymond G. Kuhlen (1959, p. 892) says: "Studies of factors related to adjustment in old age leave much to be desired, but they tend to emphasize the importance of positive self-images and age identification." The complexity of the issue is shown by the conclusion reported by Clark and Anderson (1967, p. 84): "studies of age differences within a geriatric group show no inexorable loss of feelings of self-worth due to advancing age."

[10] Jeffers, Eisdorfer, and Busse (1962, p. 439) suggest there may be regional differences in the use of the terms "middle-aged," "elderly," "old." We do not agree with this interpretation, for there do not seem to be systematic regional peculiarities among the groups we compared.

people with an "older" self-image tend to retire and the others
continue working. Therefore, before we investigate the effects
of retirement itself on subjective age-identification, we can ask
if the persons who consider themselves "older" actually do
retire earlier. It is clear from the data in Table 36 that whether
our male respondents considered themselves "old" or "middle-
aged" in 1952 did not seem to have much bearing on how long
they remained at work. Our "middle-aged" female respondents,
however, indicate some tendency to retire later than earlier.

Table 36. Distribution of 1952 subjective ages by sex and
retirement category (in per cent)

Sex and age	R'54	R'56	R'57	R'58	WW'58	RW
Men						
Late middle-aged, old,						
elderly ($N = 503$)	26	13	9	12	19	21
Middle-aged ($N = 976$)	25	15	10	10	19	20
Women						
Late middle-aged, old,						
elderly ($N = 121$)	23	10	16	12	21	19
Middle-aged ($N = 362$)	20	15	8	20	19	17

Men: $X^2 = 2.74$ / $p < .80$.   Women: $X^2 = 11.28$ / $p < .05$.

Does retirement itself make a difference in our respondents'
age identification? Since we asked the question of the respondents at each contact we can look at the net changes in the
groups. Turning to Table 37 and examining the aggregate data
for men and women separately for the four points of time (last
column on right), we find that, at the first contact, 33 per cent
of the men were self-classified as "older." At each subsequent
contact, the number increased, rising to 43, 51 and finally to 67
per cent. Thus, at the end of the study, more than twice as many
men classified themselves in the "older" category. The pattern
for women is similar, although a smaller percentage of women
classify themselves as "older" at any time point, ranging from

24 per cent at the beginning of the study to 53 per cent at the end. (There is one exception in the ten categories—namely among the R'58 women in the period 1954–1956: there is a two per cent decline in the percentage who identified themselves as "older." It is clear, then, that as our respondents age, there is a definite trend for larger proportions to think of themselves as older. This trend, along with other data, suggests that our respondents tend to take a realistic view of the aging process.

Table 37. Effect of retirement on subjective age identification, by sex and retirement category (in per cent saying old, elderly, late middle-aged)

Sex and year	R'54	R'56	R'57	R'58	WW'58	Total
Men	(373)	(216)	(153)	(166)	(282)	(1,190)
1952	36	30	30	37	34	33
1954	47	42	44	38	45	43
1956	53	53	53	47	49	51
1958	66	69	73	67	67	67
Women	(103)	(67)	(48)	(87)	(94)	(399)
1952	27	18	39	16	26	24
1954	32	27	48	31	31	32
1956	40	45	52	29	42	40
1958	50	50	63	53	54	53

Note: Crucial before and after comparisons, showing percentages before retirement and in the year of retirement, are shown in boldface.

The data in Table 37 also allow us to examine the proposition whether retirement is a key factor in altering people's age identification. Here, again, investigators like Blau, employing cross-sectional data, have perhaps incorrectly overestimated the impact of retirement on age identity. The Cornell data clearly show that the proportions of persons in the various retirement categories who classified themselves as "older" was about the same at the initial point of observation. Further, when we compare the categories in longitudinal perspective, we see at the end of the study the same proportion of persons classified themselves as "older," no matter whether they had retired or continued working. One can also compare the polar categories— those who retired at the beginning of the study and those who worked throughout the study. Thus, if R'54 is compared with WW'58, it is noted that the longitudinal pattern of age identification is almost identical. This is true for both men and women. To sum up the data at this point, we see that the analysis by retirement-categories shows the same relationship between aging and age identity as was found in the aggregate data. In all of the categories, about twice as many people classified themselves as "older" when they had chronologically aged seven years.

Finally, turning to the examination of the immediate impact of retirement on age identity, we are able to examine the way in which retirees viewed themselves in the crucial year after retirement. We note that there is no marked shift to rate themselves as "older" in comparison to those who continued to work. Looking again at Table 37 and making comparisons of the "retirement impact year" (the lower of the paired figures in boldface) we note among the men in R'54 that there was an 11 per cent increase in those who classified themselves as older in the year after retirement. But approximately the same increase in age identity is noted in three of the four categories who continued to work between the first and second interview. Similar data are found when we compare the critical impact years for other groups.

Some gerontologists have pointed out the tendency of the old to misperceive and misclassify themselves as being younger than they are. These researchers have undoubtedly relied on cross-sectional data, which may lead to erroneous inferences about age identity as people grow older. The over-all picture of the Cornell respondents is one of realism in that they eventually recognize the fact that they are growing old. However, if one looked only at the 1952 responses in Table 37, in which only 16 to 39 per cent of the respondents placed themselves in the "older" category, he might conclude that these people were denying reality. It is only by a longitudinal study that one can note in successive years the steady increase in the number and proportion of those who rate themselves as "older."

We wished to probe further whether retirement increases feelings of older age identification and thereby verify or disprove the cultural evaluation that "retirement makes you old." When the participants were asked the direct question, "Do you think stopping work has made you think of yourself as

Table 38. Subjective evaluation of the effect of retirement upon age identification (in per cent responding to the question "Do you think stopping work has made you think of yourself as older or younger?")

Year and evaluation	Men				Women			
	R'54 (373)	R'56 (216)	R'57 (153)	R'58 (166)	R'54 (103)	R'56 (67)	R'57 (48)	R'58 (87)
1954								
Older	23				22			
Younger	5				6			
No difference	72				72			
Total	100				100			
1956								
Older	20	23			22	18		
Younger	6	5			5	4		
No difference	74	72			72	76		
Total	100	100			99	98		
1958								
Older	25	27	22	31	22	25	42	29
Younger	4	3	3	3	1	4	0	1
No difference	70	69	74	65	75	70	58	70
Total	99	99	99	99	98	99	100	100

older or younger?" only about a fourth of the retirees said it made them think of themselves as older (Table 38). The response pattern was the same for men and women and was practically the same for each retirement cohort. Moreover, there was little change in the aggregate proportion who report feeling older because of retirement as the length of retirement increased. Thus, we see that at each point in time practically three-fourths of the Cornell respondents indicate that retirement made no difference as to feeling older or younger.

Age Identification in Prospect

The longitudinal design makes it possible to ask respondents to predict future trends and the possible consequences of impending events such as retirement, and then enables the investigator to follow up later and to determine whether the respondent's predictions were borne out. We asked our respondents before retirement, "Do you think that stopping work would make you think of yourself as older or younger?" We see in Table 39 that a quarter to a half of the respondents think re-

Table 39. Pre-retirement evaluation of the effect of retirement upon subjective age identification (in per cent responding to the question "Do you think stopping work would make you think of yourself as older or younger?")

1956 evaluation	Men			Women		
	R'57 (153)	R'58 (166)	WW'58 (282)	R'57 (48)	R'58 (87)	WW'58 (94)
Older	28	45	51	29	36	42
Younger	0	0	0	0	0	0
No difference	60	43	38	54	54	47
Don't know	12	10	9	17	10	10
Total	100	98	98	100	100	99

Men: $X^2 = 23.71$ / $p < .001$.   Women: $X^2 = 3.68$ / $p < .50$.

tirement will make them feel older. None said they thought it would make them feel younger. A more pessimistic prediction concerning the impact of retirement is more likely to be found among those who continue to work longer.

In Table 40 we observe a before-after comparison of two retirement cohorts concerning the effect of retirement on age identity. A substantial majority before retirement said retirement would make no difference—and an even larger percentage *after retirement* said it had made no difference in their subjective age identification. In the case of the men, for both cohorts, there was a tendency to overestimate the negative effect of retirement. For example, in the R'58 category, 45 per cent said retirement would make them think of themselves as older, but after retirement only 31 per cent said this had actually occurred.

Table 40. A comparison of pre- and post-retirement evaluations of the effect of retirement upon subjective age identification (in per cent responding to the statements)

Pre-retirement (1956): Stopping work *would* make me think of myself as			Post-retirement (1958): Stopping work *has* made me think of myself as		
Response	R'57	R'58	Response	R'57	R'58
Men	(153)	(166)	Men	(153)	(166)
Older	28	45	Older	22	31
Younger	0	0	Younger	3	3
No difference	60	43	No difference	74	65
Don't know	12	10			
Total	100	98	Total	99	99
Women	(48)	(87)	Women	(48)	(87)
Older	29	36	Older	42	29
Younger	0	0	Younger	0	0
No difference	54	54	No difference	58	70
Don't know	17	10			
Total	100	100	Total	100	99

Age Identity and Occupational Category

It is important to examine whether the aggregate results we have reported concerning age identification remain the same or are modified by occupational position. It could be argued that persons who have higher positions in the occupational structure with accompanying greater amounts of recognition, prestige, and esteem are more likely to maintain a younger self-image than persons who are lower in the structure and may have worked harder physically during their lifetime. In Table 41 the data are presented for men for six occupational categories for the various cohorts of retiree-worker for four points in time.

When we compare the six occupational categories in 1952 we observe that although there are some variations in the percentage of people whose self-identity is "older," there is no consistent marked difference from one occupational category to another. It is also significant to note that for all occupational levels and for all retiree or worker categories, there is a gradual increase in the percentage of people who classify themselves as "older." Moreover, at the last point of observation, some six years after the first, we note that again all occupational groups, regardless of skill or prestige level, evidence almost the same proportions of persons classifying themselves as elderly. At the beginning of the study roughly a fifth to one-half in all occupational types classified themselves as elderly and at the end from two-thirds to three-fourths classified themselves in the older age category. Clearly, occupational status does not alter the fact that as people age chronologically, they gradually change their self-image accordingly. For illustrative purposes, it can be noted that the skilled worker category shows the pattern in the most consistent fashion. It is important to stress that when we compare the people who worked throughout the study with those who retired, there is no difference in the general trend or pattern of responses concerning age identity.

Finally, we need to examine again the question of whether

Table 41. Subjective age identification of men, by occupational types, for various time periods (in per cent saying, old, elderly, late middle-aged)

Occupational type and year	R'54	R'56	R'57	R'58	WW'58
Professional					
1952	37	47	63	38	35
1954	**47**	60	56	51	56
1956	74	**73**	37	51	51
1958	74	80	**75**	**69**	65
Managerial					
1952	33	19	44	29	42
1954	**55**	43	44	52	50
1956	53	**52**	44	43	45
1958	69	71	**69**	**43**	74
Clerical					
1952	19	27	31	44	29
1954	**22**	36	37	31	21
1956	47	**45**	50	56	50
1958	59	73	**69**	**81**	64
Skilled					
1952	34	33	23	24	**28**
1954	**43**	39	45	27	30
1956	48	**58**	66	41	44
1958	59	71	**77**	**65**	61
Semiskilled					
1952	42	31	16	35	20
1954	**53**	45	19	31	33
1956	56	**57**	45	54	33
1958	56	71	**77**	**73**	80
Unskilled					
1952	42	23	30	57	48
1954	**53**	40	70	39	63
1956	61	**34**	63	43	59
1958	86	54	**67**	**74**	78

Note: Figures in boldface are for the impact year of retirement.

the impact year of retirement has a "shock effect" on age identity; that is, do we find a sudden shift in age identity in the year of retirement? The data clearly show that there is no negative effect in the impact year. Those who continue to work and those who retire have the same tendency to consider themselves older. In every occupational category this general pattern is found.

These data clearly show that occupational position does not differentiate age identity in this study population. The evidence for this generalization can be most easily verified by comparing the polar groups of the occupational hierarchy—namely, the professionals and the unskilled workers.

Summary

Investigators like Blau have written that retirement seems to increase the likelihood that one will consider himself old. The implication is that the change of role caused by retirement is a traumatic experience which drastically affects the self-image of the elderly. Data from this longitudinal study indicate that whether people worked or retired does not increase an older age identity. Chronological age rather than the impact of retirement seems to be the determining factor. In all categories, approximately a third of the people considered themselves middle-aged at age 70, regardless of whether they were working or retired. Furthermore, an analysis of pre-retirement and post-retirement evaluations of age identification suggest that respondents tended to overestimate the negative effect of retirement on age identity.

An analysis of age identification by occupational category substantially confirms the trend for the aggregate data. Again, no sudden shift was noted during the year of retirement. The data gathered from retirees in this study do not support the commonplace that "retirement makes you old."

CHAPTER 8

The Social Psychology
of Retirement:
Satisfaction with Life

In Chapter 5 we discussed the nature of the relationship between retirement and our respondents' subjective evaluation of their physical health. We assume that a retiree's evaluation of his physical health includes some aspects of psychological health. The assumption behind some of the writing concerning the relationship between health and retirement seems to be that, at the very least, physiological symptoms emerge, are aggravated, and are exaggerated because of psychological difficulties which the individual experiences as an immediate result of retirement. The general impression, for example, of the effects of retirement which one receives from *The Encyclopedia of Mental Health* is that it is a psychological depressant. For example, Dr. Douglass W. Orr writes, "Retirement is a mental health hazard under any circumstances." Discussing situations leading to reactive depressions, Dr. Felix Von Mendelssohn lists "forced retirement" along with such situations as "crippling accidents and diseases, totally hopeless situations . . . and loss of skills." Perhaps the strongest position is asserted by Dr. Kenneth Soddy: "Many men find their most important identity in their career, which, being relinquished, establishes a strong tendency toward early breakdown and death." [1]

[1] Orr in *The Encyclopedia of Mental Health,* edited by Albert Deutsch

The negative consequences of retirement mentioned repeatedly in this standard source book are not documented with reference to any empirical studies of the authors or other investigators. It is likely that the bases for the statements are observations of patients seen by psychiatrists in the course of treatment. We are not questioning the validity of these observations for this special subtype of retiree, but rather the applicability of the assertions to many, most, or all retirees. The discrepancy between the reports of clinicians or physicians who observe a small sample of retirees in a specific therapeutic context and the reports of more broadly based surveys employing data from larger and more representative populations is, of course, not peculiar to studies of retirement.

The observations of psychiatrists and other clinical investigators and our theoretical orientation suggested the importance of ascertaining the psychological and social-psychological consequences of stopping or continuing to work: how people *felt* about retirement. Therefore the questionnaire included items not only about the respondents' physical health, but also about their psychological health.

Measures of Satisfaction with Life

At each period of the study we asked all our respondents three questions which we then combined into a Guttman-type measure of "general satisfaction with life":

1. "In general, how would you say you feel most of the time —in good spirits or in low spirits?" (Positive answer: "I am usually in good spirits.")

2. "How often do you find yourself feeling 'blue'?" (Positive answer: "hardly ever or never.")

3. "On the whole, how satisfied would you say you are with your way of life today?" (Positive answer: "very satisfied.")

(6 vols.; New York: Franklin Watts, 1963), I, 126; Von Mendelssohn in ibid., II, 463; Soddy in ibid., III, 832. The index lists 18 references to retirement; Each time the notion of retirement from work is discussed in a meaningful context, its depressive or negative effects are emphasized.

This measure is quite general; but that very characteristic may index the manifold variables that enter into a subjective evaluation of one's psychological health.[2] The respondents were categorized according to their scale scores into (a) "satisfied"; i.e., those who said they were usually in good spirits, hardly ever or never felt "blue," and were very satisfied with their way of life; and (b) "not satisfied"; i.e., all others. This is, of course, an extreme dichotomization but for that very reason may offset the tendency for respondents to give the satisfied answer more readily than the unsatisfied answer. However, this fact also suggests caution in interpreting the over-all percentages.

Table 42. Distribution of 1952 general-satisfaction-with-life scores of respondents by sex and retirement category (in per cent)

Sex and attitude	R'54	R'56	R'57	R'58	WW'58	RW
Men						
Satisfied ($N = 672$)	27	13	10	11	19	20
Not satisfied ($N = 814$)	24	16	11	10	19	19
Women						
Satisfied ($N = 250$)	22	13	9	20	21	15
Not satisfied ($N = 233$)	21	15	10	15	18	19

Men: $X^2 = 4.38$ / $p < .50$.   Women: $X^2 = 3.91$ / $p < .70$.

It is possible that depression occurring after retirement is simply an indication that those who are depressed retire and that therefore the influence is the reverse of what it may seem. We can investigate this relationship very generally as we did in the case of physical health. If we consider our respondents' scores in 1952, there seems to be no relationship between psychological health as we measured it and length of work life. The retirement pattern is the same whether the respondents were satisfied or not satisfied with life generally.

[2] The items are related in a Guttman scalar pattern with the first item most frequently answered positively and the third, the least frequently so answered.

The data in Table 42 show, for example, that approximately a quarter of both the satisfied and not satisfied retired in 1954. Equal percentages of those classified as satisfied or dissatisfied were found in succeeding retirement cohorts. The pattern is the same for men and for women.

If retirement were generally a psychological depressant, this should show up in our longitudinal analysis. If our Guttman-type measure is an indicator of psychological health, then it should be possible to test the hypothesis that, in general, retirement leads to a decline in psychological health. Specifically, we hypothesize that relative to the nonretiring control groups, retirement leads to a greater decline in the proportion of those in the retiring groups who are scored "satisfied with life." In other words, given a certain condition of psychological health in 1952 among older employed men and women, is a decline in psychological health more likely among those who retire than among those who continue to work?

Table 43. Effect of retirement on satisfaction with life, by sex and retirement category (in per cent scored "satisfied")

Sex and year	R'54	R'56	R'57	R'58	WW'58	Total
Men	(373)	(216)	(153)	(166)	(282)	(1,190)
1952	**48**	41	44	45	46	45
1954	**35**	**35**	37	42	43	39
1956	43	**41**	**40**	**44**	45	43
1958	39	35	**41**	**40**	47	40
Women	(103)	(67)	(48)	(87)	(94)	(399)
1952	**52**	49	46	57	56	53
1954	**52**	**42**	36	52	44	46
1956	48	**48**	**48**	**52**	52	50
1958	42	33	**33**	**59**	48	44

Note: Crucial before and after comparisons, showing percentages before retirement and in the year of retirement, are shown in boldface.

The over-all impression that emerges from the data is one of little change, particularly among the men (Table 43). Time itself does seem to lead to a small decrease in the over-all proportion of men and women who are scored satisfied. However, the decline is not steady, and two groups (men of WW'58 and women of R'58) show a slight increase in the years between 1952 and 1958. It seems also that a slightly higher proportion of women than men in most groups are scored satisfied.

Impact Year Analysis

We are interested specifically in net changes in the proportion of those reporting life satisfaction which occurred between the time just *before* retirement and the time just *after*. The crucial "before and after" comparisons in Table 43 (shown in boldface) indicate very clearly that our hypothesis is not confirmed. For example, though Men R'54 show a 13 per cent net decline in the proportion scored satisfied after retirement, R'56 show a 6 per cent increase; Women R'54 show no change and R'57 show a 15 per cent decrease. Other control comparisons (periods of no change in work status) show the same inconsistency. If the data can be considered to indicate a general tendency, it might be concluded that changes in psychological health that occur among older persons cannot be directly attributed to retirement itself, but rather to the process of aging.

In order to find out how our respondents themselves evaluated the effect of retirement we asked those who retired: "Do you think stopping work has made you less satisfied with your way of life today?" The responses are shown in Table 44. The great majority, three-fourths or more, of the retired respondents said "no" in answer to the question. The rest of the respondents are about evenly divided between those who said "yes" and those who said "I don't know." Very few of the retired respondents are willing to attribute a decline in satisfaction to retirement. There is little or no difference between men and women in this regard. Thus the answers to this question as a measure of

satisfaction with life confirm our finding that retirement itself
is not a psychological depressant.

Table 44. Subjective evaluation of the effect of retirement upon
satisfaction with life (in per cent responding to the question
"Do you think stopping work has made you feel less
satisfied with your way of life today?")

Year and evaluation	Men				Women			
	R'54 (373)	R'56 (216)	R'57 (153)	R'58 (166)	R'54 (103)	R'56 (67)	R'57 (48)	R'58 (87)
1954								
Yes	10				9			
No	80				83			
Don't know	10				9			
Total	100				101			
1956								
Yes	17	18			15	19		
No	72	67			77	67		
Don't know	11	15			8	12		
Total	100	100			100	98		
1958								
Yes	11	11	13	14	9	13	15	14
No	76	71	75	75	76	73	75	77
Don't know	12	17	12	11	15	13	10	9
Total	99	99	100	100	100	99	100	100

Retiree Reports

To illustrate this point more vividly, we offer once again quotations from two of the qualitative interviews conducted after
many of the respondents had retired. One man stated:

I like retirement. I take life easy! [Big smile.] You can sleep as long
as you want. Go to bed if you want to. I had three heart attacks so
I quit work. But the doctor says I have 25 more years to go! I have
no trouble keeping busy—I have been doing some painting. I
worked a few hours a day—did the lower part of the house. I have

a big yard—60 feet by 60. I like to monkey around in the basement. I go visiting in the afternoon. I have five children in Milwaukee and 13 grandchildren. They are all glad to see me. My children treat me pretty good—all of them. I am "Grandpa" to all the neighbors. I have a good family—my daughters are very close. They always have a big gathering. When it was my 69th birthday, they had a big gang there.

I've got to take it easy. I don't do any more drinking—no taverns. I don't take any big trips—it's too tiring. No hunting or fishing. I know my limits. But I go to the ball games.

I have no money problems—I get 210 dollars a month pension including Social Security. I own my home, and my daughter, her husband and their family live here and pay rent.

I'm happy all the time! The children are good to me. All the relatives want me to visit them—they say, "The sooner you come, the better we like it."

Another retiree said:

I take it easy. But I keep busy—a man has to do something. I cut the grass, and pull the weeds. I monkey around—keep reading. I like to read the Reader's Digest. I take a walk—go one and a half miles. Then sometimes I go fishing with a couple of fishing partners —I went three times this year to an inland lake. I watch the ball games every night on TV. I walk over to my daughters' houses three or four times a week and see them and their families. We all go on picnics sometimes.

It would be hard to make a go of it if we didn't live with our son. His wife moved in with us during the war, and when he came back, they just stayed. We moved to the present house three years ago. My son wouldn't ever let us move out—he wants us to stay with them. I used to talk a lot with the men at work. Now it keeps me busy chattering with my wife and the kids. [The grandchildren were 16 and 13 years old.] I don't notice much difference.

It is obvious that retirement was not a psychological depressant to these two men. Both were friendly and gregarious, and found enough social interaction with their families, friends, and neighbors to satisfy them. Of the fifty cases personally interviewed by the senior author about three-fourths were similarly cheerful and adjusted.

Satisfaction with Life in Prospect and Retrospect

Since the same respondents were contacted at different times it was possible to ask them *before* retirement what they thought the effect of retirement would be and compare this to what they said *after* retirement. In 1956 we asked those respondents who were still working (R'56, R'58, WW'58) whether they thought that stopping work would make them feel less satisfied with

Table 45. Pre-retirement evaluation of the effect of retirement upon satisfaction with life (in per cent responding to the question "Do you think stopping work would make you feel less satisfied with your way of life?")

	Men			Women		
1956 evaluation	R'57 (153)	R'58 (166)	WW'58 (282)	R'57 (48)	R'58 (87)	WW'58 (94)
Yes	20	37	55	21	25	55
No	56	45	30	54	48	28
Don't know	23	18	15	25	26	17
Total	99	100	100	100	99	100

Men: $X^2 = 51.66$ / $p < .001$.   Women: $X^2 = 23.87$ / $p < .001$.

their way of life. Table 45 shows their responses to this question. There is quite clearly a relationship between a negative view of the effects of retirement and length of work life. Those who foresee negative effects tend to stay at work longer. Over half of both men and women in the WW'58 group (55 per cent) thought that stopping work would make them feel less satisfied with their way of life, whereas only 20–21 per cent of R'57 do so. The pattern of responses among men and women are remarkably similar.

Table 46 shows a comparison of the responses of R'57 and R'58 before retirement and after retirement. About half of the respondents seem to have had an accurate idea of the effect of retirement upon their feelings of satisfaction with life. However, in each case the proportion who said they thought retirement would make them feel less satisfied or who didn't know what it would do is greater before retirement than after. The adverse effects of retirement were overestimated by about one out of five retirees.

Table 46. A comparison of pre- and post-retirement evaluations of the effect of retirement upon satisfaction with life (in per cent responding to the statements)

Pre-retirement (1956): Stopping work *would* make me feel less satisfied with my way of life			Post-retirement (1958): Stopping work *has* made me feel less satisfied with my way of life		
Response	R'57	R'58	Response	R'57	R'58
Men	(153)	(166)	Men	(153)	(166)
Yes	20	37	Yes	13	14
No	56	45	No	75	75
I don't know	24	18	I don't know	12	11
Total	100	100	Total	100	100
Women	(48)	(87)	Women	(48)	(87)
Yes	21	25	Yes	15	14
No	54	48	No	75	77
I don't know	25	27	I don't know	10	9
Total	100	100	Total	100	100

Summary

No consistent change in psychological health was observed as measured by the questionnaire items. The changes which were observed were not clearly attributable to retirement. The respondents themselves did not attribute a decline in satisfaction to retirement. While nearly half did not expect retirement to make them feel less satisfied, a sizable proportion of our respondents overestimated the adverse effect of retirement on this feeling of satisfaction. Those who tend in larger proportions to think of retirement as a depressant tend not to retire.

These findings confirm the observations of Havighurst and his fellow researchers that life satisfaction does not decrease with age.[3] Although role loss may occur with increasing age, the older person is apparently able to adapt to these changes, and, while he regrets the loss of role, he is able to maintain a positive evaluation of himself and satisfaction with life as a whole.

[3] Havighurst, Neugarten, and Tobin, 1968, esp. p. 168.

CHAPTER 9

The Social Psychology of Retirement: Feelings of Usefulness

One of the intriguing aspects of retirement is the way in which it can be studied in relation to the changing nature of an industrialized bureaucratic society, and the way in which work and nonwork are viewed within this complex and changing context. The transformation of Western societies in the last 200 years from traditional, agricultural and religiously oriented societies to those which are industrialized, bureaucratized, and secular was accompanied by increasing differentiation and much greater occupational specialization. These changes were also accompanied by modifications of attitudes and values toward religion, family, and work.

One of the major themes running through this transformation is a shift from an other-worldly asceticism to a this-worldly asceticism which emphasized work as a duty or "calling" in which work and usefulness and achievement became signs of virtue and sources of personal satisfaction. This has sometimes been labeled the Protestant ethic. Indeed, the need for meaningful work in the burgeoning industrialized nations was the concern of many analysts and critics of industrialization. It was pointed out that work is one of the important segments of a person's life and when work conveys meaning and significance, people are less apt to become alienated.

In the last fifty years, many changes have taken place that affect attitudes toward work: the higher productivity of the economy, the increasing security for workers through unionization, the shorter work week, pension plans, Social Security—all these factors have created a different economic and social milieu. In addition, the religious motivations associated with the Protestant work ethic have been lost for many persons. Yet residues of these ideas remain and influence attitudes toward working and retirement. The persons interviewed in the Cornell Study were born in the late nineteenth century, and were socialized in a period of expanding industrialization, when the work ideology was dominant. We wanted to find whether they could adjust to comparatively early retirement with more leisure than they had previously had. We assumed that many of these people have found work to be more effective than play in providing self-respect and in gaining for them the respect of others. We also assumed that some would maintain this self-respect after retirement by their reputations as long-time, successful workers, and would feel that retirement was a reward for a well-spent lifetime of work. We wanted to find if others, however, would be more likely to interpret retirement as a sign that they were no longer needed, useful, or productive, and would harbor residual feelings of guilt about not working. Thus we asked questions designed to elicit their feelings about the meaning of working and not working.

When all the participants were still gainfully employed, we asked them about their feelings of usefulness and uselessness. In Table 47, we sorted out the polar groups of those who said they often or sometimes felt their life was not very useful, and those who hardly ever or never had such feelings, to see if there were any differences in the subsequent retirement patterns of these two categories. The data show that there is a tendency for those who said they often or sometimes felt useless to retire in the early retirement period. The differences are very slight when we

look at the various cohorts. The patterns for the men and
women are quite similar.

Table 47. Distribution of 1952 reported feelings of usefulness by sex
and retirement category (in per cent answering "How often do
you get the feeling that your life today is not very useful?")

Sex and response	R'54	R'56	R'57	R'58	WW'58
Men					
Often or sometimes					
(N = 154)	38	22	12	10	18
Hardly ever or never					
(N = 1,036)	30	18	13	14	24
Women					
Often or sometimes					
(N = 64)	28	12	19	17	24
Hardly ever or never					
(N = 335)	25	18	11	23	23

Men: $X^2 = 8.94$ / $p < .10.$ Women: $X^2 = 4.60$ / $p < .50.$

Attitudes about Usefulness

Of course some people may feel not very "useful" most of their
lives and it may have nothing to do with retirement or aging.
By asking the same respondents the same question at different
time periods we can perhaps control this. We might expect a
higher proportion of respondents in the retired groups to report
having this feeling often or sometimes than in the groups that
continue to work. This relationship is examined in Table 48,
where it can be observed that the overwhelming majority do *not*
feel useless. Examining the various retirement cohorts, we note
that there is a slight tendency among the males for those who
retire earlier to express feelings of uselessness. This small difference is probably related to the fact that some of the R'54
group retired because of poor health. In Table 48 we have set
off in boldface type the year before retirement and the impact

year immediately following retirement; there is a marked increase in the proportion of persons who express a feeling of uselessness in the impact year. Among those persons who continue to work, however, there is no change in reported feelings of uselessness. Moreover, the retirees tend to remain at the higher level of reported uselessness in subsequent post-retirement years.

Table 48. Effect of retirement on feelings of usefulness by sex and retirement category (in per cent saying they "often" or "sometimes" feel that their lives today are not very useful)

Sex and year	R'54	R'56	R'57	R'58	WW'58	Total
Men	(373)	(216)	(153)	(166)	(282)	(1,190)
1952	**16**	16	12	9	10	13
1954	**21**	**15**	10	10	9	14
1956	28	**30**	**10**	**16**	10	20
1958	26	34	**22**	**28**	12	24
Women	(103)	(67)	(48)	(87)	(94)	(399)
1952	**18**	13	25	13	16	16
1954	**26**	**18**	27	14	17	20
1956	29	**40**	**27**	14	17	25
1958	31	40	**46**	**19**	14	28

Note: Crucial before and after comparisons, showing percentages before retirement and in the year of retirement, are shown in boldface.

In general, there is little difference between men and women. However, it is interesting that fewer men than women report experiencing at least sometimes the feeling that their lives are not very useful. Other data in our studies have shown that women are more willing to express psychological complaints, such as "feeling blue" and being despondent.

Two cohorts of women (R'56 and R'57) report a somewhat

higher proportion of feelings of uselessness than the other groups. And in both these cohorts the effect of the change in status seems to be operating more strongly. Though the effect of retirement is most marked in those two groups it shows up generally in the others for which we have before and after re-

Table 49. Subjective evaluation of the effect of retirement upon feelings of usefulness (in per cent responding to the question "Do you think stopping work has given you the feeling that your life today is not very useful?")

Year and evaluation	Men				Women			
	R'54 (373)	R'56 (216)	R'57 (153)	R'58 (166)	R'54 (103)	R'56 (67)	R'57 (48)	R'58 (87)
1954								
Yes	11				13			
No	78				80			
Undecided	11				7			
Total	100				100			
1956								
Yes	18	18			16	25		
No	70	73			77	65		
Undecided	12	9			8	9		
Total	100	100			101	99		
1958								
Yes	15	18	13	14	17	16	23	13
No	76	70	78	77	72	69	65	78
Undecided	9	12	9	9	11	13	12	9
Total	100	100	100	100	100	98	100	100

sponses; the proportions in groups which continue to work change very little. In no case does the proportion of those giving the less favorable response decrease with retirement. However, it is important to repeat that the over-all proportion who give the "often" or "sometimes" response is only about a fourth, and the large majority report they "hardly ever or never" experience the feeling that their lives are not very useful.

If retirement increases the proportion of those who say they often or sometimes get a feeling of uselessness, do our respondents recognize this as an effect of retirement? Table 49 shows that only a small group of both men and women attribute this feeling to retirement. For example, in almost every cohort, about three fourths of the retirees said that stopping work had not affected their feelings of usefulness. The largest percentage in any category who attribute feelings of uselessness to retirement is about 25 per cent.

Table 50. Pre-retirement evaluation of the effect of retirement upon feelings of usefulness (in per cent responding to the question "Do you think stopping work would give you the feeling that your life is not very useful?")

1956 evaluation	Men			Women		
	R'57 (153)	R'58 (166)	WW'58 (282)	R'57 (48)	R'58 (87)	WW'58 (94)
Yes	16	34	45	25	22	44
No	64	48	40	60	53	45
Undecided	20	18	15	15	24	12
Total	100	100	100	100	99	101

Men: $X^2 = 37.50$ / $p < .001$.   Women: $X^2 = 13.22$ / $p < .02$.

As we have found in other aspects of self-image, there is a tendency for our respondents to overestimate in advance the adverse influence of retirement. Table 50 gives their responses to the question asked before retirement: "Do you think stopping work would give you the feeling that your life is not very useful?" Almost half of both men (45 per cent) and women (44 per cent) in the groups which continue to work throughout the study reply in the affirmative. The groups which retire are less pessimistic. A before and after comparison of R'57 and R'58 indicates, however, that they also tend to overestimate the adverse effects of retirement on feelings of usefulness (Table 51). In spite of this tendency, the majority of the respondents showed a fairly accurate evaluation of the effect of retirement.

Table 51. A comparison of pre- and post-retirement evaluations of the effect of retirement upon feelings of usefulness (in per cent responding to the statements)

Pre-retirement (1956): Stopping work *would* give me the feeling that my life is not very useful			Post-retirement (1958): Stopping work *has* given me the feeling that my life today is not very useful		
Response	R'57	R'58	Response	R'57	R'58
Men	(153)	(166)	Men	(153)	(166)
Yes	16	34	Yes	13	14
No	64	48	No	78	77
Undecided	20	18	Undecided	9	9
Total	100	100	Total	100	100
Women	(48)	(87)	Women	(48)	(87)
Yes	25	22	Yes	23	13
No	60	53	No	65	78
Undecided	15	24	Undecided	12	9
Total	100	99	Total	100	100

Retiree Reports

The data obtained by self-administered questionnaires permit statistical analysis but there are obvious limitations to the method. Unstructured personal interviews have a flexibility and utility which may uncover nuances that had not been anticipated. In formulating our structured instruments, the notions of usefulness were defined primarily in terms of the work experience. This assumption did not reflect the situation for everyone, however. In two cases of the fifty people personally interviewed by the senior author, for example, the respondents welcomed retirement because it meant that they could take care of their invalid spouses—a reason for favorable attitudes to retirement that we had not anticipated.

I like retirement. When I worked I had to have a housekeeper for my wife. Now I do everything—I like it. I do the cooking, cleaning —everything. The only thing is, we can't take a trip. But you take the good with the bad. We own our home. I do all the fixing up. I retired at 65 but I could have stayed until 70. I did more work with one hand than lots of the men did with two. [This man had lost an arm 37 years ago in an accident.] Adjusting to retirement doesn't bother me much. It came gradually. Things are always changing and you have to adjust. I know a lot of people say they don't know what to do when they stop working. But a fellow slows up. You have to be patient. I'm fortunate because I have my health.

Another respondent said:

I'm awful glad to be retired. As long as you can take care of yourself, it's fine. If not, it is a different thing. My wife has been sick the last 5 months and so I've been very busy—I do the housekeeping, the shopping and housework. We don't go out much since my wife has been sick. But I keep up with sports—watch hockey on TV. We don't have many friends—you know you can have too many close friends. They get too close and then they want something. I've got a nice pension and Social Security and so we do all right.

These two cases obviously had great feelings of usefulness and did not look back longingly at their work situation and its social satisfactions. Their devotion to their invalid wives superseded other considerations.

There are many other ways that people expressed a feeling of usefulness after retirement. Another retiree obtained his sense of involvement from his neighboring and community activities. He observed:

I like retirement just fine. I keep adjusted—keep busy. Sometimes I haul wood from the place where my son works. I watch the neighborhood kids from the front porch. There are about 15 kids in the neighborhood that I keep an eye on. It is a busy street. I know all my neighbors. They'll be asking who you were. It's a friendly neighborhood. Then I'm very busy with my church work. I am president of a study group. I've been an officer of the church for 18 years, and 12 years in another church before this one. I do some welfare work—in the evenings there is a ball league one night a week. I coach one of the teams. I've been very busy.

Another man obtained his feelings of usefulness in retirement mainly through kin activities. He said:

I spend lots more time visiting relatives than I used to. We have 6 children and 20 grandchildren. One of the grandchildren is staying with us now on a visit. My wife gets along fine with our youngest daughter. We just spent a month with them in Milwaukee. She has six-month-old twins and my wife helped out. We go for a day or two and then it stretches out to a month. The children are always wanting us to come and see them. They come and visit us a lot. Then we have two children in town. We baby-sit at our son's house occasionally.

Another retiree had a gloomier view. He said:

When you retire, you're put on the shelf. Even if you had money, it wouldn't help. You want to be of use until you pass on. It's too bad I'm 70. If I didn't have a heart condition, I'd stay on working. I don't like being useless. I'd like to find a litle job that would keep me occupied—maybe accounting, or taking orders—a sit-down job. Maybe answering the telephone. I can't earn over $100 a month. I do more sleeping now—my wife keeps looking at me. I'd like to get out from under.

This man's feelings of uselessness were compounded by his poor health and an apparently unsympathetic wife.

Summary

The negative view held by many that aging and particularly the retirement period is marked by feelings of uselessness is not verified by the questionnaire information gathered in this longitudinal research. Over three-fourths of the retired respondents report feelings of usefulness *after* retirement. There is a reported difference concerning these feelings among those who continued to work as compared to those who retired. Those persons who work longer tend to feel that retirement would have a negative effect upon them. Retirement does have some negative effect upon feelings of personal usefulness of a small minority, but the majority are unaffected. An analysis of the impact period reveals that the year of retirement is marked by a small decrease in feelings of usefulness and the subsequent post-retirement years tend to remain at this new level. The changes, however, are inconsistent in the different categories, ranging from 5 per cent to 22 per cent reporting greater feelings of uselessness.

These items concerning usefulness are obviously more directly related to the meaning of work and its cessation than are other questionnaire items which we have previously analyzed. Perhaps the cultural emphasis on the value of work is responsible for the finding that some of our respondents *before* retirement tend to overestimate the negative impact of retirement upon their feelings of usefulness. This area for some older workers is more threatening in prospect than it is in reality.

CHAPTER 10

Adjustment to Retirement: Prospective and Retrospective Views

The preceding analyses have been concerned with the effect of retirement on fairly general attitudes toward retirement and self-image. We will now look at a more specific measure of post-retirement satisfaction with retirement. The means of ascertaining whether or not individuals have adjusted to retirement is to have our respondents look back upon the work experience. The rationale behind this approach is that the retirement role in real-life terms is the absence of gainful employment. Hence the way persons view the components of the work role give us an index of how they adapt to the retirement role. This approach to retirement may tend to cast the retirement role in a negative light. However almost every retiree tends to conceive of his role in these terms. It would be difficult to try to mask this basic aspect of the retirement role by the direct questionnaire techniques that we had to employ with our study population. Researchers who are able to employ more indirect methods —for example, the use of projective techniques—might be able to ascertain some of the covert aspects of attitudes toward retirement.

Our analysis involves the comparison of standard categories in relation to attitudes toward adjustment: men compared to women, blue-collar categories compared to white-collar. What we have been able to do—perhaps in a simple manner—is to assess the relative impact of the retirement situation and the pre-retirement attitude of the retiree on his satisfaction with retirement. Further, by means of our longitudinal data we are able to compare on selected items the "before and after" outlook of our subjects, and also to determine the effects of retirement itself by analyzing their attitudes toward retirement.

Satisfaction with Retirement

As a general measure of post-retirement satisfaction with retirement, a score was developed which was based on the responses to four questions: (1) How often do you miss being with other people at work? (2) How often do you miss the feeling of doing a good job? (3) How often do you feel that you want to go back to work? (4) How often do you worry about not having a job? The respondents were dichotomized into two categories: "satisfied" and "dissatisfied." An individual was considered "satisfied" with retirement only if he answered "hardly ever" or "never" to each of the questions. Thus, if he did not often miss the feeling of doing a good job, did not often feel he wanted to return to work, did not often miss his former work mates, and hardly ever or never worried about not having a job, he was rated as "satisfied." The "dissatisfied" answered these questions by saying "often" or "sometimes." As with the general satisfaction scale, we used only the most extreme "favorable" answer as the best cut-off point for purposes of dichotomizing. It is entirely possible, of course, that an individual could say he often missed being with other people at work and still be normally adjusted to retirement. However, with such qualifications understood, it does seem that this score is a reasonable measure of post-retirement satisfaction with retirement.

Table 52 shows that more of those who retire earlier are satisfied than those who retire later. Almost half of the women who retired by 1954 were scored satisfied with retirement at that time. If only the later retirees are compared, it is clear that fewer of the women are satisfied than men. Neither difference, however, is large enough to be more than an indication. If those who retired in 1954 are compared over time, the trend for both men and women is the same: an initially high level of satisfaction, a drop at the next period, and then a climb back up. This observation tends to agree with the general "stage" notion of adjustment proposed by Havighurst.[1] However the data for R'56 do not support the stage thesis, for we note that a larger proportion of both men and women stated they were satisfied with retirement at the second contact than at the first.

Table 52. Satisfaction with retirement by sex and retirement category (in per cent scored "satisfied")

Sex and year	R'54	R'56	R'57	R'58
Men	(373)	(216)	(153)	(166)
1954	37			
1956	31	20		
1958	36	32	33	30
Women	(103)	(67)	(48)	(87)
1954	49			
1956	36	25		
1958	42	28	27	28

What are some of the factors affecting this "satisfaction" score? As measured before retirement, some of the respondents were scored "willing to retire," and others "reluctant to retire." And, as has been indicated previously, some of the respondents retired because they chose to do so, and others retired because their employers decided they should retire. These have been designated as voluntary and administrative retirees, respectively. It has been pointed out that not all administrative retirees were reluctant to retire, nor were all those respondents who chose to retire willing to retire. These respondents have been called

[1] Havighurst, 1955.

"willing administrative" and "reluctant voluntary" retirees, respectively. It might be expected that a differential reaction to retirement would appear according to situation (voluntary or administrative) and prior attitude (willing or reluctant).[2] The general tone of the literature on the matter of compulsory as opposed to some sort of graduated or voluntary retirement tends to argue that compulsory retirement (what we are calling "administrative") has more disadvantages than advantages and is a crucial determinant of adjustment in the post-retirement period.[3] Donahue, Orbach, and Pollack suggest, however, that the effect of prior attitude toward retirement has been somewhat neglected in studies of retirement. It is our suggestion that prior attitude is actually more important than the mode of retirement. As indicated in this analysis the attitude and situation tend to reinforce each other so that "willing voluntary" are most satisfied and "reluctant administrative" are least satisfied as a group.

Table 53 shows the relationship of attitude or the retirement situation upon satisfaction with retirement. In every case the difference in the proportion of willing over reluctant who are satisfied is larger than the difference between the voluntary and administrative. In each cohort except women R'57, the proportion of voluntary who are satisfied exceeds that of the adminis-

[2] Actually this set of dichotimizations yields four retiree types: willing administrative, willing voluntary, reluctant administrative, reluctant voluntary. We would like to compare the satisfaction of these four types, but the numbers in the cells become too small to make analysis intelligible. The comparison was made, however, for earlier waves of the study in Thompson, 1956, ch. iv, "The Effects of Retirement," pp. 86–133, and in Schneider, 1964, ch. vi, "Attitude and Situation," pp. 124–140.

[3] For example, Donahue, Orbach, and Pollack, 1960, pp. 355–368. A different approach is suggested by Orr (1963, p. 142), who argues that compulsory retirement can be "known" and can therefore be planned for. Thompson, 1958, reports that the most important factors related to satisfaction with retirement are an accurate preconception of retirement and a favorable pre-retirement attitude.

trative, and in every cohort the proportion of willing who are satisfied exceeds that of the reluctant. In general, there are more willing than voluntary who are satisfied and fewer reluctant than administrative. This indicates, we think, that the influence of prior attitude on adjustment after retirement is greater than the effect of the retirement situation.

Table 53. Situation and attitude and satisfaction with retirement by sex and retirement category (in per cent scored "satisfied")

	R′54	R′56	R′57	R′58	Total
Men	(373)	(216)	(153)	(166)	(908)
Voluntary	43	21	39	39	35
Administrative	33	16	23	22	26
Willing	47	27	42	43	41
Reluctant	22	13	22	25	20
Women	(103)	(67)	(48)	(87)	(305)
Voluntary	49	27	26	33	35
Administrative	48	23	29	24	33
Willing	60	31	37	44	48
Reluctant	32	22	21	21	24

The professionals show a higher proportion of satisfied retirees than any other group of both men and women, as is shown in Table 54. (We pointed out earlier, however, that a larger proportion of professionals did not retire.) Fewer of the skilled and semiskilled women retirees were satisfied, but more women in each of the other categories were satisfied than men.

It is significant, but difficult to explain, that the women have a much greater variation in satisfaction scores than the men. The percentage difference in the male categories ranges from 27 to 37 per cent—a 10 per cent range. The women, on the other hand, have a 25 per cent range—from 19 per cent to 44 per cent. The pattern is clearly not monotonic up or down the skill level.

The five degrees of skill level employed here suggest that the tentative findings of Stokes and Maddox, who employed a white-collar–blue-collar dichotomy with only 53 male blue-collar retirees, are "illustrative rather than conclusive," as they say.[4] These authors found that, in the short run, blue-collar workers adapt to retirement more successfully than white-collar workers.

Table 54. Satisfaction with retirement by sex and occupation

	Men		Women	
Occupation	% *	No.	% *	No.
Professional	37	89	44	101
Managerial, clerical	29	208	34	98
Skilled	31	282	21	24
Semiskilled	27	165	19	31
Unskilled	31	154	37	43

* Percent scored "satisfied" in retirement year.

In considering some of the reasons why professionals show a higher satisfaction with retirement, we speculate that many of them may have made plans. For example, a teacher who was going to retire soon, told the interviewer:

I don't view retirement with worry or fear. I look forward to an interesting way of using my time. I have not had enough time all my life to do the things I wanted, and I imagine retirement will be the same. I have half a dozen subjects to keep busy for years. I have published quite a bit. I'm going to spend lots more time in travel— I hope to travel around the world. The main change will be that what I do will be self-motivated. I won't be under obligation to re-

[4] Stokes and Maddox, 1967, p. 333. It should be pointed out that the second contact in the research conducted by Stokes and Maddox was six years after the first interview. Our data suggest that the situation is somewhat more complicated. In this study "short run" includes persons contacted two years after retirement. The data of the two studies are not precisely comparable.

port to students. You know when you carry out your work, it's not interesting all the time. Retirement won't affect me financially. I have my teacher's pension and Social Security, and my home is paid for. And then I have income property.

This case clearly indicates a very positive attitude toward retirement plus precise plans for the new leisure time available and the intellectual, psychological, and economic resources to carry them out.

Just as the effect of prior attitude upon satisfaction with retirement is greater than the effect of the retirement situation, so the same seems to be the case with satisfaction with life, as shown in Table 55. (For a description of our measurement of

Table 55. Situation and attitude and satisfaction with life by sex and retirement category (in per cent scored "satisfied")

	R'54	R'56	R'57	R'58	Total
Men					
Voluntary	42	46	45	49	45
Administrative	35	33	37	34	35
Willing	47	54	49	57	50
Reluctant	26	28	32	32	29
Women					
Voluntary	53	49	35	57	49
Administrative	52	46	29	59	51
Willing	62	46	31	68	55
Reluctant	39	49	34	55	46

satisfaction with life, see Chapter 8 above.) Again, prior attitude means attitude toward retirement in the year before retirement and satisfaction with life means satisfaction in the retirement year. The greater effect of prior attitude than of situation is more clearly shown among the men than among the women.

Now we would like to investigate in more detail the respondents' pre- and post-retirement evaluations of the effect of retirement for specific items.

Being with people and doing a good job are two important noneconomic motives for working. The respondents were asked in 1956 and again in 1958 about these aspects of their work. It is possible to compare pre- and post-retirement responses for R'57 and R'58. We worded the questions in this way: "How often would you miss being with other people at work if you stopped working?" for those who were still working; and "How often do you miss being with other people at work?" for those who were retired. Table 56 gives the proportion of each group who responded "often." The responses to the question: "How often would you (do you) miss the feeling of doing a good job?" are also given in Table 56. More women than men said they would and do often miss being with other people at work and would and do often miss the feeling of doing a good job. The second finding, that women more than men say they would and do often miss the feeling of doing a good job, tends to confirm our previously reported findings on the importance of work for older women.

In all cases the post-retirement assessment results in fewer reporting they often *do* than reported they often *would*. Among the R'57 and R'58 women the change between pre- and post-retirement is most marked. Again it would seem that the adverse effects of retirement are overestimated before retirement is actually experienced.

It is also interesting to compare the answers of the men and the women. In answers to all four pre-retirement questions by the 1957 retirees, the women are more apt to express apprehension about the effects of retirement. For example, only 25 per cent of the men say they expect to miss the other people at work in comparison to 63 per cent of the women.

An examination of two items in Table 56 that we have not considered before shows again the tendency we have already noted for persons to overestimate the adverse effects of retirement. In 1956 and 1958, respondents were asked, "How often would you (do you) feel you want to go back to work?" and

Table 56. The effect of retirement on selected attitudes (in per cent responding "often")

Pre-retirement (1956)

Question	Men R'57 (153)	Men R'58 (166)	Women R'57 (48)	Women R'58 (87)
How often *would* you miss being with other people at work?	25	42	63	56
How often *would* you miss the feeling of doing a good job?	26	48	44	54
How often *would* you feel you want to go back to work?	12	32	21	21
How often *would* you worry about not having a job?	8	21	15	14

Post-retirement (1958)

Question	Men R'57 (153)	Men R'58 (166)	Women R'57 (48)	Women R'58 (87)
How often *do* you miss being with other people at work?	16	25	29	28
How often *do* you miss the feeling of doing a good job?	14	21	27	20
How often *do* you feel you want to go back to work?	8	13	8	8
How often *do* you worry about not having a job?	0	4	0	2

"How often would you (do you) worry about not having a job?" While these two items seemed to elicit fewer apprehensions in advance, the reported reality again turns out to be less stressful than many anticipated.

Should Older People Stop Working?

In the early phases of the research, respondents were asked whether they would stop working or continue to work if it were up to them alone. The early results suggested some ambiguity because it was not clear whether or not the question assumed that a person had an adequate income. Since economic considerations might enter into a person's response to the question, the researchers attempted a clarification of the question in 1956 and

Table 57. Effect of retirement upon attitude toward stopping work (in per cent agreeing with the statement, "If they can afford it, when people get older they ought to stop work and take things easy")

Sex and year	R'54	R'56	R'57	R'58	WW'58
Men					
1956	84	80	71	54	38
1958	86	84	82	71	44
Women					
1956	66	63	42	37	28
1958	78	76	71	60	42

1958. Respondents were asked whether they agreed or disagreed with the statement, "If they can afford it, when people get older they ought to stop work and take things easy." Table 57 shows the distribution of those respondents who agreed with the statement. In general, fewer women agree than men, both before and after retirement. There is a tendency for persons who retired earlier to express a favorable attitude toward "stopping work and taking things easy," while those who continued working

were much less apt to agree with our statement. Those people
who continued to work throughout the study evidenced the
greatest hostility to stopping work, even when the hypothetical
situation specified that economic needs are met. As the respondents get older they tend to agree in higher proportions, but
the retirement experience itself effects greater changes in the
proportions who say people should stop working if they can
afford it.

In further questioning about the impact of retirement, we
asked respondents whether they found not working was a diff-
ficult experience. As shown in Table 58, from two-thirds to
three-fourths of the various categories reported that they *did not*

Table 58. Proportion of respondents who did
not find not working difficult (in per cent)

Sex and year	R'54	R'56	R'57	R'58
Men	(373)	(216)	(153)	(166)
1954	70			
1956	75	68		
1958	79	71	73	69
Women	(103)	(67)	(48)	(87)
1954	76			
1956	79	71		
1958	79	74	73	81

find it difficult to be retired. The pattern is the same for women
as men and there is a slight tendency for the percentage of those
retirees reporting no difficulty to increase with age.

By now it seems clear from the data that our respondents do
not think that retirement is a terribly difficult experience and
that men and women do not differ very much in their response
to that experience. As a final check on their general attitude
toward retirement, at each time period all the respondents were
asked, "Would you say that retirement is mostly good for a
person or mostly bad?" The distribution of responses is given

in Table 59. Generally, fewer women than men, both before
and after retirement, say that retirement is mostly good for a
person, though the differences are not great. The group that did
not retire at all during the study period is least optimistic. This
confirms other findings, since it is clear that actual retirement
makes a difference in how a respondent evaluates retirement.
Except for men R'56, the changes in the proportion who say
"retirement is mostly good for a person" in the year after retirement are quite dramatic (20 to 40 per cent increases).

It seems clear most of the retired respondents have come to
terms with the actual fact of retirement. For whatever reason,
as a group they do not define it negatively. In order to illustrate
the point, let us select one cohort—those men and women who
retired in 1954—as an example. We asked, "Would you say that
not working has turned out better or worse than you expected?"

Table 59. Pre- and post-retirement attitudes toward
retirement (in per cent saying retirement
is mostly good for a person)

Sex and year	R'54	R'56	R'57	R'58	WW'58
Men	(373)	(216)	(153)	(166)	(282)
1952	**44**	53	52	41	31
1954	**83**	**67**	53	40	28
1956	83	**70**	**65**	44	34
1958	87	85	**81**	**75**	38
Women	(103)	(67)	(48)	(87)	(94)
1952	**62**	52	35	44	36
1954	**81**	**46**	40	34	22
1956	81	**67**	**44**	46	32
1958	85	76	**77**	**76**	33

Note: Crucial before and after comparisons, showing
percentages before retirement and in the year of retirement, are shown in boldface.

About a third (31 per cent) of both men and women say that retirement has turned out better than they expected, only 4 (women) or 5 (men) per cent say it has turned out worse, and nearly two-thirds (64 per cent of 373 men and 65 per cent of 103 women) say it turned out about the way they expected. Perhaps our respondents are coming to terms with what is an unpleasant experience by some process such as that outlined by the theory of cognitive dissonance. This could be tested to some extent by the reaction of those who themselves chose to retire. But we have found that prior attitude was more important than whether they were retired by administrative decision or whether they chose to retire. In any event these older persons seem to have adjusted to the change in status effected by retirement.

Retiree Reports

The aggregate survey data give an over-all picture of satisfaction or dissatisfaction with retirement, but behind the thousands of replies to the questionnaires are complex, functioning human beings whose attitudes and behavior are difficult to describe in summary statistical form. Again, the case study material from a random sample of retirees offers striking impressions of how various respondents acted quite differently in coping with retirement.

The over-all view of the questionnaire results indicates that many of the respondents had adapted successfully to their retirement situation. Yet popular literature, newspaper accounts, and public hearings often describe the bitter, hostile retiree who dislikes his life situation in retirement. An example of this type of person was interviewed in the sample follow-up. He said:

I dislike retirement. Personally I think it is better to keep busy. When you are not occupied and not useful, you feel like a back number. The world gets along without you. Sometimes I think about suicide. There is nothing to do but read—it's hard keeping occupied. I used to bowl, golf, but I have a coronary and can't shovel snow or golf or mow the lawn. But I haven't slowed down mentally.

Yesterday I answered an ad—80 dollars a month, answering a phone, nine to five, six days a week. Or I may get my old job back. The man who replaced me is not working out satisfactorily. Retirement is the bunk. I had two years to go. But I quit. I could have worked longer. Circumstances made me discouraged. [Interviewer: "Do you belong to any clubs or social groups?"] Not any more. I just drifted away.

This man's responses must be viewed in the context of other facts in his life. He reported that he had married for the first time in his middle fifties, as he had lived with his mother and supported her until her death. He felt considerable hostility toward a younger brother whom he helped to put through school, but later the brother never helped in support of the mother. He sees his brother rarely, and when they do meet, the visit usually ends in a dispute. This case of poor adjustment to retirement shows the complexity of the variables which affect one's response and adaptation. This man's low morale was due not only to retirement, but also to poor health, quarrelsome relatives, absence of social groups, and lack of children or grandchildren.

Another case which would be classified toward the negative end of the retirement adjustment continuum illustrates the way in which family relationships can be a compounding factor in the retirement equation. This man had four children by his first wife. He then married a woman with three small sons. At the time of the interview they were all in their twenties, all unmarried and living at home. Although they had good jobs, they paid only $10 a week for room and board, which the respondent felt was not enough. He expressed the opinion that they should be "on their own," and that they were mainly interested in his money. In speaking about his retirement situation, he said:

When a man retires, management should not belittle him. They should keep him at an interesting job, and show him that he is valuable. The last thirty to sixty days that I was working, I was a nobody. Gradually they phased me out. They did not make me feel valuable.

The only thing I don't like about retirement is that it means I am getting old. When you are young, you plan to get married, get a home, have kids, be happy. I'm content here, but my daughter keeps wanting me to come out to California where she lives. What should I do—sell my house? How can a retired man satisfy his kids' demands? My kids are good. But they don't want to get ahead. They are just waiting for my money. They don't want my help—just my money. An older person is in everyone's way. If you have money, then it's fine. You need to pay your way.

One had the impression that this man had time to brood over his family situation now that he was retired. His feelings that he was being exploited by his children obviously colored his view of retirement.

Then there were those cases whose attitudes toward retirement were ambivalent—sometimes negative and sometimes positive. One man said:

I don't like it. I like to work. But then, some days I get up and maybe I don't feel so well, and the weather is bad outside, and then I think it might not be so bad after all to stay in bed! The main problem is finding something to do. In the summer I have the yard and the house. And then I do a little cabinet work—cupboards, tables, and repairs, but you can't do that all the time. It's mainly in the winter that I'm concerned about what to do. I guess I'll watch TV more. Then I have a lot of reading to do. I may do more work around the house. [The respondent's wife added, "He likes to cook and bake, and he's a wonderful cook!"]

Then I'll probably do a little decorating. My daughter says she will keep me busy. I see all my daughters very regularly. I used to stop in three or four times a week to see my grandchild on the way home from work. [Wife added, "He's French, and you know how they are said to be close families."]

Then in the back of my mind is the thought that I'll get a job, part time. In my work, I tested cement and materials for companies who deal with the state. I could get something part time, and mostly in the summer.

One is left with the impression that this man is uncertain whether he will adjust to retirement or not, but that his wife and family will give him a great deal of emotional support and help him in the transition.

Another man who was lukewarm about retirement said:

Retirement is all right. The only thing is there is not enough money and I've got nothing to do with my time. But you can't work all the time. I cut down on expenses—eat cheaper food. I *have* to like it—what else can I do? Look for work? You can't get work. Past 50, they don't want to hire you. But my family is always glad to see me. My son built a new home. So I moved in his old house. Of course I pay rent. I've got a good daughter-in-law and three fine grand-children.

Finally, we found many people who were frankly enthusiastic about retirement:

Retirement means everything to me! I'm so happy about the whole set-up. When I was 68 I was retired. I was pleased. I'm having a good time. [Interviewer: "Do you have problems keeping occupied?"] No! I'm getting along just fine. But then I've never worried. I am not the worrying type. There is no use kicking against bricks! I just got back from a two-week vacation and I'm returning there in October. I don't have any trouble keeping busy. On Monday I gardened. On Tuesday I played 18 holes of golf. Sometimes I bowl. On Wednesday I did yard work all morning. On Saturday I went fishing. I read a lot. In the winter I go to my lodge, and play cards. I get in more golfing and bowling than when I worked. I've had several job offers but I don't want to work. I've read the Bible through twice in less than a year since I retired. I pray a lot.

One thing I would like to say again—I say it to my wife several times a day. I'm so thankful. We have such a good life. We have our home—our family—we're taken care of with my pension—we go when we want to. It's *very nice.*

Another respondent gave this reply:

I like retirement! I'm 69 and I figure I got about 10 years to live, and I'm going to enjoy myself. Now my brother—he won't quit. He's a salesman. But I worked until I was 68. Then I figured it was time to get out. I'm not bothered by not working—I just don't worry about it. Oh, I probably would go back if I get enough money, like a supervisor's job. But why work? I'm happy and contented. I do a lot of sitting around—clean up the house—do some reading—help my wife. Take a walk. I'm enjoying life. I got a wonderful wife. We get along fine. She never bothers me. She helps to make my life happy.

Still another respondent, who was clearly at the poverty level economically, was contented:

I'm tickled to death I'm retired. You can do as you please. You can get up at five A.M. or at eleven o'clock. We get along pretty well financially although we get kind of a raw deal on Social Security— we get only 147 dollars a month for the two of us. I would have gladly stayed on working but I was not eligible for a pension. I do different things to keep busy—I read a lot more and watch more TV. I cut down smoking to half what I used to, and cut out drinking. But I can still get in the jalopy and go—we have 11 children and 27 grandchildren. Once a year we have a big reunion. I'm all right—I'm still active.

Summary

In this chapter we have tried to assess the effect of not working upon attitudes toward retirement itself. This was indexed by having respondents estimate how much they missed various aspects of work. About a third of the retired respondents could be classified as "satisfied" on our four-item scale. There is a tendency for those persons who retire early to be more satisfied than those who stop work later.

In an attempt to compare the relative influence of the prior attitude (willingness to retire) and the situation of retirement (whether administrative or voluntary), we concluded that the prior attitude is more influential in determining satisfaction than is the actual mode of retirement.

Our data also show that respondents tend to overestimate the adverse effects of retirement. There is a distinct trend for retirees to say that retirement is "mostly good for a person," while a much lower percentage of those who continue working express such an evaluation.

CHAPTER 11

Rejection of the Retiree Role: Why Do Some Retirees Return to Work?

We have now examined a number of important issues related to the retirement role: the reasons why some people retire initially, the importance of health and economic factors in retirement, and the role played by social-psychological factors such as age identity, satisfaction with life, and feelings of usefulness. Another important issue which has interesting sociological considerations as well as personal and policy implications is why some retirees return to work. We know that many retirees are hostile to retirement and yet over time many become adjusted to their role as retirees. However, some people do return to the labor force and thus reject the retiree role. It is of sociological interest to analyze the process of role rejection and role transition for those persons who change from the role of retiree to that of "retired-worker."

Once again, it is pertinent to point out that a longitudinal study permits the analysis of role change in a more rigorous fashion than would be possible in cross-sectional studies. We have information before the persons stopped work, and thus we can examine how these characteristics may be related to returning to full-time gainful employment.

The general focus of the analysis is indicated in Diagram 1. Our central interest is in the factors which may explain why some persons rejected the retiree rule while most remained in it. Thus the analysis is a comparison of the retired (1956) and the retired-working (1956). The data are for males only in the first three waves of the study. We shall examine indices on which we have observations for 1954 and 1952 in order to determine whether antecedent factors influenced a person to continue as a retiree or to return to a worker role.

Diagram 1. Longitudinal analysis of staying retired or returning to work

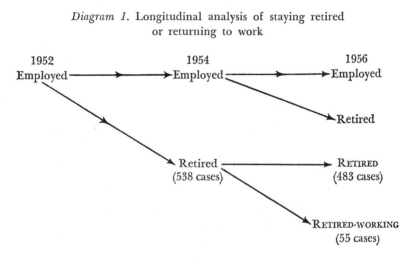

Two major clusters of variables will be investigated in order to determine whether they played a part in influencing persons to remain in the retiree role or to return to the worker role. The first cluster is called motivating factors and the second enabling factors. The first can be considered to be more directly causative in structuring the role of retiree or retired-worker.

Motivating Factors

Orientation to the Retiree Role

One of the crucial factors involved in role acceptance and role change is orientation toward the role itself. We shall examine the orientation which the actor holds specifically toward the role of retiree and how evaluation of the role may be a significant factor influencing the person to give it up.

The advantages of longitudinal design are clearly demonstrated when one tries to analyze the process of role evaluation and role change through time. In this study it was possible to obtain the respondent's evaluation of the retiree role *before* retirement (in 1952). In Table 60 the data are presented which show that before retirement the retired-working already had a negative orientation toward the retiree role. These persons were more likely to say that retirement is "bad" for a person and that they would continue working if they had the power to decide whether to stop work and retire or whether to continue working. In anticipation of the new role, the retired-working had a negative orientation, for almost one-half of the retired-working compared to less than one-fifth of the retired had unfavorable attitudes toward retirement *before they retired.*

How did the two categories of persons view the retiree role *after* they had retired? About eighteen months after retirement, we obtained information to determine the ways in which the retirees defined the role they were then enacting. The last three items in Table 60 show that the retired-working were more likely to define the retiree role negatively than the persons who continued in retirement. We note, for example, that almost three-fourths of the retired compared to one-half of the retired-working were "satisfied" with retirement. Moreover, about one in ten in the former category as compared to about three in ten in the latter said they found not working "very difficult." A similar pattern is noted for the answers to the question: "About how long would you say it took you to become used to not working?" Approximately 53 per cent of the retired-working compared to 29 per cent of the retired reported that they were still not used to retirement. Thus, we see that a negative pre-retirement evaluation of the retiree role was confirmed by the reality of retirement and must have been one of the major determinants resulting in the role change.

Orientation to Work and Change in Role

The acceptance or rejection of a particular role is affected also
by the general cultural context of which the role is a part. When
we analyze why older persons remain in retirement or why they
return to work, one of the important variables we must examine
is the way in which work is viewed in the general constellation
of values and activities in the society. A number of observers of
American society have pointed out that work ranks high in the
hierarchy of values.[1] There is a growing body of empirical evidence which shows quite consistently that work is generally considered a major life activity which is positively valued. Weiss

Table 60. Indices of dissatisfaction with retiree role for
those who continued in retirement and those who
returned to work (in per cent)

Index	Retired (483)	Retired-working (55)
Attitudes-toward-retirement scale: "Unfavorable" (1952)	19	45
Satisfaction-with-retirement scale: "Satisfied" (1954)	72	51
Difficulty in not working: "Very difficult" (1954)	11	31
Time required to get used to not working: "Not used to it" (1954)	29	53

Note: Tests of statistical significance have not been used
because of the question of the relevancy of such tests for the
kinds of data analyzed here and because of the exploratory
nature of the research. For a discussion of the factors which
determine when significance tests are too weak, too strong,
or irrelevant see Seymour Martin Lipset, Martin Trow, and
James Coleman, *Union Democracy* (Garden City, N.Y.,
Doubleday Anchor Books, 1962), pp. 480–485.

[1] Williams, 2d; 1960, p. 423.

and Morse, for example, report in their study on the meaning of work that 80 per cent of a sample of male workers say they would continue working even if they were financially independent.[2] Friedmann and Havighurst conclude their study of older persons in five different occupations by observing: "Work is important as a source of interesting, purposeful activity and as a source of intrinsic enjoyment for all five groups."[3] Although contradictory findings have been reported by Dubin, his research was based on a study population of younger persons of whom the majority were women.[4]

Is a positive orientation toward work a factor associated with the change in role from retiree to retired-worker? In a culture which places great importance upon work as a source of recognition and satisfactions, in addition to the economic rewards, one would expect considerable emphasis upon work as a central life value among older workers. Our questionnaire permits us to discover whether work is differentially valued by the use of a question in which respondents were asked to check those items which were the source of major comforts and satisfactions in life. The data show that a larger proportion of those persons who return to work (73 per cent) state work is a major source of satisfaction compared to those who remain in retirement (55 per cent). Thus, it appears that an emphasis upon the positive meanings of work is another factor associated with changing from the retiree to the worker role among older men.

Another important aspect to consider in examining the retiree's orientation to work is whether he was compulsorily retired by his employer or retired voluntarily. Data show that a much larger percentage of the retirees who returned to work were compulsorily retired (84 per cent) as compared to those

[2] Morse and Weiss, 1955.

[3] Friedmann and Havighurst, 1954, p. 174.

[4] Dubin, 1956. The sex and age distributions do not appear in the publication. Professor Dubin kindly reported them to G. F. Streib in personal correspondence.

retirees who stayed in retirement (65 per cent). The evidence presented above which showed that the retired-worker found more satisfaction in his work is given additional support by this finding.

Another facet of the orientation toward the role of the retiree is the person's attitude toward his economic situation. We must emphasize here that the attitude one has toward his economic position may not reflect the actual economic situation, which will be discussed later in this chapter.

To measure subjective orientation toward one's economic position we employed a scale of economic deprivation. Our findings show that the retired-working are more likely to indicate feelings of deprivation (46 per cent of 55 cases) than those who remained retired (31 per cent of 483 cases). These data, along with those previously discussed, indicate the importance of orientation toward objective means in influencing a role change. Two persons with approximately the same income and assets may view their situation in quite different terms. For one person an income of a certain amount may be quite adequate to meet all needs, while another in the same objective situation may define this amount as inadequate. Therefore, it would seem that although objective determinants may play a part in bringing about a change in role, there must also be an orientation toward one's economic situation which is consonant with the role change.

Thus we have presented evidence which indicates that motivating factors such as orientation to the retiree role, orientation to work, and feelings about one's economic position have a definite effect on one's acceptance or rejection or the retiree role.

Enabling Factors

Health

Another set of factors that affect an individual's return to work are what we have called the "enabling factors": health status and actual socio-economic position. Biological or constitutional factors cannot be taken for granted, particularly when the respondents are older persons. One of the inexorable aspects of life is that the older organism is more prone to illness. Hence, health is a significant enabling factor which needs to be examined in a study of persons who return to the labor force after having retired.[5]

In Table 61 data are presented on the health status of the two categories of retirees. On three of the indices we observe that the retirees who returned to work were rated as better in their health than those persons who continued as retirees. The retirees were more likely to report deterioration of their health as measured by the health deterioration scale, and they were also more likely to report that they stopped working and retired for reasons of health. These data suggest that those persons who returned to work were more likely to be in better health. This does not necessarily mean they returned to work because of their health, but that their health condition *permitted* them to return to work. It is necessary to point out, however, that the "objective" measure of health, which we have for a subgroup of our study population, indicates that a slightly larger percentage of those who stayed in retirement were in better health than those who returned to work.

Although the data for this "objective" index tends to contradict the evidence for the three other indices, it must be interpreted with caution. In the first place, the physicians' health ratings were available for only 32 per cent of the retired and for 25 per cent of the retired-working. In the latter category, this constituted only 14 cases. Further, published data from the Cornell study have shown that health questionnaires are measures of "perceived" health—how the individual "feels" about his health—and that such measures show a significant relationship to attitudinal and behavioral correlates of health.[6] Thus, among the determinants of this role change, perhaps one's perception of

[5] Streib, 1956. See also Thompson and Streib, 1958.
[6] Suchman, Phillips, and Streib, 1958.

health is more significant, than the medically determined state of health.

Socioeconomic Factors

A second enabling factor comprises a cluster of variables which we have designated socioeconomic. Although there is considerable range in the economic resources of older persons, the later years are usually marked by a decline in income and a

Table 61. Health indices for retirees and for those who returned to work (in per cent)

Index	Retired (483)	Retired-working (55)
Health scale: Self-appraisal "good" or "excellent"	57	73
Health deterioration scale: "Deterioration"	20	7
Poor health given as reason for stopping work initially	15	2
M.D. health rating: "Satisfactory" *	84	79

* Based upon M.D. rating for 32 per cent of retired ($N = 153$) and 25 per cent of retired-working ($N = 14$) categories.

tendency toward dissavings. For the purposes of analysis we have somewhat arbitrarily classified the indices under three categories: (1) Economic: income and home ownership; (2) Occupational-educational: type of occupation before retirement and level of education; (3) Subjective: class identification. The pertinent survey data on these five socioeconomic characteristics are summarized in Table 62.

First, let us examine the way in which income and home ownership are related to changing to the worker role. We have used $150 a month as a cut-off point for income. This amount is roughly approximate to that which Steiner and Dorfman called a "standard" budget in 1957 for an urban couple not living with relatives.[7] In Table 62, the data show that about equal proportions of both the retired and retired-working have incomes of less than $150 per month. On the second objective indicator of economic position, home ownership, there is a tendency for the retired to be more affluent than those who return to the labor force. Several writers on the economics of aging have suggested that home ownership may be one of the reasons that some older persons are able to maintain a modicum of economic independence, particularly with a sharp decrease in income upon retirement. The data on home ownership do point up the fact that those who remain in the retiree role may be in a somewhat more advantageous economic position than those persons who

Table 62. Socioeconomic characteristics of the retired and retired-working (in per cent)

Characteristics	Retired (483)	Retired-working (55)
Economic		
Less than $150/month income	34	36
Own home	77	64
Occupational-educational		
Occupation		
Clerical	8	20
Skilled	35	33
Semiskilled	18	13
Unskilled	20	18
Education		
Grade school or less	33	18
Some college or more	10	22
Subjective		
"Working-class" identification	63	47

[7] Steiner and Dorfman, 1957, p. 71.

return to work. However, we must emphasize that the two categories of retirees do have about the same percentages with a "standard" income or less per month, but, as pointed out previously, a larger percentage of the retired-working *feel* economically deprived.

Turning to the second set of items, occupational status and educational attainments, we note a more advantageous level on both items for those who return to work. The retired-working are more likely to have engaged in white-collar clerical occupations than those who stayed retired; this higher proportion is probably a reflection of a higher level of education. White-collar occupations and higher educational attainments combine to aid an older person who wants to return to the labor market. In the first place, the greater amount of education implies skills in job seeking—answering advertisements, writing letters, using the telephone for business purposes, employing interpersonal skills advantageously—which are essential in order to obtain employment when one is an older person and perhaps discriminated against because of age. It is also possible that the more highly educated white-collar people have a wider range of occupations open to them. On the one hand, persons who have engaged in heavier work are not as likely to seek re-employment; the release from hard and debilitating work is undoubtedly welcome. On the other hand, persons who have held clerical jobs in which physical strength is less important may continue to work with greater ease and with probably less harmful effects upon their health.[8]

We observe another striking difference between the two categories when we examine subjective socioeconomic position: the retired-working are much less likely to identify with the working class than are the retired. The tendency to identify with the middle class is probably a reflection of the higher educational attainments and the greater proportion of clerks among the retired-working. It also suggests that the person is more likely to

[8] Dublin, Lotka, and Spiegelman, 1949, esp. pp. 212–235.

seek individual rather than collective solutions for his economic problems.[9] In the later years persons who identify with the middle class are, therefore, more likely to seek employment in order to maintain a middle-class standard of living. Seeking work after retirement is also a reflection of the importance of motivations related to the Protestant ethic and the importance of meeting economic needs in individualistic, rationalistic, work-oriented terms.

Thus we see a complex pattern of health and socioeconomic determinants which influence the role change: an identification with the middle class, plus higher educational and occupational skills which are useful in obtaining and holding a job compatible with one's physical condition in the later years of life.

It should be emphasized that the preceding analysis is based on people who returned to full-time work. In addition, some of the respondents engaged in occasional part-time work. The conclusions from a nationwide study of Social Security recipients agree with the Cornell findings that only a small percentage of older persons leave the labor force and then re-enter it. A major constraining factor which inhibits the return to full-time employment is the loss of Social Security benefits. The Social Security regulations at the time of this study provided that if a person's income from employment exceeded $1,200 a year, his benefits would be proportionately reduced. Hence, a person would have to be very strongly motivated to return to work and would have to feel that the economic gains would offset the cut in Social Security benefits.

There are two other considerations which may influence the return to the labor force: the number of job opportunities and the availability of transportation. While we did not gather sys-

[9] An interesting finding in relation to class identity and downward mobility in old age is reported in Tissue, 1970. He found that the aged poor from middle-class backgrounds are more likely to cling to their beliefs in the equity and propriety of the larger social system than persons of working-class origins.

tematic data in the primary surveys on the job opportunities available, we were able to obtain some information on this matter from the personally-conducted interviews. Generally, the available jobs are reduced because of discrimination on the basis of age. Employers often do not want to hire older workers because of fear that they will not be able to keep up with the work, that they will get injured, have higher absenteeism, etc. Also, the reduced ability to drive a car and the nonavailability of public transportation may hamper a return to work. Because of these factors, old people are more likely to seek part-time employment.

Retiree Reports

The follow-up survey, in which a sample of the retirees were interviewed personally by the senior author, revealed that a number of the participants had engaged in part-time work. For example, one man said:

I work in a gas station sometimes—not for pay, but he gives me gas, oil, a grease job, etc. Then I do some work for the landlady, like sprinkle her lawn. What I'd really like to do is get an easy job —one with a lot of walking. I stayed in St. Petersburg one winter— I got a job for a rich lady. I was her chauffeur from December to April. But my brothers and sisters are up North so I came back. I have applied for a kitchen job in a government hospital. I would get room, board, and pay. If I got it I would be able to save quite a bit.

Another case seemed to feel the need to do outside work. He said:

I've been working for a real estate company that my son works for— trying to sell new houses. I haven't sold any yet, but I have four or five deals cooking. I'll get a commission when I sell them. So far I've spent 30 dollars on gas. The boss loaned me his car to drive around. I've also worked at fairs and at the voting booth at election time. I have no steady job. Maybe I'll clerk at the hardware store— I like that kind of work.

One senses that this man does not really need work, and will not make a serious effort to seek a steady job. He seems to indicate that he likes to "remain involved" and make plans. However, he later recounted warmly the visits to his children's homes in other cities, and one felt that he would not sacrifice them for a steady job.

In constrast, a man who stopped work suddenly three years previously because of an acute attack of arthritis was very resentful. He said:

I don't like retirement. If I could get out and get a job, I would. It means a lot to a man to work. I don't like this—I feel forced out. I'm going to lick this—I'm going to get a job. I have a cataract on my right eye so I can't read. But I am going to find *something*.

Other retirees mentioned the desire to find occasional work, or a few hours a day on a steady basis. They spoke of such jobs as parking cars, answering telephones, working seasonally as at Christmas or at fair time, and so on. Women in particular could find occasional work as babysitters or homemaking aides if they desired and their health permitted. Another man said:

I work until I have made 1200 dollars. I have my engineer's license and worked in a theater until I made the maximum allowance of 1200 dollars. I had to refuse 395 dollars for excess earnings last year. Another year I worked for a detective agency as a guard. I have no trouble getting work and will get a regular job again after the first of the year.

Summary

In this chapter we have examined the factors which influence a change in role—namely, rejecting the retiree role and returning to the labor force. We considered two sets of factors: motivating and enabling. In the first category we found that a person's orientation toward work may influence him to change from retiree to worker. The data also show that among the most important factors determining a change in a person's role are the actor's orientation toward the role before he enters it and his evaluation of the role after it has been imposed upon him. The data suggest that role changes are a crescive process which is strongly affected by social and personal factors. Health and socioeconomic condition are enabling factors which may determine whether a person changes his role from retiree to worker.

CHAPTER 12

Summary and Interpretation

Overview of Major Findings

It is useful to summarize the major findings of our research and to examine their implications for students and scholars concerned with problems of an aging population.

The findings show that there are two age foci for retirement: age 65 and age 70. Our data indicate that both men and women of higher income levels, higher educational attainments, and higher levels of the occupational structure tend to work longer than their counterparts with lower socioeconomic status. Among women we find that those who are living with their spouse are more likely to retire earlier than those who are widowed, divorced, or separated.

The social-psychological aspect of retirement—namely, whether persons are "willing" or "reluctant" to retire—indicates, as one might expect, that those persons who are favorably disposed toward retirement are much more likely to retire than those persons who are psychologically reluctant to do so.

In the latter part of the life cycle health looms as an important part of one's personal life, and in studies of aging and retirement the analyst must include health as a variable. Our results show that there is a moderate decline in subjectively rated health as the respondents age from 65 to 70. However this decline in reported health does not seem to be the result of retirement per se, for those respondents who continued to work showed about the same kind of decline in the self-assessment of their health as did those who retired. The "myth" that retirement causes a decline in health does not appear to be supported. The respondents themselves seem to be captured by this myth for there is a tendency *before* retirement for them to overestimate the adverse effects of stopping work upon their health. The examination of the health information by occupational categories shows that some subgroups—the clerical and semiskilled—had a slightly greater decline in reported health than those who kept on working. However among the unskilled—those who presumably engaged in harder physical work—there is a trend toward a slight improvement in health after retirement.

In any study related to aging and the aged, one must take account of economic factors and attitudes toward monetary matters. The respondents in this longitudinal study reported a sharp drop in actual dollar income which was approximately a 50 per cent reduction from pre-retirement levels. However when we turn to subjective income—the way older persons evaluate their income—we found that the indices show a decline in feelings of income adequacy and then a leveling off after the first year of retirement. Even after a severe cut in income, about two-thirds of the respondents reported that their income was "enough." Indeed about one-fourth of the retirees said their standard of living in retirement was better than it had been in earlier periods of their lives. Among those who continued to work beyond age 65 we find no decline in subjective income over time.

Age identification was employed as a crude index of self-image in later life to determine whether retirement has a critical effect upon this dimension of the social-psychological aspects of aging. The pattern of an increasingly older age identification was found, whether a person retired or continued working, and the pattern for women followed the trend for men. There was also a tendency for women at all points in the study to classify themselves as "younger" compared to men of the same age.

It should be stressed that when we compare the older persons who work with those who retired we find about the same shift in age identification over time in both worker and retiree categories. These longitudinal data suggest that our respondents hold a realistic view of the aging process.

Another important gauge of the effect of retirement from a social-psychological perspective is our measure of feelings of usefulness. A comparison shows that over time the older person who works is more likely to have feelings of usefulness than the person who retires. However the proportion of retired older persons who have feelings of uselessness is, in general, less than one-quarter of the study population. There is a tendency for feelings of uselessness—unlike age identification—to increase somewhat in the impact year of retirement. More surprising is the fact that women who retire report a sharper increase in feelings of uselessness than do their retired male counterparts. This finding certainly suggests that further research is needed to examine the stereotyped idea that the male retiree will find it harder to occupy his time than the older woman who retires.

In assessing an older person's psychological health by means of questionnaire data, complex psychological states may easily be oversimplified. We employed a three-item, Guttman-type measure of "general satisfaction with life." Time itself does have a slight over-all negative effect upon life satisfaction in this older population. More specifically we wanted to assess more precisely the effect of retirement in the period just after retirement and compare it with feelings reported before retirement. The data suggest that change in psychological health (as measured by this scale) cannot be directly attributed to retirement itself. There is a very slight decline, but retirement does not cause a sudden deterioration in psychological health as has been asserted by other writers.

Another social-psychological dimension which was assessed was the direct effect of retirement itself upon attitudes toward retirement. This was accomplished by asking the respondents to state what they missed about not working. The data showed that early retirees were somewhat more likely to be "satisfied" than those who retired later. This was also found about an item which asked persons to say whether retirement is mostly good for an older person. Retirees were much more optimistic about their retirement; in contrast, persons who continue working were the most negative about the effect of retirement. Retirees do tend to overestimate the adverse effects of retirement. This type of information can be obtained more precisely in a longitudinal study because estimates of the effect were obtained before retirement and reports of the impact of retirement were secured after it had happened. The data tend to support the proposition that one's prior attitude is more important than the mode of retirement (administrative or voluntary) in determining whether a person is "satisfied" with retirement or with life in general.

Retirement and Role Theory: A Reinterpretation

Role theory—both structural and social-psychological—is the theoretical perspective that was employed in the Cornell Study of Occupational Retirement. We have examined the consequences of dropping or disrupting a major role in the latter part of the life cycle. At the outset of the study, we considered retirement—the dropping of the worker role—as having deleterious consequences to the individual's social-psychological adjustment. Thus our approach to role theory has been to analyze roles in old age in real-life terms. This is similar to what Merton and Barber describe as the sociographic approach to roles: viewing them as categories taken from everyday life and not as abstract concepts from sociological theory.[1]

[1] Merton and Barber, 1963, distinguish three kinds of role analysis: depictive, sociographic, and analytical. They also emphasize that their work in this particular paper is mainly sociographic.

A summary overview of the data shows that retirement does not have the broad negative consequences for the older person that we had expected. The cessation of the work role results in a sharp reduction in income, but there is no significant increase in "worry" about money in the impact year of retirement. There is no sharp decline in health, feelings of usefulness, or satisfaction in life after retirement. Neither do respondents suddenly think of themselves as "old" when they stop working. How can we account for the disjuncture between the hypothesized relationship of the factors and the actual data?

First, it is useful to point out that from the perspective of the sociology of knowledge, the original formulation of the relationship between the retirement and the consequential variables was developed in a period when studies of aging and retirement were viewed by researchers from a social and personal problems point of view, which tended to stress the dysfunctional and pathological aspects of a phenomenon. At the start of this research, this perspective influenced the theoretical formulation of the problem.

Another and perhaps more fundamental explanation for the broad results which are summarized here is that the theoretical orientation—role theory—was inadequately and imprecisely formulated for studies of the latter part of the life cycle. Although there were a few writings on role theory in relation to old age, the early thinking and empirical studies employing this theoretical perspective were developed essentially for children and young people.[2] Cooley, Mead, and their latter-day expositors, such as Lindesmith, Strauss, and others, were primarily concerned with the important problems of early socialization in relation to role taking, role changes, role crises, role adaptation, and so on.

Some of the writers who have employed role theory in rela-

[2] A notable exception was the pioneering paper of Cottrell, 1942, in which age was an explicit kind of role. It is interesting to note, however, that only one of his nine references to age and sex roles was concerned with the latter part of the life cycle.

tion to the latter part of the life cycle, such as Ruth S. Cavan and Arnold Rose, have utilized role concepts inflexibly in studying aging and older persons. In some instances there may be a sound basis for assuming a "good fit" of the theory for older age groups, but in other instances—for example, role ambiguity—the concept may not be applicable to the experience of retirees. One of the basic propositions of role theory is that clarity of role definition facilitates positive adjustment.[3] But clarity of role definition is precisely what is lacking in the retirement role, according to sociologists and social psychologists. In summarizing a large body of knowledge pertaining to retirement, Donahue, Orbach, and Pollak state: "Indeed, one might well say that the fundamental social-psychological problem of the retirement role is the lack of clarity and the ambiguity which currently characterize it."[4] Other sociologists, such as Havighurst, Parsons, and Tibbitts have emphasized this point.[5]

Wilbert Moore has expressed the problem of role ambiguity and adjustment in old age in broad sociological perspective:

Perhaps the fundamental problem of the aged in industrial societies is that they have no definite place in the social structure. That is, there are no regular, institutionally sanctioned responsibilities for their care and social participation which square with both traditional values and the requirements of an industrial system.[6]

Burgess epitomizes this point of view when he speaks of the "roleless role" of the retired:

In short, the retired older man and his wife are imprisoned in a roleless role. They have no vital function to perform. . . . This roleless role is thrust upon the older person at retirement and to a greater or lesser degree he has accepted it or become resigned to it.[7]

[3] *Ibid.*, pp. 618–619.

[4] Donahue, Orbach, and Pollak, 1960, p. 334.

[5] For example, Havighurst, 1952; Parsons, 1954; Tibbitts, 1954.

[6] Moore, 1951, p. 530.   [7] Burgess, 1960, p. 20.

In designing the Cornell Study of Occupational Retirement, we accepted the proposition that role clarity was important, and it guided the design of the study and the gathering of the data. However, our findings suggest a more positive set of consequences to retirement than had been hypothesized. Older people seem to be able to tolerate ambiguous role definitions in retirement and to adjust to them adaptively, given a situation in which deceleration and disengagement is a factual base. We conclude that propositions derived from concern with younger age groups and research on their social adjustment, which stress the need for clarity of role definition, may not be precisely applicable to a study of retirement.

Furthermore, Burgess' characterization of retirement as a "roleless role" is a somewhat simplistic conception. This viewpoint has been expanded and improved upon by later theoretical discussions of position, status, and role by writers such as Frederick L. Bates and Robert K. Merton who have pointed out that a position may have multiple roles associated with it.[8] For example, the status (position) of the older person has a distinctive role set which includes a complement of role relationships such as worker, husband, father, grandfather, neighbor, church member. The increased specification of the status-role concepts also includes a dynamic or processual aspect—status sequence—which refers to a series of positions a person occupies over a period of time and role sequence which refers to role performance in successive time periods. In our analysis of retirement we can conceive of the worker status sequence which is followed by retiree status sequence at a given time A, and this is followed by a retiree status sequence at a later time B, and so forth. Thus the retiree, say in 1954, has a distinctive role set relating to his wife, children, neighbors, relatives, etc. It is important to emphasize that part of his role set in retirement may no longer include his relationship to his employer, his immediate supervisor, his fellow workers, and others. These role

[8] Bates, 1956; Merton, 1957a, and 1957b, pp. 368 ff.

relationships may be included, of course, if the retiree has contact with them in other contexts than at the place of work, such as in the neighborhood, union hall, church or synagogue. The point to be stressed is that although the work relationships are of great importance—indeed for some they may be of commanding significance in his totality of role relationships—they are only *one* part of the role set. It is possible that upon retirement the person's role relationships may become somewhat blurred by the attenuation or even the complete cutting off of significant relationships of long standing. However, as was suggested previously, many retirees are able to tolerate this attenuation of roles which may cause role ambiguity and will ultimately result in the restructuring of their role sets over time. For some older persons the trauma may be greater than for others, but the findings summarized here suggest that many retirees are able to cope with role realignment which is one aspect of the total process of disengagement.

The "roleless role" approach has also been congruent with the thinking and emphasis of sociologists and gerontologists who view retirement primarily from a "problems perspective." This point of view also tends to be activity-oriented and concerned with sharp role distinctions and clear role demands. This may be highly desirable for earlier stages of life, but may not be so essential for later stages. In fact, in an industrial society the blurring of roles—the "roleless role" of the old—may prove to be functional for the old. While some sociologists, such as Arnold Rose, would argue that this is "putting the old on the shelf," this is precisely what many old people expect and desire.[9] Most want dignity and respect, but they may at the same time wish to avoid activity and involvement because the demands are too great.

Thus, the retiree's role expectations and those of others may be vague, but this very vagueness may be a protective mechanism which reduces demands and make explicit role perfor-

[9] Rose, 1954, p. 23.

mance more difficult to ascertain. Some might argue that this is undesirable in an achievement-oriented society with specific role demands. However, the opposite position may be taken: namely, that when the person is less capable of meeting explicit and demanding role expectations, his adaptation and his acceptance of his physical decline and his disengagement may be assisted by role ambiguity.

There is a further reason why having a clearly defined role is not as important to older persons as to younger persons. As one of the authors has written:

A clearly-defined role facilitates activity and gives a sense of security to a person involved in a network of impersonal universalistically-oriented judgments and evaluations. This may not be the kind of world in which many older people live. In the later years of life, the important persons in one's life—friends and relatives—know who the older person is and therefore he moves in a world that is familiar to him, and with which he is familiar. He may not need a sharply defined extra-familial "role" to give him an identity or to facilitate his own activity in his everyday world. We suggest therefore that so far as the older person himself is concerned, his willingness to leave the work force and perhaps his satisfaction with other aspects of life are not dependent upon whether he has a clearly-defined alternative role or not.[10]

Thus we see that the old, unlike the young and youthful, have lived a lifetime with a relatively fixed set of roles which have been internalized and enacted throughout the course of their life. The fact of role reinforcement—of enacting a role set and its components—constitutes a major anchorage point for the elderly, in contrast to younger persons who are still "finding themselves" in relation to important roles. The continuity of the major components of the role set of the aged may involve considerable gratification, esteem, prestige, etc. Butler's concept of the "life review" "as a naturally occurring, universal

[10] Schneider, 1964, p. 56.

mental process characterized by the progressive return to consciousness of past experiences" suggests how the old may relive in memory important roles and situations which may be gratifying and sustaining.[11] Indeed, if we follow role theory to its logical development, the elderly are able to relive roles and obtain gratification without actually engaging in former roles which were meaningful. Needless to say, it might be argued that the mental re-enactment of a previous role may not be as gratifying as the actual enactment.

In concluding the re-examination of role theory, we refer to the work of Sarbin and Allen in analyzing roles in earlier and later periods of the life cycle.[12] They assert that the process of learning roles in childhood is distinguished from that in adulthood by three characteristics: (1) adult roles elicit a higher degree of motivation; (2) adult roles can be superimposed upon or added to on-going roles; (3) adult roles are more likely to involve anticipatory socialization. It should be pointed out that Sarbin and Allen, like so many analysts and researchers in the role-theory tradition, are primarily concerned with early childhood and early adulthood; they give little if any attention to adulthood beyond the period when occupational roles are being learned.[13]

In the first place, roles in old age are similar to those in childhood in that there is not as high a level of motivation as is present in early adulthood. Like the child, the older person does not have the high motivation for achievement, or success, or perhaps even for economic survival that the young adult has. Low motivation for many persons in later maturity is not only a matter of perception but is also due to the fact that the

---

[11] Butler, 1968, p. 487.   [12] Sarbin and Allen, 1968.

[13] In Sarbin and Allen's long and detailed review of role theory with almost 200 references to the literature, there is only one or possibly two citations which deal with the latter part of the life cycle (*ibid.*, pp. 558–567).

reality of achievement in career or monetary terms is not great. For the older person motivation must be primarily *internal,* since society and its subgroups does not impose stringent requirements (role definitions) particularly in the occupational and economic spheres.

Secondly, in late adulthood new roles may be added or superimposed, but the more commonly observed phenomenon is the deletion or retrenchment of roles. However this fact should not distract from the related observation that the decline in roles and role obligations may provide role opportunities—in some instances almost a role vacuum—to which roles may be added or old roles expanded in new areas of behavior. One facet of the learning of roles in old age—some might describe it as an advantage—is that older persons have many anchorage points for roles when they learn new ones or expand old ones. However it should be noted that the older adult may exhibit greater rigidity of thought and behavior in adapting to new roles or modifying roles to new requirements or situations. The point to be emphasized is that older persons may take a longer time to learn new roles but many persons, if given sufficient time, will learn them as well as younger persons.[14] Moreover, the continuity with older roles, and the integration of the new, affords considerable psychic gratification to the individual involved and increases predictability of behavior.

Finally, roles in later maturity would ideally involve anticipatory socialization, since often the worker knows the exact time at which he will retire. Many older persons, however, delay making specific plans for retirement. At the present time there is not as much institutionalized anticipatory socialization for new roles in later life as in earlier periods of the life cycle.

[14] For example, a study of the retraining of tram drivers reported that up to age 60 almost all older drivers (93 per cent) could be retrained to the new job if given a few extra weeks of training (Riley, Foner, *et al.*, 1968, p. 443).

However as retirement and associated activities become increasingly institutionalized through formal courses and informal retirement planning, there will be more anticipatory socialization in this sphere.

Role theorists and researchers must give more attention to the latter part of the life cycle; most theorizing is still based upon its early phases and is thus inappropriate. The need to specify role theory for later life will hopefully stimulate more empirical research guided by new conceptualizations and theoretical orientations.

CHAPTER 13

New Perspectives
on Retirement

Retirement—A Form of Differential Disengagement

Since the data for this study were gathered, a new theoretical orientation has appeared in the gerontological literature—namely, disengagement thory.[1] It has stimulated considerable discussion and controversy, and various aspects of the theory have been adapted and tested by other researchers. It is useful at this point to discuss the theory briefly and indicate how our findings relate to it.

Retirement may be considered as one aspect of the disengagement process in later life and thus a "narrowing" of the life processes. Retirement has also been considered a loss of role and therefore a negative phenomenon. More specifically, retirement may be viewed as a withdrawal from society on the part of the individual if he initiates the process. On the other hand, society may withdraw from the individual under conditions of administrative retirement. Sometimes the process is mutually initiated.

Before discussing how disengagement theory offers new insights about the Cornell Study of Occupational Retirement, it is desirable to recount briefly the origins and development of the theory and to consider some of its implications. The so-

[1] An initial statement of the theory is given in Cumming *et al.*, 1960; a further exposition appears in Cumming and Henry, 1961.

ciological and social-psychological studies of aging and the aged in the years before the formulation of the theory of disengagement were marked by a provincial, middle-class paradigm. This paradigm could be called "activity theory" or a kind of adjustment model. The ideas in the paradigm tended to emphasize that the life span undergoes steady expansion. Even infirmity and poor health were supposed to be overcome. The basic attitude of the activity theorists was optimistic to the point of rarely, if ever, including the idea of death. Withdrawal from social interaction was considered to be a sign of "failure"; signs of deceleration were generally minimized. Retirement was considered to be an unfortunate event in the life of the older person.

When the Cornell Study of Occupational Retirement was planned and designed, its basic theoretical orientation was influenced by activity theory, like so many other studies prior to the publication of *Growing Old* in 1961. It was anticipated that retirement, i.e., cessation of work activity, would have potentially deleterious effects on morale, satisfaction with life, and ultimately physical health, and would lead to dysfunction and maladjustment in many cases.

Cumming and Henry offered a new paradigm which attracted investigators away from existing conceptual systems and at the same time was sufficiently flexible and heuristic that a new group of practitioners found many issues to resolve. Disengagement theory opened new vistas and in a sense marked a turning point in studies of the middle aged and the old. In fact, the seminal quality of the theory is evidenced by the number of empirical studies which it has stimulated.[2]

That we may have a common understanding of disengagement theory, we offer a brief summary statement in the words of Cumming and Henry:

In our theory, aging is an inevitable mutual withdrawal or disengagement, resulting in decreased interaction between the aging person and others in the social systems he belongs to. The process

[2] For example, Carp, 1968; Kleemeier, 1964; Youmans, 1967.

may be initiated by the individual or by others in the situation. The aging person may withdraw more markedly from some classes of people while remaining relatively close to others. His withdrawal may be accompanied from the outset by an increased preoccupation with himself; certain institutions in society may make this withdrawal easy for him. When the aging process is complete, the equilibrium which existed in middle life between the individual and his society has given way to a new equilibrium characterized by a greater distance and an altered type of relationship.[3]

Some writers have questioned whether disengagement theory is a genuine theory. In the words of the authors it was labeled a "tentative theory"—meaning a provisional or a trial theory. Further refinements by the original authors and others have revealed the tentative nature of the original statement.[4]

We assert that disengagement theory is not a genuine theory in a scientific sense because a theory is an inclusive set of cognitive ideas involving "conceptualizations, hypotheses, generalizations of fact and of relationship, and a system of laws." [5] It might be more accurately labeled a frame of reference or a theoretical orientation, for it is not a tightly reasoned, rigorous proposition. Like so many other theories in the field of sociology and social gerontology, it is a prisoner of the phenomena with which it deals. It could not be much more rigorous because it is concerned with concepts which can give the investigator only a rough identification of what is being studied. The originators of disengagement theory were limited because they were forced by the nature of what they studied to utilize *sensi-*

[3] Cumming and Henry, 1961, pp. 14–15.

[4] Cumming, 1963; Streib, 1968. In this chapter we have not been concerned with another important issue that has been part of the controversy concerning disengagement theory—namely, that of successful aging. The authors of *Growing Old* devoted some attention to the question and concluded that demoralization may only be a temporary phenomenon. They also stated that their findings may be a function of the instruments employed. Among the critics of disengagement theory are Maddox, 1964; A. M. Rose, 1964.

[5] Larson, 1966, p. 41.

tizing and not *definitive* concepts. The distinction between these two concepts was clearly made by Herbert Blumer, who said: "Whereas definitive concepts provide prescriptions of what to see, sensitizing concepts merely suggest directions along which to look." [6]

The Distinction between Disengagement and Alienation

The lack of conceptual precision of disengagement theory needs to be acknowledge in dealing with its use and implications.[7] Some of the controversy and ambiguity concerning disengagement arises because of the confusion in the minds of some sociologists and gerontologists in separating disengagement from alienation. These two processes and their theoretical systems are distinct in some basic respects, but they may also have some degrees of overlap. In fact, the authors of *Growing Old,* and their colleagues Dean, Newell, and McCaffrey, have confused disengagement as an aging process with processes which are more strictly sociocultural or socioeconomic in their origins. Disengagement is *biosocial* in its origins. Alienation is *sociocultural* and *socioeconomic* in its origins and can occur at any time in the life cycle. The biological roots of disengagement must be pointed out in order to differentiate it clearly from other aspects of the latter part of the life cycle. The focus of disengagement theory is upon the psychological and social-psychological effects of the biologically rooted universal fact that human organisms get old and decline.

Disengagement as a result of the aging process may also be related to alienation because of the structure of a society—particularly a modern, urban, industrial society which gives a high value to gainful employment. Thus, alienation is a concomitant of other processes which are not necessarily age related but are more clearly a consequent of the nature of modern industrial

[6] Blumer, 1954.

[7] It should be noted that Damianopoulos, 1961, is a formal statement of disengagement theory.

society, such as retirement and perhaps the resulting economic deprivation.

Perhaps a greater degree of clarity can be obtained if we distinguish between the origins and consequences of the theories of disengagement and alienation. Disengagement as a sensitizing concept is based on the fact that all people get old and decline in their capacities. By virtue of the fact that disengagement is linked conceptually and empirically to aging—growing old—it has a certain clarity that the concept of alienation does not have. Alienation is multifaceted and has many different dimensions as Feuer, Seeman, and others have shown.[8] Indeed one of the multiple meanings of alienation is indicated by the fact that the originators of disengagement theory employed alienation as a dependent variable—a consequence of disengagement. They argued that the theory of disengagement postulates that there is more alienation among the old because they have a smaller life space. Alienation, according to these writers, is a failure to conform to the dominant optimistic values of our culture.[9] This is one operational way to define and use alienation, but such usage may lead to misunderstanding if one assumes that this simplistic form of alienation is the total picture. Alienation has many facets—powerlessness, isolation, self-estrangement are three of the dimensions employed by Seeman. Thus, to sum up briefly, disengagement and alienation are quite distinct from an analytical perpsective, but they may sometimes occur simultaneously. In the Cornell study we observed one form of disengagement—in this case, cessation of the worker role. However, we did not find that it was accompanied by a high degree of loss of morale, feelings of powerlessness, or alienation.

[8] Feuer, 1963; Seeman, 1959.   [9] Cumming and Henry, 1961, p. 95.

The Cornell Study and Disengagement Theory

Disengagement theory has stimulated many social gerontologists and social psychologists to re-examine old studies and has challenged prospective researchers to be aware of its theoretical implications. We wish to examine the general findings of the Cornell study in the light of disengagement theory and also to suggest new directions for understanding retirement as a major kind of role change and a stage of disengagement of the elderly in industrialized societies. As Cumming and Henry state, "retirement is a visible point in the transition between engagement and disengagement." [10]

The activity theorists would lead us to believe that retirement is a traumatic experience and is accompanied by lower morale, loss of health, lower self-esteem, and general decline. As we have shown, in general these results were not observed in the respondents in this study. In attempting to find an explanation for our findings we may turn to a significant remark of Cumming and Henry: "Retirement is society's permission to men to disengage." [11] Thus, if disengagement is an expected characteristic of aging, and if retirement is a "normal" component of disengagement, it is not surprising that the majority of people make the adjustment without undue traumatic effects.

In other words, retirement both as a process and as an event is a result of a number of voluntary and involuntary actions. Some persons are automatically and administratively retired; similarly, others are forced to retire because of poor health. A minority stop working because of choice. Many people have advance notice and can make plans for their retirement ahead of time. Whatever the causes of retirement—and they are complex and varied—when a person retires, society redefines his roles so that fewer demands are made upon him, and he may reduce his social involvement if he wishes. Defining retirement as "per-

[10] *Ibid.*, p. 149.   [11] *Ibid.*, p. 146.

mission to disengage" enables us to view retirement as a way
of preserving self-esteem in old age. The traditional outlook
has been that retrenchment and decline in social and economic
activities may lead to a loss of self-esteem. However, an opposite view is possible: that those who view retirement as "permission to disengage" are free to lower their level of activity
and still preserve their self-esteem. They are released from com-
peting in the job situation, which, with its possibility of in-
ordinate demands upon mental and physical capacities, could
very possibly result in recognition of decreased abilities by
others in the work group and thus cause embarrassment and
loss of self-esteem.

Furthermore, disengagement in the sphere of gainful employment may permit the older person to *remain engaged* in other
spheres of life—interacting with children and grandchildren,
visiting relatives, pursuing hobbies, traveling, and the like.

Another departure point for the re-examination of our findings is a proposition from the formal statement of disengagement theory by Ernest Damianopoulos: "Because the abandon-
ment of life's central roles—work for men, marriage and family
for women—results in a dramatically reduced social life space,
it will result in crisis and loss of morale unless different roles,
appropriate to the disengaged state, are available." [12] There are
several issues in this proposition which require qualification
and criticism in the light of our general findings. Work and
family are central roles for men and women respectively, but
the assertion that, for men, retirement results in a sharp decline in social life space is not tenable for persons in many
occupations. The disengagement theorist incorrectly assumes
that work for most people is an interesting and stimulating
social experience, but this is not the case for many persons who
may tolerate the social side of work with their associates but
consider it unimportant in the long run. One has little—if any
—choice in the selection of work mates, and one's fellow em-

[12] *Ibid.*, p. 215.

ployees are usually selected for reasons other than social compatibility. In special and restricted circumstances, interpersonal compatibility and group cohesion may be an important ingredient from the standpoint of job productivity and efficiency. For example, it was found during World War II that compatible flying partners made more efficient bombing teams. However, in most work situations there is not this opportunity to control the selection of work partners through the allocation of a large pool of manpower.

Secondly, Damianopoulos asserts that the loss of the work role, because it leads to loss of social life space may result in a *crisis*. We have already challenged the assertion that the loss of work role is necessarily loss of life space. Hence it seems questionable whether loss of the work role may lead to a crisis for most older workers. Our longitudinal studies of the impact year point to the fact that retirement is usually not a crisis. Damianopoulos' use of the word "crisis" in discussing retirement indicates he views it as a potential trauma. This point of view is consistent with that of other theorists and writers who have stressed the negative results and ignored the flexibility and adaptability of many people.

Finally, Damianopoulos and others suggest lowered morale in retirement will result unless *different* roles are available to the retired person. Here again we think the disengagement theorists are asserting a unitary consequence of retirement which is not warranted. This view of retirement is similar to the older and somewhat looser statement of Ernest Burgess when he wrote about the "roleless role of the retired." We have granted the centrality of the work role for men and women who were gainfully employed in later life. However, it must be stressed that the worker role is only one of many in a person's role set. Other roles of significance are present and exercise considerable effect upon morale and feelings of role crisis. These other roles—parent, spouse, neighbor, club member, etc.—obviously vary in different persons and in various socioeconomic strata. These roles have been enacted along with the work role for most of adulthood. The problem of the retiree is often to expand engagement in those on-going roles, rather than find different roles. Other roles may have been latent and need to be reactivated, and for some persons the mere presence of latent roles, even though they are rarely enacted, may be sufficient to reduce role crisis.

Many critics of disengagement theory have come to accept the practically universal retrenchment and decline in a variety of activities by older persons. This aspect of aging appears to be almost universal. Hence one must view the related and somewhat controversial issue emerging from disengagement theory— the idea of optimum or successful aging—within this broadly accepted and well-established process of disengagement.

Disengagement, like other social and social-psychological aspects of the life of the older person, can be more precisely and more realistically analyzed by the concept of *differential disengagement*. By this term we mean that disengagement occurs at different rates and in different amounts for the various roles in a person's role set.[13] Cessation of work activity does not necessarily result in automatic disengagement in familial, friendship, neighborhood, and other role spheres. Disengagement operates unevenly in terms of role demands and in its pace. It has been assumed by those who view retirement as a crisis that retirement was the precipitant for a series of retrenchments in role activities. This may occur in some instances—indeed it may be the only kind which comes to the attention of physicians, social workers, psychiatrists, clergymen, and other therapists— but these dramatic instances should not be used as the modal pattern. The use of the dramatic case study as the basis for generalization leads only to the oversimplification of a complex

[13] In interpreting the data from a cross-national study, Neugarten and Havighurst, 1969, point out the varying patterns involved in the interactions of 12 different roles of 300 retired men. They also indicate the importance of the sociocultural setting.

process. While we do not deny the reality and poignancy of such cases, we emphasize that one must look for the modalities and major trends.

By way of summary we may say that disengagement theory employing sensitizing and not definitive concepts is useful in shedding new light on the findings of the Cornell Study of Occupational Retirement. Our data suggest that disengagement theory must be further refined to emphasize that in real life, differential disengagement is the common pattern. The research results lead us to conclude that disengagement in one sphere, such as retirement, does not signal withdrawal and retrenchment in all spheres.

New Roles for the Aged: Activity within Disengagement

We have criticized an earlier formulation of role theory because as elaborated it is not congruent with the situation of the older person under conditions of deceleration and disengagement. Therefore, from a real-life perspective we may ask: Is there a possibility of new roles emerging for the aged? The concepts of role and role sets are still valid, but they must be more clearly specified for the elderly.

As we have pointed out, the activity approach to aging tends to have a middle-class, middle-age bias in which there is an implicit notion that work or work substitutes are essential for the optimum adjustment of an older person. The disengagement approach, on the other hand, tends to have a pessimistic and negative orientation because it focuses on the intrinsic and inevitable nature of decline. Both of these points of view have elements of validity as applied to older persons. Certainly the evidence from a great variety of sources suggests the physical, psychological, and social deceleration of older people. On the other hand there is clinical evidence that suggests that physical, social, and mental activity is conducive to the well-being of persons at all stages of the life cycle, including the old. There is clearly a need to take account of these well established empirical observations which have been interpreted from the point of view of either activity or disengagement.

We propose a third approach as a means of recognizing the slowing down of the old and at the same time acknowledging the necessity for optimum activity and remaining engaged with life. What is needed is the creation of new roles for older people which take account of these key facts. Such activities should not be mere "busy work" but should be satisfying in social-psychological terms, and they must be recognized as valid pursuits that are prestigeful or socially useful by other members of society, old and young.

Before discussing possible new roles, it is desirable to set forth the working assumptions which underlie our thinking.

1. Deceleration or disengagement is inevitable in the human organism. However, it may occur quickly at the end of life, or slowly over one or two decades.

2. For optimum morale, most people need some kind of activity.

3. Older people have a strong desire for autonomy and independence, and this should be respected.

4. Old age is devalued in the United States today, for there is a cultural bias in favor of youth and youthful activities.

5. Old people possess a commodity which is in short supply in the United States—a daily supply of free time.

6. The available resources in any community are limited and thus there is keen competition for them. Power determines their allocation, and the aged are relatively weak. Hence, it is unrealistic to expect that they will ever receive all the resources they desire.

We believe that it is possible that new roles for the old can develop within these parameters. First, modern society does not require that retirees and other older persons meet societal needs in the same way that younger persons are expected to do so;

providing for one's financial needs, getting ahead, looking to the future, raising a family are all in the past. New roles are possible because the societal demands either are diminished or have changed considerably. Counterbalancing the structural possibility of new roles for the old are, of course, the obvious and important factors that the old in general have less physical and psychic energy and they have fewer material resources. But undue emphasis should not be placed upon these limiting factors. Even with the social, personal, and financial limitations, many elderly people—particularly early retirees—have the potential to develop new roles *if they wish to do so.* Moreover new roles in later life, developed and enacted by the old, can offer the opportunity to exercise the autonomy and independence which so many older persons say they want.

The new roles of "activity within disengagement" which are developing seem to fall into two main categories: the leisure role and the citizenship-service role. The leisure role is based on the assumption that the later years of life are a time of leisure, and therefore different from the middle years, just as the early years are different from the middle years. To conceptualize the later years of life as "leisure years" not only puts a positive connotation upon them, but sets them apart from the work years. This means that they can be studied on their own merits. The retiree need not merely try to seek the same satisfactions and rewards of the work years. Thus the leisure years must not be considered as simply less of the same kind of life lived in the work years. They are years for which such concepts as "usefulness" and "achievement" have a changed meaning.

Leisure is not easy to define. Kaplan discusses six aspects of leisure:

. . . (1) an antithesis to work as an economic function; (2) a pleasant expectation and recollection; (3) a minimum of involuntary social-role obligations; (4) a psychological perception of freedom; (5) a close relation to values of the culture, and the inclusion of an entire range from inconsequence and insignificance to weightiness and importance and (6) often, but not necessarily, an activity characterized by the element of play.[14]

This "theory" of leisure has been criticized for being vague and all-embracing—more of a philosophy than a description of a role. But if leisure is to be a useful analytical concept in the study of the behavior of older persons then it must not be needlessly restricted to the meaning it could have in the work life of an individual. Thus it would seem that the crucial aspects of the concept of leisure time would be, psychologically, a sense of freedom and, sociologically, an actual freedom from involuntary social-role expectations. For leisure is free time; its organization and use are not prescribed for the individual by the society or subgroups in which he lives. A real appreciation by society of the luxury of having a nonresponsible supply of time would seem to enhance the prestige of the old and make him an object of envy rather than pity.

A second major kind of new role in which some older people may engage with their new supply of time may be called the citizenship-service role. These role activities are in some instances continuations of roles carried on in previous periods. For example, the research of Norval D. Glenn indicates that older persons maintain more interest in national and international events, and have more knowledge of public personalities than younger groups in the population.[15] Moreover, the evidence cited by Glenn and others shows that until very advanced

14 Kaplan, 1961, p. 392. See also the comments on Kaplan's paper in Anderson, 1961. Anderson's main criticism of the "theory" as proposed by Kaplan is that it is not a scientific theory but a philosophy of aging. We would suggest that it is no more a philosophy than either the activity approach or the disengagement approach. Kaplan's leisure theory is another example of the lack of definitive concepts in social science. Within this basic limitation, all three "theories" can be specified and operationalized.

15 Glenn, 1969.

ages the old do not decline in turnout in elections.[16] These pieces of evidence and others of a similar character suggest that there is already some base upon which to build new citizen roles for the old.

In other instances, new kinds of behavior or increased involvement in citizenship-service activities bring a new sense of usefulness to the individual—different from the usefulness he felt as a member of the labor force, but no less valid. In recent years a number of new and imaginative programs have been initiated by private and governmental agencies which offer opportunities for older citizens to engage in service roles. For example, one of the more successful of these government-sponsored plans is the Foster Grandparents Program in which senior citizens become "grandparents" for young children who do not have any relatives who are giving them love and attention.[17] Churches and senior citizens' councils and other voluntary agencies have established other programs such as "Dial-a-Friend" in which older citizens have a list of housebound older people whom they call every day in order to check on their health and welfare and determine whether they need any immediate assistance. Another example is the hospital visiting program in which older citizens regularly visit people in mental hospitals, nursing homes, and homes for the aged. Many of these activities have a reciprocal help pattern in that one older person receives visits and care which he needs, and the other older person who is rendering the service obtains feelings of usefulness and purpose which may have been lacking in his life. One of the problems involved in such programs is in institutionalizing roles and activities which have traditionally been defined as "family" or "friendship" roles.

Some studies suggest that new roles involving mutual help patterns are evolving in many segments of American life. Some

[16] For a summary of the data pertaining to political roles and political participation, see Riley, Foner, et al., 1968, pp. 464–479.
[17] Saltz, 1968.

of these roles are facilitated by ecological or residential factors; when the proper conditions are present, the potential for the emergence of new roles is greater. For example, Rosow's study of apartment dwellers in Cleveland clearly shows that when the density of older persons is higher in a neighborhood, the possibility of receiving help and assistance from neighbors is increased. Where the density is low, the possibility is less.[18]

Another consideration in the recognition of new roles for the older citizen in industrialized societies is that some of the incentive and responsibility for creating and implementing new role opportunities will have to come from the old themselves. In the postwar period the social gerontologists and others concerned with the plight of the elderly developed a sort of minority-group psychology and strategy: the aged were viewed as a rejected, segregated category, and society was supposed to provide them with more opportunities, money, and services. This point of view influenced the research perspectives and the programmatic developments in the field. In recent years, as a result of a complex set of factors, these essentially negative outlooks about the situation of the elderly have changed somewhat, but, there are still many residues of the earlier forms of thinking.

Granted the necessity and indeed in many instances the urgency to provide more adequate pensions and insurance benefits for older citizens, there are still many opportunities for older people themselves to improve the social climate in which they live. It is an obvious and inexorable fact that the ability of the community and its organizations to supply funds and resources is limited. Demand always exceeds supply. Hence, the older citizens will have to use their skill and ingenuity to improve their social climate without making excessive demands on the community. There is much concern about alienated older men and women as if they were mere puppets and had no options as to their social integration. A complex modern society can be demanding and at times rather imperious; still the in-

18 Rosow, 1967.

dividual does have opportunities to take the initiative and change the mode of his social life. Freedom of choice may be reduced, particularly for some categories of the old, but minority-group psychology does not fully explain the situation or the behavior of many older persons. There is a price which must be paid for involvement and commitment, and some older persons do not wish to pay the price; they would prefer to remain free of demands and social responsibilities. This is an essential aspect of disengagement. As Wilbert Moore states: "some of the phenomena of alienation can be attributed to the attempt by individuals to reduce the cost of 'tied-in' role demands." [19] Further, there are those who have been isolated, and in some cases alienated, throughout most of their lives. It would be grossly naïve to expect suddenly that in old age these people would emerge as dedicated and involved citizens. Thus the possibility of developing new roles in old age must be viewed in realistic terms. There will be no sudden shift, particularly to citizenship roles. It is more likely that the higher educated groups will become more involved, in addition to those blue-collar persons who have been active in trade unions or other voluntary organizations.[20]

Institutional and Societal Perspectives on Retirement

Up to this point the summary and interpretive analysis has relied primarily upon the theoretical orientation of the social psychologist, for we have considered retirement as a major point of role transition and role adaptation. We have presented our empirical results in terms of the adaptation of role theory and we have speculated about the possibilities of viewing re-

[19] Wilbert E. Moore, 1969, p. 294.

[20] Gordon and Anderson (1964, p. 415) report that in their survey of the literature and in their own exploratory research on blue-collar workers they found little tendency for them to develop in their new leisure time such things as "a higher esthetic sense, greater civic participation, and more sophisticated political and ideological orientation."

tirement in terms of new roles in a changing industrial society. But retirement can and should be viewed in broader perspective, that is, from the institutional and societal points of view. Much of the literature on retirement has been concerned with the process from the standpoint of the individual carrying out his roles, and many writers have stressed the negative aspects. This attitude has also been characteristic of some persons who view retirement in institutional terms; that is, as a *social problem,* not just a personal problem. However, retirement may also have positive and negative consequences for the operation of organizations, institutional structures (such as the economy), and the society itself. Business, governmental, trade-union, and academic organizations function more effectively, in part, as a result of having retirement programs.

For example, a modern industrialized society requires mobility of the labor force. Older members must relinquish their positions so that the young who have been trained can be inducted and offered some possibility of advancement. Without the orderly and phased retirement of the old, the opportunities for entry and promotion of younger persons would be much reduced in many organizations. Thus retirement as an institutionalized aspect of a modern society makes it possible for new leaders to emerge and assume positions of influence and power; it also increases the probability that new ideas will be developed.

Another example of the beneficial effect of retirement can be seen in trade unions. In this instance, retirement performs an important positive function in counteracting the effects of seniority, which insures that older members will have priority for preferred opportunities, such as more desirable work shifts and more pleasant working conditions. A retirement system acts as a check and balance to the seniority system so that the older union members are transferred into retirement and the young trade unionists are offered more opportunities. A seniority system without the balancing effect of retirement could become sclerotic, and would undoubtedly increase the possibility of frustration and disillusionment of younger members.

Thus, retirement in present-day society has become institutionalized; it has become routinized and formalized by rules and roles. Standard procedures have been widely adopted to facilitate the transfer of persons out of active participation in the labor force. These new rules, roles, and practices show that retirement is now an integral part of the American institutional structure. It is accepted that schooling is a central activity in the roles of childhood; similarly, the norms of an industrialized society now prescribe retirement as an institutionalized, "normal" role in late adulthood.

Institutionalized retirement has come about as a result of a demographic revolution in which people live longer so that now about 10 per cent of the population of the United States consists of people over 65 years of age. Furthermore, the emergence of a more efficient and more productive technological system means that it is not necessary to rely on the total employment of manpower throughout the life cycle. This permits the economy to support a larger number of older dependents. A concomitant development is a new political and social order which assumes many of the traditional family activities for the care of the old.

The institutionalization of retirement is only one phase in the emergence of an urban industrialized society in which men have exchanged one set of traditional patterns of living and coping with human needs for a new and different set of patterns. Persons in complex societies have "solved" some problems but they confront some new ones. The emergence of new "problems" in later maturity can be compared to the emergence of other kinds of "problems" at other stages in the life cycle. For example, the widespread attention to the operation of the public school system—concern for discipline and the motivation of the unwilling learner, the escalating costs of education, the attempt to make the curriculum more flexible to meet the varying needs of the students—all these issues come to the fore only in complex societies in which universal compulsory education is institutionalized. Similarly, in later life, the economic costs of dependency, the drawbacks of phased retirement, and the resulting social and psychological stress and personal maladjustment experienced by some persons are results of institutionalized retirement. Less developed societies obviously do not have these institutionalized patterns and the consequent maladaptations at both earlier and later phases of the life cycle.

In recent years some newer developments have been taking place which are causing additional changes in retirement as an institutionalized part of society. We regard the most important of these to be those developments in the sociomedical and economic areas. The broadening of coverage under Old Age and Survivor's Insurance and the increased benefits which have been made available are highly significant. Another important change is the passage of federal health and medical legislation, such as Medicare and supplementary state legislation, which has increased the health and medical insurance coverage for many older people. There have also been some improvements in various private retirement and health insurance plans for older persons. Some of these changes have made it possible for some empolyees to retire earlier than the normal retirement age. For example, the United Automobile Workers has increased economic benefits for those members who choose to retire early. The facts clearly demonstrate that when pension plans are improved, more auto workers choose early retirement.[21]

Other developments include the establishment of many new

[21] There is convincing evidence about the members of the United Automobile Workers union which clearly shows that when improved financial benefits are available, early retirement is more acceptable to industrial workers (Orbach, 1967).

retirement communities and the growth of those established previously.[22] Some communities have also seen the establishment of centers and programs for aging persons.[23] These changes have contributed to the broader and deeper institutionalization of retirement. Moreover it has meant that the situation of retirees and other aging persons has changed from that which prevailed when the Cornell Retirement Study was initiated. For one thing, there is now greater general and age-specific awareness of retirement, and there are more options available to the individual. In summary, the trends demonstrate the institutionalization of retirement as an important permanent ongoing part of the social structure.

These structural changes should not be confused with the positive or negative emotions that persons may have toward the latter part of the life cycle. Individuals will always have problems of coping with declining physical and mental functions, and adaptations will be required when one stops work and one's income is reduced decisively. These individual social-psychological problems remain and in some regards are probably very similar to those which retirees faced in earlier periods when institutionalized retirement was not as firmly fixed in the social structure.

The sociologist studying retirement does not regard it as a unitary problem or process. Varying strata of the class and occupational system perceive, prepare for, and adapt to retirement differentially.[24] The higher educational and professional strata have the most positive attitudes and the most resources to cope with their new circumstances. The unskilled and uneducated are the least prepared and have the least personal, economic,

[22] It is estimated for example that about 200,000 persons over 60 reside in various kinds of retirement housing facilities in California alone (Walkley et al., 1965).

[23] For a listing of the variety of activities developed in recent years for retirees to engage in, see Wray, 1969.

[24] For detailed information on a variety of retirement phenomena carefully analyzed by occupational strata see Simpson et al., 1966, pp. 45 ff.

and social resources to meet the challenge of retirement. Obviously the latter strata, more than the former, require the concern and support of private and governmental programs if they are to adapt creatively to the retirement role.

Retirement has often been regarded as a severe role crisis— and perhaps this definition is accurate for some people in the present generation of retirees. In future generations, with more role models of retirees, greater preparation for retirement, and better economic provisions, the concept of role crisis may not be so salient. Furthermore, retirees form a greater percentage of the population every year, and the older perspectives on the lifetime virtue of work may be altered, with new and satisfying roles emerging. Both old and young need to understand differential disengagement: that retirement is only part of the deceleration which accompanies aging and that retrenchment in one sphere does not imply retrenchment in all areas. Greater knowledge and acceptance of differential disengagement may result in more older persons being stimulated to explore and develop alternate social patterns than was true in an earlier period before retirement became institutionalized. It is anticipated that the retiree of the future will be better able to spend his declining years in comfort, dignity, and self-respect.

Publications of the Cornell Study of Occupational Retirement

Publications in each category are listed in chronological order.

Papers Published in Professional Journals

Barron, M. L., G. Streib, and E. A. Suchman.
  1952. "Research on the Social Disorganization of Retirement." American Sociological Review 17: 479–482.

Young, C. M., G. F. Streib, and B. J. Greer.
  1954. "Food Usage and Food Habits in Older Workers." *A. M. A. Archives of Industrial Hygiene and Occupational Medicine* 10: 501–511.

Barron, M. L.
  1955. "Occupational Roles." *Public Health Reports* 70: 854–856.

Streib, G. F.
  1956. "Morale of the Retired." *Social Problems* 3: 270–276.

Taietz, P., and G. F. Streib.
  1956. "Retirement Problems in Rural New York." *Farm Research* 22: 5.

Suchman, E. A., B. S. Phillips, and G. F. Streib.
  1958. "An Analysis of the Validity of Health Questionnaires." *Social Forces* 36: 223–232.

Thompson, W. E., and G. F. Streib.
  1958. "Cornell Study of Occupational Retirement." *Industrial and Labor Relations Review* 11: 658–659.

Thompson, W. E., and G. F. Streib.

1958. "Situational Determinants: Health and Economic Deprivation in Retirement." *Journal of Social Issues* 14: 18–34.

Streib, G. F., W. E. Thompson, and E. A. Suchman.
1958. "The Cornell Study of Occupational Retirement." *Journal of Social Issues* 14: 3–17.

Thompson, W. E.
1958. "Pre-Retirement Anticipation and Adjustment in Retirement." *Journal of Social Issues* 14: 35–45.

Streib, G. F.
1958. "Family Patterns in Retirement." *Journal of Social Issues* 14: 46–60.

Streib, G. F., and W. E. Thompson.
1958. "Cornell Longitudinal Study of Occupational Retirement." *Public Health Reports* 73: 1119–1120.

Thompson, W. E.
1960. "Health and Retirement." *Journal of the Michigan State Medical Society* 59: 756–758.

Thompson, W. E., G. F. Streib, and J. Kosa.
1960. "The Effect of Retirement on Personal Adjustment: A Panel Analysis." *Journal of Gerontology* 15: 165–169.

Streib, G. F.
1965. "Intergenerational Relations: Perspective of the Two Generations." *Journal of Marriage and the Family* 27: 469–476.

Streib, G. F.
1966. "Participants and Drop-Outs in a Longitudinal Study." *Journal of Gerontology* 21: 200–209.

Monographs and Chapters in Books

Barron, M. L.
1955. "A Survey of a Cross-Section of the Urban Aged in the United States." Pp. 340–349 in *Old Age in the Modern World.* London: E. and S. Livingstone.

Taietz, P., G. F. Streib, and M. L. Barron.
1956. *Adjustment to Retirement in Rural New York State.* Bulletin 919. Ithaca, New York: Cornell Agricultural Experiment Station.

Barron, M. L.
1956. "The Dynamics of Occupational Roles and Health in Old

Age." Pp. 236–239 in J. E. Anderson, ed., *Psychological Aspects of Aging.* Washington, D.C.: American Psychological Association.

Streib, G. F., and W. E. Thompson.
1957. "Personal and Social Adjustment in Retirement." Pp. 180–197 in W. Donahue and C. Tibbitts, eds., *The New Frontiers of Aging.* Ann Arbor: University of Michigan Press.

Streib, G. F.
1958. "Research on Retirement: A Report on the Cornell Longitudinal Study." Pp. 67–87 in F. C. Jeffers, ed., *Proceedings of Seminars: 1957–58.* Duke University Council on Gerontology. Durham, N.C.: Duke University.

Streib, G. F., and W. E. Thompson.
1960. "The Older Person in a Family Context." Pp. 447–488 in C. Tibbitts, ed., *Handbook of Social Gerontology.* Chicago: University of Chicago Press.

Streib, G. F.
1962. "The Pros and Cons of Flexible Retirement." Pp. 146–152 in H. I. Wells, Jr., ed., *Proceedings, Second National Conference to Improve the Health Care of the Aged.* Chicago.

Streib, G. F.
1963. "Longitudinal Studies in Social Gerontology." Pp. 25–39 in R. H. Williams, C. Tibbitts, and W. Donahue, eds., *Processes of Aging,* Vol. II. New York: Atherton Press.

Related Publications on Retirement and Aging

Barron, M. L.
1953. "Minority Group Characteristics of the Aged in American Society." *Journal of Gerontology* 8: 477–482.

Phillips, B. S.
1957. "A Role Theory Approach to Adjustment in Old Age." *American Sociological Review* 22: 212–217.

Streib, G. F.
1959. "Foreword." Pp. v–ix in E. H. Moore, *The Nature of Retirement.* New York: Macmillan.

Thompson, W. E., and G. F. Streib
1961. "Meaningful Activity in a Family Context." Pp. 177–212 in R. W. Kleemeier, ed., *Aging and Leisure.* New York: Oxford University Press.

Thompson, W. E., and G. F. Streib.
    1962. "Meaningful Activity in a Family Context." Pp. 905–912 in
    C. Tibbitts and W. Donahue, eds., *Social and Psychological
    Aspects of Aging.* New York: Columbia University Press.
Streib, G. F.
    1965. "Are the Aged a Minority Group? Some Conceptual and
    Empirical Considerations." Pp. 311–328 in A. Gouldner and
    S. M. Miller, eds., *Applied Sociology: Opportunities and Prob-
    lems.* New York: The Free Press.
Streib, G. F., and H. Orbach.
    1967. "Aging." Pp. 612–640 in P. F. Lazarsfeld, W. Sewell, and
    H. Wilensky, eds., *The Uses of Sociology.* New York: Basic Books.
Streib, G. F.
    1968. "Disengagement Theory in Socio-Cultural Perspective." *In-
    ternational Journal of Psychiatry* 6: 69–76.

Cornell University Ph.D. Dissertations

Thompson, W. E.
    1956. *The Impact of Retirement.* Ann Arbor, Mich.: University
    Microfilms. No. 17,012.
Phillips, B. S.
    1956. *A Role Theory Approach to Predicting Adjustment of the
    Aged in Two Communities.* Ann Arbor, Mich.: University Micro-
    films. No. 18,284.
Martel, M. U.
    1956. *Situations of Aging in American Society.* Ann Arbor, Mich.:
    University Microfilms. No. 20, 418.
Cicourel, A. V.
    1957. *Organizational Structure, Social Interaction, and the Phe-
    nomenal World of the Actor.* Ann Arbor, Mich.: University Mi-
    crofilms. L.C. Card No. Mic 58–850.
Schneider, C. J.
    1964. *Adjustment of Employed Women to Retirement.* Ann
    Arbor, Mich.: University Microfilms. Order No. 65–3352.
Knox, W. E.
    1965. *Filial Bonds: The Correlates of the Retired Father's Per-
    ception of Solidarity with his Adult Children.* Ann Arbor, Mich.:
    University Microfilms. Order No. 65–14, 697.

Sample Questionnaires

WHAT THIS IS ALL ABOUT

This is not a "test." There are no right or wrong answers. Just answer the questions in the way you, yourself, feel about them. Give YOUR OWN HONEST OPINIONS.

The information you give us will be kept strictly confidential. Nothing you write will be shown either to the company or to the union. Both the company and the union have agreed not to look at your answers.

Read every question carefully. Then be sure you check the answer which best gives your opinion. Be sure to answer every question. If you are not sure, guess. It is important that you answer them all.

Some of the questions will have special instructions which you should follow. If you do not understand what to do at any time, ask for help.

Pay no attention to the numbers printed in front of the answer spaces. They are for coding purposes.

Thank you for your cooperation.

[200]   **APPENDIX II**

CONFIDENTIAL

-2-

1. When were you born? Month_____   Day_____   Year_____

2. Sex: Put a check in front of your answer like this:__✔__.

    0_____Male

    X_____Female

3. Check the one statement below that best describes your present marriage. (CHECK ONE)

    1_____I have never been married.

    2_____I am married and living with my wife (or husband).

    3_____I am married but separated from my wife (or husband).

       How long have you been separated? _____years.

    4_____I am widowed.

       How long have you been a widower (or widow)? _____years.

    5_____I am divorced.

       How long have you been divorced? _____years.

4. Who are the people who live in the house or apartment with you? Tell us who they are by putting a check before your answers. Tell us how many there are by writing the number in the space after "How many?"
For example, if you have two sons who live with you, write 2 in the space after "How many?" and so on.
Check all who live with you.

    The people living with me are:

    1_____I live alone.

    2_____Wife (or husband)

    3_____Sister(s): How many? _____

    4_____Brother(s): How many? _____

    5_____Daughter(s): How many? _____

    6_____Son(s): How many? _____

    7_____Daughter(s)-in-law: How many? _____

    8_____Son(s)-in-law: How many? _____

    9_____Grandchild(ren): How many? _____

    0_____Other relatives such as uncles, cousins, in-laws: How many? _____

    X_____Other people such as boarders: How many? _____

CONFIDENTIAL

(11-17)   -3-

5. a) How many living children do you have? (WRITE THE NUMBER IN THE BLANK)

        I have _____ living children. IF NO CHILDREN, GO TO QUESTION 6.

    b) How many of your children do you see every week or oftener? (WRITE
        THE NUMBER IN THE BLANK)

        I see _____ of my children every week or oftener.

6. How many of your relatives other than your children do you usually see
    every week or oftener? (WRITE THE NUMBER IN THE BLANK)

        I see _____ of my relatives every week or oftener.

7. About how many really close friends do you have here in town with whom
    you talk over personal matters? (CHECK ONE)

        1_____Many close friends
        2_____Some close friends
        3_____Few close friends
        4_____No close friends

8. How many of your close friends are people from your place of work?

        1_____All my close friends are from my place of work.
        2_____Most of my close friends are from my place of work.
        3_____Some of my close friends are from my place of work.
        4_____None of my close friends are from my place of work.

9. Now think of the one friend that you see most often — how often do
    you see that friend?

    I see this friend: (PLEASE CHECK ONLY ONE)

        1_____Three times a week or more
        2_____Once or twice a week
        3_____Every two or three weeks
        4_____Once a month or less

10. Have you lost any close friends recently through their death? (CHECK
    ONE)

        0_____Yes
        X_____No

CONFIDENTIAL

(19-23)   -4-

11. How well do you get along with your family? (CHECK ONE)

     1_____We get along very well

     2_____We get along fairly well

     3_____We get along poorly

     4_____We get along very poorly

12. How often do you worry about your family? (CHECK ONE)

     1_____Often

     2_____Sometimes

     3_____Hardly ever

13. Have you lost any member of your family recently through death? (CHECK ONE)

     1_____No

     _____Yes: Who? _____

14. Which of these things give you the most satisfaction and comfort in life today? (CHECK AS MANY AS YOU NEED TO TELL ALL THE THINGS THAT GIVE YOU THE GREATEST COMFORT AND SATISFACTION)

     1_____Just being with my family at home

     2_____Working around the house and yard

     3_____Having relatives visit me

     4_____Doing things I like to do by myself at home

     5_____My religion or church work

     6_____My work

     7_____Spending time with close friends

     8_____Just sitting and thinking about things

     9_____Reading

     0_____My recreation outside the home

     X_____Getting out to visit relatives

     Y_____Visiting with my neighbors

15. How do you think of yourself as far as age goes — do you think of yourself as: (CHECK ONE)

     1_____Elderly

     2_____Middle-aged

     3_____Late middle-aged

     4_____Old

CONFIDENTIAL

(25-43)   -5-

16. How often do you do each of the following things: (PUT A CHECK IN FRONT
    OF EITHER "OFTEN," "SOMETIMES," OR "HARDLY EVER OR NEVER")

    a. See your children   ___OFTEN ___SOMETIMES ___HARDLY EVER OR NEVER

    b. See your grandchildren ___OFTEN ___SOMETIMES ___HARDLY EVER OR NEVER

    c. Go visiting   ___OFTEN ___SOMETIMES ___HARDLY EVER OR NEVER

    d. Attend church   ___OFTEN ___SOMETIMES ___HARDLY EVER OR NEVER

    e. Attend club, union or
       lodge meetings   ___OFTEN ___SOMETIMES ___HARDLY EVER OR NEVER

    f. Go to see sports
       events   ___OFTEN ___SOMETIMES ___HARDLY EVER OR NEVER

    g. Read   ___OFTEN ___SOMETIMES ___HARDLY EVER OR NEVER

    h. Listen to the radio   ___OFTEN ___SOMETIMES ___HARDLY EVER OR NEVER

    i. Watch television   ___OFTEN ___SOMETIMES ___HARDLY EVER OR NEVER

    j. Go to the movies   ___OFTEN ___SOMETIMES ___HARDLY EVER OR NEVER

    k. Talk with friends   ___OFTEN ___SOMETIMES ___HARDLY EVER OR NEVER

    l. Take walks by yourself ___OFTEN ___SOMETIMES ___HARDLY EVER OR NEVER

    m. Work in the garden or
       yard   ___OFTEN ___SOMETIMES ___HARDLY EVER OR NEVER

    n. Play cards   ___OFTEN ___SOMETIMES ___HARDLY EVER OR NEVER

    o. Take rides in the
       country   ___OFTEN ___SOMETIMES ___HARDLY EVER OR NEVER

    p. Go to a tavern or bar ___OFTEN ___SOMETIMES ___HARDLY EVER OR NEVER

    q. Go hunting, fishing,
       or other outdoor
       sports   ___OFTEN ___SOMETIMES ___HARDLY EVER OR NEVER

17. Which one of the above activities which you do "OFTEN" is the most
    important to you?

                ENTER THE LETTER HERE: _____

CONFIDENTIAL

(45-51)   -6-

18. How happy is (or was) your marriage? (CHECK ONE)

     1_____I have never been married

     2_____Very unhappy

     3_____Unhappy

     4_____Average

     5_____Happy

     6_____Very happy

NOW WE WOULD LIKE TO ASK YOU SOME QUESTIONS ABOUT YOUR WORK.

19. What is your job here now?

_____

20. How long have you been doing this kind of work? _____ years

21. How good a place would you say this is to work in? (CHECK ONE)

     1_____Very good

     2_____Fairly good

     3_____Not very good

     4_____No good at all

22. How much do you enjoy your work at present? (CHECK ONE)

     1_____I enjoy it very much

     2_____I enjoy it fairly much

     3_____I don't enjoy it so much

     4_____I don't enjoy my work at all

23. Would you like to change to some other job in the company if given a chance? (CHECK ONE)

     1_____Yes, I would like to

     2_____No, I would not like to

     3_____Undecided

24. How well do you get along with your immediate supervisors (foremen)? (CHECK ONE)

     1_____We get along very well

     2_____We get along fairly well

     3_____We get along poorly

     4_____We get along very poorly

CONFIDENTIAL

(53-57)   -7-

25. How well do you get along with the people you work with? (CHECK ONE)

       1_____We get along very well
       2_____We get along fairly well
       3_____We get along poorly
       4_____We get along very poorly

26. Have you ever had a job on a higher level than your present job?
    (CHECK ONE)

       1_____No
       2_____Yes: When? _____

27. How much do you earn now from your job? (CHECK ONE)

       1_____Less than $25 a week
       2_____More than $25 but less than $45
       3_____More than $45 but less than $65
       4_____More than $65 but less than $85
       5_____More than $85 but less than $100
       6_____More than $100

28. Do you have any income besides what you earn at work?

       1_____No
       2_____Yes: From Where? (CHECK AS MANY AS YOU HAVE INCOME FROM)

          3_____Other members of the family
          4_____Social Security
          5_____Pension
          6_____Old age assistance (public or private welfare)
          7_____Savings
          8_____Bonds or investments
          9_____Income from property
          0_____Insurance annuities
          X_____Some other source. What is it? _____

29. Do you consider your present income enough to meet your living expenses?
    (CHECK ONE)

       0_____It is enough
       X_____It is not enough

CONFIDENTIAL

(59-63)   -8-

30. How do you feel about the pension plan this company has?   (CHECK ONE)

    1_____My company has no pension plan

    2_____It's a very good plan
    3_____It's a fairly good plan
    4_____It's not so good
    5_____It's no good at all
    6_____I don't know about it

31. Has your company tried to do anything to help you prepare for retirement aside from pensions?   (CHECK ONE)

    0_____No
    X_____Yes: What? _____

NOW WE WOULD LIKE TO ASK YOU SOME QUESTIONS ABOUT RETIREMENT.

32. Does your company have a special age for retirement?   (CHECK ONE)

    1_____There is no special age for stopping work and retiring.
    2_____There is a special age but I can stay on if I am able and the company wants me to.
    3_____There is a special age and everyone must stop working.
    4_____I don't know.

33. During the next five years will you reach the retirement age of your company?   (CHECK ONE)

    1_____There is no special age

    2_____Yes
    3_____No

34. If it were up to you alone, would you continue working for your present company?   (CHECK ONE)

    0_____I would continue working.

    X_____I would stop working.

CONFIDENTIAL

(65-68)   -9-

35. What are your prospects for the next five years in regard to your work? (CHECK ONE)

    1_____I expect to continue in my present work

    2_____I plan to stop work and retire

    3_____I plan to change to another job in this company

    4_____I plan to get a job someplace else

    5_____I plan to do something else. What are you planning to do?

    _____

36. If you plan to continue working for the next five years, why are you planning to continue working? (CHECK THE MOST IMPORTANT)

    1_____I do not plan to continue working

    2_____Because I do not have enough money to retire on

    3_____Because I am afraid of not keeping occupied

    4_____Because I like my work so much I don't want to give it up

37. If you are planning to retire, why are you planning to retire? (CHECK THE MOST IMPORTANT)

    1_____I do not plan to retire

    2_____Because of my health

    3_____Because I have difficulty in doing my job

    4_____Because I am not able to work as well as younger men

    5_____Because I want more leisure time

    6_____Because my company says I have to retire

38. If you are planning to change to some other type of work, why are you planning to change? (CHECK THE MOST IMPORTANT)

    1_____I do not intend to change my work

    2_____Because of my health

    3_____Because I have difficulty in doing my job

    4_____Because I am not able to do my present work as well as younger men

    5_____Because I want more leisure time

    6_____Because my company will not keep me at my present work

    7_____Because I have always wanted to do this

    8_____I have another reason. What is it? _____

CONFIDENTIAL

(70-73)   -10-

39. If you plan to do something else, why are you planning to do this?
     (CHECK THE MOST IMPORTANT)

     1_____I have no other plans

     2_____Because of my health

     3_____Because I have difficulty in doing my job

     4_____Because I am not able to do my present work as well as
           younger men

     5_____Because I want more leisure time

     6_____Because I have always wanted to do this

     7_____I have another reason. What is it? _____
     _____

40. We'd like to know how you will meet your financial problems in the
     future. When you stop working, will you have any income from the
     following? (CHECK AS MANY AS YOU WILL HAVE INCOME FROM)

     1_____Social Security

     2_____Pensions from industry or government

     3_____Old age assistance (public or private welfare)

     4_____Savings

     5_____Bonds and investments

     6_____Income from property

     7_____Insurance annuities

     8_____Other: What? _____
     _____

41. About how much do you expect this income will amount to per month?
     (CHECK ONE)

     1_____Less than $100 per month

     2_____More than $100 but less than $150

     3_____More than $150 but less than $200

     4_____More than $200 per month

     5_____I don't know

42. Do you expect to receive any support from members of your family,
     friends, or anyone else?

     1_____No: IF YOU ANSWER NO, GO TO QUESTION 43.

     _____Yes: Who will they be? (CHECK AS MANY AS YOU WILL RECEIVE
                SUPPORT FROM)

          4_____My children

          5_____My brothers or sisters

          6_____My grandchildren

          7_____My other relatives

          8_____My friends

          _____Other: Who? _____

     2_____I don't know

CONFIDENTIAL

(75-80)   -11-

43. Some people say that retirement is good for a person, some say it is
    bad. In general, what do you think? (CHECK ONE)

        0_____Retirement is mostly good for a person
        X_____Retirement is mostly bad for a person

44. Who do you think should make the decision as to when a person should
    retire? (CHECK THE ONE YOU THINK SHOULD HAVE THE MOST SAY)

        1_____The person himself
        2_____His employer
        3_____A doctor
        4_____His family
        5_____His supervisor
        6_____His union
        7_____Someone else: Who? _____
        8_____I don't know

45. How do you think it is best for a person to retire -- all at once, or
    gradually, by working fewer and fewer hours? (CHECK ONE)

        0_____At once
        X_____Gradually

46. Do you mostly look forward to the time when you will stop working and
    retire or in general do you dislike the idea? (CHECK ONE)

        1_____I look forward to it
        2_____I dislike the idea
        3_____Undecided

47. Have you made plans for anything you would like to do after you stop
    working? (CHECK ONE)

        0_____No
        X_____Yes: What? _____

48. How often do you worry about being able to do your job? (CHECK ONE)

        1_____Often
        2_____Sometimes
        3_____Hardly ever

CONFIDENTIAL

(6-11)   -12-

49. At what age would you say you were able to do your best work?

When I was _____years old.

50. Are you more able to do your work well now or were you better able to do it when you were 50 years old? (CHECK ONE)

1_____I am more able now
2_____There hasn't been any change
3_____I was more able at 50

51. Which one of these things is MOST important to you in your work? (CHECK ONLY ONE)

1_____Mixing with good friends on the job
2_____New things happening on the job
3_____The respect that it brings from others
4_____It keeps me from being bored
5_____It gives me a feeling of being useful

52. Does an older person or a younger person tend to do a better job on your kind of work? (CHECK ONE)

1_____An older person does a better job
2_____A younger person does a better job
3_____Age does not make any difference

53. Do you feel younger employees are "pushing" for your job? (CHECK ONE)

0_____No
X_____Yes

54. Does your supervisor give you any special consideration as an older employee? (CHECK ONE)

0_____No

X_____Yes

(13-26)   -13-

55. Here are some statements that people have different opinions about.
Read each one carefully and decide whether you tend to agree or disagree with it. If you tend to agree with a statement, check YES. If
you tend to disagree, check NO. Remember there are no right or wrong
answers.

	IF YOU AGREE	IF YOU DISAGREE	
a. Older employees have a hard time keeping up with the work.	___YES	___NO	___UNDECIDED
b. Older employees keep to themselves and don't mix with the younger employees.	___YES	___NO	___UNDECIDED
c. Younger employees are more willing to try new ways of doing things.	___YES	___NO	___UNDECIDED
d. I work under a great deal of tension.	___YES	___NO	___UNDECIDED
e. Every year I get more able to do my job better.	___YES	___NO	___UNDECIDED
f. I find I tire more easily these days.	___YES	___NO	___UNDECIDED
g. Physical strength is important in my job.	___YES	___NO	___UNDECIDED
h. The work I do can best be done by an older, mature person.	___YES	___NO	___UNDECIDED
i. Employees should be encouraged to retire at 65.	___YES	___NO	___UNDECIDED
j. People lose respect for a man who no longer works.	___YES	___NO	___UNDECIDED
k. These days I find myself giving up hope of trying to improve myself.	___YES	___NO	___UNDECIDED
l. The government ought to take care of a person when he is out of a job.	___YES	___NO	___UNDECIDED
m. Generally speaking, Negroes are lazy and ignorant.	___YES	___NO	___UNDECIDED
n. Nowadays a person has to live pretty much for today and let tomorrow take care of itself.	___YES	___NO	___UNDECIDED

APPENDIX II

(28-33)   -14-

If you tend to agree with a statement, check YES. If you tend to disagree, check NO.

	IF YOU AGREE	IF YOU DISAGREE	
o. In spite of what some people say, the situation of the average man is getting better, not worse.	___YES	___NO	___UNDECIDED
p. It's hard to respect a person who lives off the government.	___YES	___NO	___UNDECIDED
q. Almost everything these days is a racket.	___YES	___NO	___UNDECIDED
r. If people knew what was really going on in high places these days, it would blow the lid off things.	___YES	___NO	___UNDECIDED

NOW WE WOULD LIKE TO ASK YOU SOME QUESTIONS ABOUT YOUR HEALTH.

56. How would you rate your health at the present time? (CHECK ONE)

    1_____Very poor
    2_____Poor
    3_____Fair
    4_____Good
    5_____Excellent

57. Has your health changed during the past year? (CHECK ONE)

    1_____No: IF YOU ANSWER NO, GO TO QUESTION 58.
    _____Yes: IF YES: Has it become better or worse? (CHECK ONE
            AND TELL IN WHAT WAY)

       3_____It is better. In what way? _____
       _____
       4_____It is worse. In what way? _____
       _____

CONFIDENTIAL

(35-37)   -15-

58. Do you have any particular physical or health problems at present?
    (CHECK ONE)

        1_____No: IF YOU ANSWER NO, GO TO QUESTION 59.
        _____Yes: IF YES: What are they? _____

                          _____

                          _____

            Are any of these problems because you're getting older?
            (CHECK ONE)

            3_____No: NOW GO TO QUESTION 59.
            _____Yes: Please explain _____

                      _____

59. Have you been seen by a doctor during the past year? (CHECK ONE)

        1_____No: IF YOU ANSWER NO, GO TO QUESTION 60.
        _____Yes: IF YES: Why? (CHECK AS MANY AS APPLY TO YOU)

            3_____For regular examination by company doctor
            4_____For regular examination by my own doctor
            5_____For illness, seen only in doctor's office
            6_____For illness, seen at home
            7_____For first aid or an accident
            8_____Admitted to hospital

60. During the past year have you had to change or cut down your daily
    activities such as driving, gardening, taking walks, and the like,
    because of your health or physical condition? (CHECK ONE)

        0_____No
        X_____Yes: IF YES: Please explain _____

                          _____

                          _____

CONFIDENTIAL

(39-41)   -16-

61. Has your health or physical condition ever interfered in any way with your ability to do your job? (CHECK ONE)

    1_____No: IF YOU ANSWER NO, GO TO QUESTION 62.

    _____Yes: IF YES: Please explain _____

                    _____

Were you given some other job? (CHECK ONE)

3_____Yes: NOW GO TO QUESTION 62.

_____No: IF NO: Do you think you should have been given some other job? (CHECK ONE)

    5_____Yes

    6_____No

62. Has your job ever had any bad effects upon your health? (CHECK ONE)

    1_____No: IF YOU ANSWER NO, GO TO QUESTION 63.

    _____Yes: IF YES: Please explain _____

                    _____

Were you given some other job? (CHECK ONE)

3_____Yes: NOW GO TO QUESTION 63.

_____No: IF NO: Do you think you should have been given some other job? (CHECK ONE)

    5_____Yes

    6_____No

63. How often do you worry about your health? (CHECK ONE)

    1_____Often

    2_____Sometimes

    3_____Hardly ever

(43-47)   -17-

NOW WE WOULD LIKE TO ASK YOU SOME QUESTIONS ABOUT LIFE IN GENERAL.

64. All in all, how much happiness would you say you find in life today? (CHECK ONE)

    5_____Almost none

    6_____Some, but not very much

    7_____A good deal

65. On the whole, how satisfied would you say you are with your way of life today? (CHECK ONE)

    1_____Very satisfied

    2_____Fairly satisfied

    3_____Not very satisfied

    4_____Not satisfied at all

66. Compared to other people your age, would you say you find it harder to get used to changes, or do you find it easier to get used to changes? (CHECK ONE)

    6_____I find it harder to get used to changes

    7_____I find it easier to get used to changes

    8_____I find it just about the same as others

67. How often do you feel hurt by the things that people say or do to you? (CHECK ONE)

    1_____Often

    2_____Sometimes

    3_____Hardly ever

68. When you are troubled about life and its meaning, what do you most often do? (CHECK THE ONE YOU DO MOST OFTEN)

    5_____Think it through by myself

    6_____Talk it over with my wife (or husband)

    7_____Talk it over with a friend

    8_____Pray to God for help

    9_____Talk it over with my minister, priest, or rabbi

    0_____Worry about it

    X_____Other: What? _____

CONFIDENTIAL

(49-54)   -18-

69. Do you believe in a life after death (heaven)? (CHECK ONE)

    1_____No

    2_____Not sure

    3_____Yes, I'm sure of it

70. How much comfort does religion (not just going to church) give you in times of trouble and difficulty? (CHECK ONE)

    5_____A great deal of comfort

    6_____Some comfort

    7_____Very little comfort

    8_____None at all

71. Would you say you are a religious person, or doesn't religion mean very much to you? (CHECK ONE)

    1_____I'd say I am a religious person

    2_____Religion doesn't mean very much to me

    3_____Undecided

72. Do you attend church more often or less often now than when you were 50? (CHECK ONE)

    5_____I attend church more often now

    6_____There hasn't been any change

    7_____I attend church less often now

73. How often do you get upset by the things that happen in your day-to-day living? (CHECK ONE)

    9_____Often

    0_____Sometimes

    X_____Hardly ever

74. How often do you worry about money matters? (CHECK ONE)

    1_____Often

    2_____Sometimes

    3_____Hardly ever

CONFIDENTIAL

(56-61)   -19-

75. In general, how would you say you feel most of the time, in good spirits or in low spirits? (CHECK ONE)

    5_____I am usually in good spirits

    6_____I am in good spirits some of the time and in low spirits some of the time

    7_____I am usually in low spirits

76. How often do you find yourself day-dreaming about the past? (CHECK ONE)

    9_____Often

    0_____Sometimes

    X_____Hardly ever

77. How often do you find yourself being absent-minded? (CHECK ONE)

    1_____Often

    2_____Sometimes

    3_____Hardly ever

78. When you find yourself being absent-minded, how serious a problem is this for you? (CHECK ONE)

    5_____I am hardly ever absent-minded

    6_____Very serious

    7_____Somewhat serious

    8_____Not serious

79. How often do you find yourself feeling "blue"? (CHECK ONE)

    1_____Often

    2_____Sometimes

    3_____Hardly ever

80. When you feel "blue," how serious a problem is this for you? (CHECK ONE)

    5_____I hardly ever feel "blue"

    6_____Very serious

    7_____Somewhat serious

    8_____Not serious

CONFIDENTIAL

(63-68)   -20-

81. How often do you find yourself having thoughts about dying?   (CHECK ONE)

    1_____Often
    2_____Sometimes
    3_____Hardly ever

82. How often do you have trouble in getting to sleep and staying asleep? (CHECK ONE)

    1_____Often
    2_____Sometimes
    3_____Hardly ever

83. When you have trouble in getting to sleep and staying asleep, how serious a problem is this for you? (CHECK ONE)

    5_____I hardly ever have trouble in getting to sleep

    6_____Very serious
    7_____Somewhat serious
    8_____Not serious

84. How much do you feel that the "breaks" in life were against you? (CHECK ONE)

    1_____Most of the "breaks" were against me
    2_____Some, but not most of them were
    3_____Hardly any of them were against me.

85. How often do you get the feeling that your life today is not very useful? (CHECK ONE)

    5_____Often
    6_____Sometimes
    7_____Hardly ever

86. How often do you find yourself wishing you were younger? (CHECK ONE)

    9_____Often
    0_____Sometimes
    X_____Hardly ever

CONFIDENTIAL

(70-75)   -21-

WE'D LIKE TO HAVE A LITTLE FACTUAL INFORMATION ABOUT YOU.

87. In what city and state were you born?_____
    (If not born in the United States, which country?)

88. In what state or country was your father born?_____

89. If you were asked to put yourself (your family) in one of these four
    groups, would you say you are in the: (CHECK ONE)

        1_____Upper class

        2_____Middle class

        3_____Working class

        4_____Lower class

90. What is your religion?

        6_____Protestant

        7_____Catholic

        8_____Jewish

        9_____None

        0_____Other: What?_____

91. Did you ever belong to a labor union?   (CHECK ONE)

        1_____No

        2_____Yes, I now belong

        3_____Yes, I once did, but no longer do

92. How far did you go in school?   (CHECK THE ANSWER SHOWING THE HIGHEST
    GRADE YOU COMPLETED IN SCHOOL)

        5_____None

        6_____Some grade school

        7_____Graduated from grade school

        8_____Some high school, but did not graduate

        9_____Graduated from high school or business college

        0_____Some college, but did not graduate

        X_____Graduated from college

CONFIDENTIAL

(77-78)   -22-

93. Which of the following community activities do you take part in?
     (CHECK AS MANY AS APPLY TO YOU)

     1_____Vote in last local election

     2_____Vote in last national election

     3_____Work for a political party

     4_____Civilian Defense work

     5_____Collect money for Red Cross or Community Chest

     6_____Other: What?_____

     7_____None of these

94. What is your race?   (CHECK ONE)

     9_____White

     0_____Negro

     X_____Other

(NOTE: In the questionnaire the materials below were a separate tear-out
        page.)

It is not necessary to identify your individual answers since this study is
CONFIDENTIAL. However, it is necessary to have a list of those people who
have filled in the questionnaire. So please sign your name on the line
below and tear off the slip on the dotted ling and hand it in separately
from your answer sheet. Thank you.

                    Name _____

                    Address_____

                         _____

Will you also please give the name and address of some person who will
always know where you are living.

                    Name _____

                    Address_____

                         _____

S-1 (W) 1954

No._____

WAVE II WORKING QUESTIONNAIRE

WHAT THIS IS ALL ABOUT

This is the second part of the Cornell University survey of America's older citizens in which you are a participant.

This is not a "test." You probably remember that there are no right or wrong answers. Just answer the questions in the way you, yourself, feel about them. GIVE YOUR OWN HONEST OPINIONS.

The information you give us will be kept strictly confidential.

Read every question carefully. Then be sure you check the answer which best gives your opinion. Be sure to answer every question. If you are not sure, guess. It is important that you answer them all.

If you find that a question does not fit your situation, or does not give you a chance to express your opinion, first check your answer and then please feel free to write in what you think.

Some of the questions will have special instructions which you should follow.

THANK YOU FOR YOUR COOPERATION

            *   *   *   *   *   *   *   *

1. First of all, when were you born? Month_____Day_____Year_____

2. Sex: (Just put a check in front of your answers like this: _✓_)

        0_____Male
        X_____Female

3. In what city and state were you born? _____
    (If not born in the United States, which country?)

4. Where do you live at the present? (CHECK ONLY ONE)

        1_____I own my home
        2_____I rent a house
        3_____I rent an apartment
        4_____I rent a room
        5_____Some other living arrangement. What?_____

5. What are your prospects for the next four years in regard to your work?
    (CHECK ONLY ONE)

        1_____I expect to continue in my present work
        2_____I plan to stop work and retire
        3_____I plan to change to another job in this company
        4_____I plan to get a job someplace else
        5_____I plan to do something else. What are you planning to do?
        _____

- 2 -

6. If you plan to continue working for the next four years, why are you planning to continue working? (<u>CHECK <u>THE</u> <u>ONE</u> <u>MOST</u> IMPORTANT REASON</u>)

   1_____I do not plan to continue working

   2_____Because I do not have enough money to retire on
   3_____Because I am afraid of not keeping occupied
   4_____Because I like my work so much I don't want to give it up

7. If you are planning to retire, why are you planning to retire? (<u>CHECK THE ONE MOST IMPORTANT REASON</u>)

   1_____I do not plan to retire

   2_____Because of my health
   3_____Because I have difficulty in doing my job
   4_____Because I am not able to work as well as younger men
   5_____Because I want more leisure time
   6_____Because my company says I have to retire

8. If you are planning to change your work, why are you planning to change? (<u>CHECK THE ONE MOST IMPORTANT REASON</u>)

   1_____I do not intend to change my work

   2_____Because of my health
   3_____Because I have difficulty in doing my job
   4_____Because I am not able to do my present work as well as younger men
   5_____Because I want more leisure time
   6_____Because my company will not keep me at my present work
   7_____Because I have always wanted to do this
   8_____I have another reason. What is it?_____

9. Do you live with your children at the present? (CHECK ONLY ONE)

   1_____I do not have any living children

   2_____I live with one or more of my children
   3_____I do not live with my children

10. How much would you like to be in touch with your children more than you are these days? (CHECK ONLY ONE)

   1_____I do not have any living children

   2_____I would like to be in touch with them a <u>good deal</u> more
   3_____I would like to be in touch with them <u>somewhat</u> more
   4_____I would <u>not</u> like to be in touch with them any more than I am

11. About how many really <u>close</u> friends do you have here in town with whom you talk over personal affairs (CHECK ONLY ONE)

   1_____Many close friends
   2_____Some close friends
   3_____Few close friends
   4_____No close friends

12. How many of your close friends are people from your place of work? (CHECK ONLY ONE)

   1_____All my close friends are from my place of work
   2_____Most of my close friends are from my place of work
   3_____Some of my close friends are from my place of work
   4_____None of my close friends are from my place of work

13. Now think of the one friend that you see most often -- how often do you see that friend? (CHECK ONLY ONE)

    1_____Three times a week or more
    2_____Once or twice a week
    3_____Every two or three weeks
    4_____Once a month or less

14. Would you say you take part in many, a few, or practically no activities such as card clubs, lodge, church groups, unions, community activities and the like? (CHECK ONLY ONE)

    1_____I take part in many activities
    2_____I take part in a few activities
    3_____I take part in practically no activities

15. Would you say you go around with a certain bunch of close friends who visit back and forth in each other's homes? (CHECK ONLY ONE)

    0_____Yes
    X_____No

16. As you get older, would you say things seem to be better or worse than you thought they would be? (CHECK ONLY ONE)

    1_____Better
    2_____Worse
    3_____Same
    4_____Don't know

17. Where does your income come from now? (CHECK AS MANY AS YOU HAVE INCOME FROM)

    1_____My job
    2_____Other members of the family
    3_____Social Security
    4_____Pension
    5_____Old Age Assistance (public or private welfare)
    6_____Savings
    7_____Bonds and investments
    8_____Income from property
    9_____Insurance annuities
    0_____Other: What? _____

18. About how much does this income amount to a week? (CHECK ONLY ONE)

    1_____Less than $25 a week
    2_____More than $25 but less than $45 a week
    3_____More than $45 but less than $65 a week
    4_____More than $65 but less than $85 a week
    5_____More than $85 but less than $100 a week
    6_____More than $100 a week

19. Do you consider your present income enough to meet your living expenses? (CHECK ONLY ONE)

    0_____It is enough
    X_____It is not enough

20. How much do you plan ahead the things that you will be doing next week or the week after? (CHECK ONLY ONE)

    1_____ I make <u>many</u> plans
    2_____ I make <u>a few</u> plans
    3_____ I make <u>almost no</u> plans

21. Is your standard of living better today or was it better during most of your lifetime? (CHECK ONLY ONE)

    1_____ My standard of living is better today
    2_____ My standard of living was better during most of my lifetime
    3_____ My standard of living has not changed

22. How much do you regret the chances you missed during your life to do a better job of living? (CHECK ONLY ONE)

    1_____ Not at all
    2_____ Somewhat
    3_____ A good deal

23. What are your plans for the next five or ten years? (CHECK ONLY ONE)

    1_____ I expect to keep on working at my present job
    2_____ I expect to take life easy and enjoy myself
    3_____ I expect to find some work to keep me busy
    4_____ I do not expect to live another five to ten years
    5_____ I don't know

NOW WE WOULD LIKE TO ASK YOU SOME QUESTIONS ABOUT YOUR HEALTH

24. How would you rate your health at the present time? (CHECK ONLY ONE)

    1_____ Excellent
    2_____ Good
    3_____ Fair
    4_____ Poor
    5_____ Very poor

25. Do you think continuing work has made your health better or worse? (CHECK ONLY ONE)

    1_____ Continuing work has made my health <u>better</u>
    2_____ Continuing work has made my health <u>worse</u>
    3_____ Continuing work has made <u>no difference</u> in my health

26. Do you have any particular physical or health problems at present? (CHECK ONLY ONE)

    1_____ No
    _____ Yes: If YES, what are they?_____

    _____

27. Are any of your health problems because you're getting older? (CHECK ONLY ONE)

    1_____ I don't have any health problems

    2_____ No, my health problems are <u>not</u> because I'm getting older
    3_____ Yes, my health problems are because I'm getting older

-5-

28. For what reasons have you been seen by a doctor during the past year? (CHECK AS MANY AS YOU NEED TO)

1_____ I have not been seen by a doctor

2_____ For regular examination by the company doctor
3_____ For regular examination by my own doctor
4_____ For illness, seen only in doctor's office
5_____ For illness, seen at home
6_____ For first aid or an accident
7_____ Admitted to hospital

NOW WE WOULD LIKE TO ASK YOU SOME QUESTIONS ABOUT LIFE IN GENERAL

29. All in all, how much unhappiness would you say you find in life today? (CHECK ONLY ONE)

1_____ Almost none
2_____ Some, but not very much
3_____ A good deal

30. On the whole, how satisfied would you say you are with your way of life today? (CHECK ONLY ONE)

1_____ Very satisfied
2_____ Fairly satisfied
3_____ Not very satisfied
4_____ Not satisified at all

31. How do you think of yourself as far as age goes -- do you think of yourself as: (CHECK ONLY ONE)

1_____ Elderly
2_____ Middle-aged
3_____ Late middle-aged
4_____ Old

32. Which of these things give you the most satisfaction and comfort in life today? (CHECK AS MANY AS YOU NEED TO TELL ALL THE THINGS THAT GIVE YOU THE GREATEST COMFORT AND SATISFACTION)

1_____ Just being with my family at home
2_____ Working around the house, garden or yard
3_____ Having relatives other than my children visit me
4_____ Doing things I like to do by myself at home
5_____ My religion or church work
6_____ Spending time with close friends
7_____ Just sitting and thinking about things
8_____ Reading
9_____ My recreation outside the home
0_____ Getting out to visit relatives other than my children
X_____ My job

33. In general, how would you say you feel most of the time, in good spirits or in low spirits? (CHECK ONLY ONE)

1_____ I am usually in good spirits
2_____ I am in good spirits some of the time and in low spirits some of the time
3_____ I am usually in low spirits

-6-

34. When you are troubled about life and its meaning, what do you most
    often do? (CHECK THE ONE YOU DO MOST OFTEN)

    1_____ Think it through by myself
    2_____ Talk it over with my wife (or husband)
    3_____ Talk it over with a friend
    4_____ Pray to God for help
    5_____ Talk it over with my minister, priest or rabbi
    6_____ Worry about it
    7_____ Other: What? _____

35. Do you believe in a life after death (heaven)? (CHECK ONLY ONE)

    1_____ No
    2_____ Not sure
    3_____ Yes, I'm sure of it

36. How much comfort does religion (not just going to church) give you in
    times of trouble and difficulty? (CHECK ONLY ONE)

    1_____ A great deal of comfort
    2_____ Some comfort
    3_____ Very little comfort
    4_____ None at all

37. Would you say you are a religious person, or doesn't religion mean
    very much to you? (CHECK ONLY ONE)

    1_____ I'd say I am a religious person
    2_____ Religion doesn't mean very much to me
    3_____ Undecided

38. What changes for the WORSE have taken place in your life since you
    filled out our first questionnaire over a year ago? (CHECK AS MANY
    AS APPLY TO YOU)

    1_____ Change in health
    2_____ Change in my family. What? _____
    3_____ Change in income
    4_____ Change in my job. What? _____
    5_____ Change in residence
    6_____ Death in my family. Who? _____
    7_____ Change in my outlook on life
    8_____ Other: What? _____

    9_____ No changes for the worse

39. What would you say is the MOST IMPORTANT change for the WORSE that has
    taken place in your life since you filled out our first questionnaire?
    (CHECK ONLY THE ONE MOST IMPORTANT)

    1_____ No important change for the worse

    2_____ Change in health
    3_____ Change in my family. What? _____
    4_____ Change in income
    5_____ Change in my job. What? _____
    6_____ Change in residence
    7_____ Death in my family. Who? _____
    8_____ Change in my outlook on life
    9_____ Other: What? _____

40. On this question just go down the list and check how often you do each of the following things: (PUT A CHECK IN FRONT OF EITHER "OFTEN" OR "SOMETIMES" OR "HARDLY EVER OR NEVER" FOR EVERY ITEM IN THE LIST)

HOW OFTEN DO YOU:

Feel you have lost your self respect   ___OFTEN ___SOMETIMES ___HARDLY EVER OR NEVER

Worry about your health   ___OFTEN ___SOMETIMES ___HARDLY EVER OR NEVER

Feel you deserve a good rest   ___OFTEN ___SOMETIMES ___HARDLY EVER OR NEVER

Enjoy being with other people at work   ___OFTEN ___SOMETIMES ___HARDLY EVER OR NEVER

Have times when you just don't know what to do to keep occupied   ___OFTEN ___SOMETIMES ___HARDLY EVER OR NEVER

Worry about your family   ___OFTEN ___SOMETIMES ___HARDLY EVER OR NEVER

Feel there's just no point in living   ___OFTEN ___SOMETIMES ___HARDLY EVER OR NEVER

Dislike the feeling of living by the clock   ___OFTEN ___SOMETIMES ___HARDLY EVER OR NEVER

Wish you had the chance to take life easy   ___OFTEN ___SOMETIMES ___HARDLY EVER OR NEVER

Worry about being able to do your job   ___OFTEN ___SOMETIMES ___HARDLY EVER OR NEVER

Feel lonely   ___OFTEN ___SOMETIMES ___HARDLY EVER OR NEVER

Worry about the future   ___OFTEN ___SOMETIMES ___HARDLY EVER OR NEVER

Wish you could live in a warmer climate   ___OFTEN ___SOMETIMES ___HARDLY EVER OR NEVER

Feel that you want to stop working   ___OFTEN ___SOMETIMES ___HARDLY EVER OR NEVER

Worry about not having a job   ___OFTEN ___SOMETIMES ___HARDLY EVER OR NEVER

Wish you had a hobby   ___OFTEN ___SOMETIMES ___HARDLY EVER OR NEVER

Worry about money matters   ___OFTEN ___SOMETIMES ___HARDLY EVER OR NEVER

Wish you had the chance to live your life over   ___OFTEN ___SOMETIMES ___HARDLY EVER OR NEVER

Wish you had free time to do the things you never have time to do   ___OFTEN ___SOMETIMES ___HARDLY EVER OR NEVER

Enjoy the feeling of doing a good job   ___OFTEN ___SOMETIMES ___HARDLY EVER OR NEVER

BE SURE YOU CHECKED SOMETHING FOR EVERY ITEM

41. Some people say that retirement is good for a person, some say it is
    bad. In general, what do you think? (CHECK ONLY ONE)

    0_____Retirement is mostly good for a person
    X_____Retirement is mostly bad for a person

42. Would you say that continuing to work turned out better or worse than
    you expected? (CHECK ONLY ONE)

    1_____Continuing to work has turned out better
    2_____Continuing to work has turned out worse
    3_____Continuing to work has turned out about as I expected

43. Do you think continuing work has made you feel in better spirits or
    in worse spirits? (CHECK ONLY ONE)

    1_____Continuing work has made me feel in better spirits
    2_____Continuing work has made me feel in worse spirits
    3_____Continuing work has made no difference

44. How much do you feel that the "breaks" in life were against you?
    (CHECK ONLY ONE)

    1_____Most of the "breaks" were against me
    2_____Some, but not most of them were
    3_____Hardly any of them were against me

45. Do you think that continuing work has made you more satisfied with
    your way of life today? (CHECK ONLY ONE)

    1_____Yes
    2_____No
    3_____Undecided

46. Do you think that continuing work has made you feel that you find
    less unhappiness in life today? (CHECK ONLY ONE)

    1_____Yes
    2_____No
    3_____Undecided

47. Which ONE of these things would you say you've worked hardest at in
    your life? (CHECK ONLY ONE)

    1_____Trying to get ahead in life
    2_____Trying to make the future secure
    3_____Trying to find happiness in life
    4_____Trying to be a good citizen in the community
    5_____Trying to live an upright life with nothing to regret

48. Now, how well have you lived up to what you expected of yourself in
    achieving this one thing you have just checked? (CHECK ONLY ONE)

    1_____Very well
    2_____Fairly well
    3_____Not so well

49. On this question just go down the list and check how often you do each of the following things: (PUT A CHECK IN FRONT OF EITHER "OFTEN" OR "SOMETIMES" OR "HARDLY EVER OR NEVER" FOR EVERY ITEM IN THE LIST)

HOW OFTEN DO YOU:

Just spend time with your family at home ___OFTEN ___SOMETIMES ___HARDLY EVER OR NEVER

See some of your children ___OFTEN ___SOMETIMES ___HARDLY EVER OR NEVER

See some of your grandchildren ___OFTEN ___SOMETIMES ___HARDLY EVER OR NEVER

Attend church ___OFTEN ___SOMETIMES ___HARDLY EVER OR NEVER

Take walks by yourself ___OFTEN ___SOMETIMES ___HARDLY EVER OR NEVER

Have relatives other than your children visit you ___OFTEN ___SOMETIMES ___HARDLY EVER OR NEVER

Read ___OFTEN ___SOMETIMES ___HARDLY EVER OR NEVER

Do things you like to do by yourself at home ___OFTEN ___SOEMTIMES ___HARDLY EVER OR NEVER

Watch television ___OFTEN ___SOMETIMES ___HARDLY EVER OR NEVER

Listen to the radio ___OFTEN ___SOMETIMES ___HARDLY EVER OR NEVER

Just sit and think about things ___OFTEN ___SOMETIMES ___HARDLY EVER OR NEVER

Work around the house, garden or yard ___OFTEN ___SOMETIMES ___HARDLY EVER OR NEVER

Go outside the home for recreation ___OFTEN ___SOMETIMES ___HARDLY EVER OR NEVER

Get out to visit your relatives other than your children ___OFTEN ___SOMETIMES ___HARDLY EVER OR NEVER

Do baby sitting ___OFTEN ___SOMETIMES ___HARDLY EVER OR NEVER

BE SURE YOU CHECKED SOMETHING FOR EVERY ITEM

NOW WE WOULD LIKE TO ASK YOU SOME QUESTIONS ABOUT RETIREMENT

50. How do you feel about the pension plan your company has? (CHECK ONLY ONE)

1_____ My company has no pension plan

2_____ It's a very good plan
3_____ It's a fairly good plan
4_____ It's not so good
5_____ It's no good at all

51. Do you think the pension plan of your company could be improved in any way? (CHECK ONLY ONE)

    1_____No
    _____Yes. In what way? _____

_____

52. If it were up to you alone, would you continue working for your present employer? (CHECK ONLY ONE)

    0_____I would continue working
    X_____I would stop working

53. Would you like to change to some other job in the company if given a chance? (CHECK ONLY ONE)

    1_____Yes, I would like to
    2_____No, I would not like to
    3_____Undecided

54. Here are some statements that people answer in different ways. Read each one carefully and decide whether you tend to agree or disagree with it. If you tend to agree with the statement, check YES. If you tend to disagree, check NO. Remember, there are no right or wrong answers. But be sure to check something for each one.

	IF YOU AGREE	IF YOU DISAGREE	
I get tired of being run by an alarm clock and a time clock	___YES	___NO	___UNDECIDE
Everybody ought to stop work and take things easy when they get older	___YES	___NO	___UNDECIDE
Almost everything these days is a racket	___YES	___NO	___UNDECIDE
Just staying home would drive a person nuts	___YES	___NO	___UNDECIDE
It gets harder and harder for me to keep up the pace as I get older	___YES	___NO	___UNDECIDE
These days I find myself giving up hope of trying to improve myself	___YES	___NO	___UNDECIDE
I really can't afford to retire	___YES	___NO	___UNDECIDE
Things just keep getting worse and worse for me as I get older	___YES	___NO	___UNDECIDE
It is unfair for my employer to retire older employees	___YES	___NO	___UNDECIDE

BE SURE YOU CHECKED SOMETHING FOR EVERY ITEM

55. Do you mostly look forward to the time when you will stop working and retire or in general do you dislike the idea? (CHECK ONLY ONE)

    1_____I look forward to it
    2_____I dislike the idea
    3_____Undecided

56. Have you made any plans for anything you would like to do after you stop working? (CHECK ONLY ONE)

        1____No
        ____Yes: What? _____

57. How do you expect your retirement will turn out for you? (CHECK ONLY ONE)

        1____Very good
        2____Fairly good
        3____Not so good
        4____No good at all

58. On this question just go down the list and check how often you do each of the following things: (PUT A CHECK IN FRONT OF EITHER "OFTEN" OR "SOMETIMES" OR "HARDLY EVER OR NEVER" FOR EVERY ITEM IN THE LIST)

HOW OFTEN DO YOU:

Find yourself day-dreaming about the past   ___OFTEN ___SOMETIMES ___HARDLY EVER OR NEVER

Find yourself being absend-minded   ___OFTEN ___SOMETIMES ___HARDLY EVER OR NEVER

Find yourself feeling "blue"   ___OFTEN ___SOMETIMES ___HARDLY EVER OR NEVER

Find yourself having thoughts about dying   ___OFTEN ___SOMETIMES ___HARDLY EVER OR NEVER

Have trouble in getting to sleep and staying asleep   ___OFTEN ___SOMETIMES ___HARDLY EVER OR NEVER

Get the feeling that your life today is not very useful   ___OFTEN ___SOMETIMES ___HARDLY EVER OR NEVER

Find yourself wishing you were younger   ___OFTEN ___SOMETIMES ___HARDLY EVER OR NEVER

Have physical aches and pains   ___OFTEN ___SOMETIMES ___HARDLY EVER OR NEVER

Find yourself being nervous   ___OFTEN ___SOMETIMES ___HARDLY EVER OR NEVER

Have headaches   ___OFTEN ___SOMETIMES ___HARDLY EVER OR NEVER

Have an upset stomach   ___OFTEN ___SOMETIMES ___HARDLY EVER OR NEVER

Feel hurt by the things that people say or do to you   ___OFTEN ___SOMETIMES ___HARDLY EVER OR NEVER

Get upset by the things that happen in your day to day living   ___OFTEN ___SOMETIMES ___HARDLY EVER OR NEVER

BE SURE YOU CHECKED SOMETHING FOR EVERY ITEM

CONFIDENTIAL

-12-

59. Do you think that stopping work has made you think of yourself as older or younger? (CHECK ONLY ONE)

    1_____Stopping work has made me think of myself as <u>older</u>
    2_____Stopping work has made me think of myself as <u>younger</u>
    3_____Stopping work has made <u>no difference</u>

60. Compared to other people your age, would you say you find it harder to get used to changes, or do you find it easier to get used to change. (CHECK ONLY ONE)

    1_____I find it <u>harder</u> to get used to changes
    2_____I find it <u>easier</u> to get used to changes
    3_____I find it <u>just about the same</u> as others

61. Do you think that stopping work has given you the feeling that your life today is not very useful? (CHECK ONLY ONE)

    1_____Yes
    2_____No
    3_____Undecided

62. What changes for the <u>BETTER</u> have taken place in your life since you filled out our first questionnaire over a year ago? (CHECK AS MANY AS APPLY TO YOU)

    1_____Change in health
    2_____Change in income
    3_____Change in residence
    4_____Change in my family. What?_____
    5_____Not working
    6_____Change in my outlook on life
    7_____Other: What?_____
    8_____No changes for the better

63. What would you say is the <u>MOST IMPORTANT</u> change for the <u>BETTER</u> that has taken place in your life since you filled out our first question- naire? (CHECK <u>ONLY THE ONE MOST</u> IMPORTANT)

    1_____No important change for the better
    2_____Change in health
    3_____Change in income
    4_____Change in residence
    5_____Change in my family. What?_____
    6_____Not working
    7_____Change in my outlook on life
    8_____Other: What?_____

64. Did anyone help you fill out this questionnaire? (CHECK ONLY ONE)

    1_____No
    _____Yes: Who?_____

THANK <u>YOU</u> <u>FOR</u> <u>YOUR</u> COOPERATION

S-1 (R) 1954

No._____

WAVE II RETIRED QUESTIONNAIRE
<u>   </u>

WHAT THIS IS ALL ABOUT

This is the second part of the Cornell University survey of America's older citizens in which you are a participant.

This is not a "test". You probably remember that there are no right or wrong answers. Just answer the questions in the way you, yourself, feel about them. GIVE YOUR OWN HONEST OPINIONS.

The information you give us will be kept <u>strictly confidential</u>.

Read every question carefully. Then be sure you check the answer which <u>best</u> gives your opinion. Be sure to answer every question. If you are not sure, guess. It is important that you answer them all.

If you find that a question does not fit your situation, or does not give you a chance to express your opinion, <u>first check your answer</u> and then please feel free to write in what you think.

Some of the questions will have special instructions which you should follow.

THANK YOU FOR YOUR COOPERATION.

        *   *   *   *   *   *   *

1. First of all, when were you born? Month_____ Day____ Year_____

2. Sex: (Just put a check in front of your answers like this: <u>✓</u>)

        0_____Male
        X_____Female

3. In what city and state were you born?_____
        (If not born in the United States, which country?)

4. Where do you live at the present? (CHECK ONLY ONE)

        1_____I own my home
        2_____I rent a house
        3_____I rent an apartment
        4_____I rent a room
        5_____Some other living arrangement. What?_____

5. How long ago did you stop work? (CHECK ONLY ONE)

        1_____Less than three months ago
        2_____Three to six months ago
        3_____Six months to a year ago
        4_____A year or more ago

CONFIDENTIAL

-2-

6. How did it happen that you stopped working when you did?   (CHECK ONLY ONE)

    1_____I was retired by the company on reaching retirement age
    2_____I was laid off by the company for other reasons
    3_____I just decided to stop work

7. Which one of these things had something to do with your stopping work?
   (CHECK ONLY THE MOST IMPORTANT ONE)

    1_____My health
    2_____Difficulty in doing my regular work
    3_____Not being able to do my work as well as younger people
    4_____Wanting more leisure time
    5_____None of these

8. Who decided that you should stop work when you did?   (CHECK ONLY ONE)

    0_____The company decided
    X_____I decided myself

9. It takes some people a little while to get used to not working. About
   how long would you say it took you to become used to not working?
   (CHECK ONLY ONE)

    1_____I am still not used to it
    2_____It took me a week or two (or less)
    3_____It took me about a month
    4_____It took me two or three months
    5_____It took me more than three months

10. Do you consider yourself retired?   (CHECK ONLY ONE)

    0_____No
    X_____Yes

11. Are you looking for work?   (CHECK ONLY ONE)

    1_____No
    2_____Yes, I am looking for part-time work
    3_____Yes, I am looking for full-time work

12. How difficult have you found not working?   (CHECK ONLY ONE)

    1_____I have found it very difficult
    2_____I have found it fairly difficult
    3_____I have not found it difficult

13. Do you live with your children at the present?   (CHECK ONLY ONE)

    1_____I do not have any living children

    2_____I live with one or more of my children
    3_____I do not live with my children

-3-

14. How much would you like to be in touch with your children more than
    you are these days? (CHECK ONLY ONE)

    1_____ I do not have any living children

    2_____ I would like to be in touch with them a good deal more
    3_____ I would like to be in touch with them somewhat more
    4_____ I would not like to be in touch with them any more than I am

15. About how many really close friends do you have here in town with
    whom you talk over personal matters? (CHECK ONLY ONE)

    1_____ Many close friends
    2_____ Some close friends
    3_____ Few close friends
    4_____ No close friends

16. How many of your close friends are people from the company where you
    used to work? (CHECK ONLY ONE)

    1_____ All my close friends are from where I used to work
    2_____ Most of my close friends are from where I used to work
    3_____ Some of my close friends are from where I used to work
    4_____ None of my close friends are from where I used to work

17. Now think of the one friend that you see most often — how often do
    you see that friend? (CHECK ONLY ONE)

    1_____ Three times a week or more
    2_____ Once or twice a week
    3_____ Every two or three weeks
    4_____ Once a month or less

18. Would you say you take part in many, a few, or practically no activities
    such as card clubs, lodge, church groups, unions, community activities
    and the like? (CHECK ONLY ONE)

    1_____ I take part in many activities
    2_____ I take part in a few activities
    3_____ I take part in practically no activities

19. Would you say you go around with a certain bunch of close friends who
    visit back and forth in each other's homes? (CHECK ONLY ONE)

    0_____ Yes
    X_____ No

20. As you get older, would you say things seem to be better or worse
    than you thought they would be? (CHECK ONLY ONE)

    1_____ Better
    2_____ Worse
    3_____ Same
    4_____ Don't know

CONFIDENTIAL

-4-

21. Where does your income come from now? (CHECK AS MANY AS YOU HAVE INCOME FROM)

    1____ Other members of the family
    2____ Social Security
    3____ Pension from my former employer
    4____ Old Age Assistance (Public or private welfare)
    5____ Savings
    6____ Bonds and Investments
    7____ Income from property
    8____ Insurance annuities
    9____ Other: What?_____

22. About how much does this income amount to a month? (CHECK ONLY ONE)

    1____ Less than $50 a month
    2____ More than $50 but less than $100 a month
    3____ More than $100 but less than $150 a month
    4____ More than $150 but less than $200 a month
    5____ More than $200 but less than $250 a month
    6____ More than $250 but less than $300 a month
    7____ More than $300 a month
    8____ I don't know

23. Do you consider your present income enough to meet your living expenses? (CHECK ONLY ONE)

    0____ It is enough
    X____ It is not enough

24. How much do you plan ahead the things that you will be doing next week or the week after? (CHECK ONLY ONE)

    1____ I make many plans
    2____ I make few plans
    3____ I make almost no plans

25. Is your standard of living better today or was it better during most of your lifetime? (CHECK ONLY ONE)

    1____ My standard of living is better today
    2____ My standard of living was better during most of my lifetime
    3____ My standard of living has not changed

26. How much do you regret the chances you missed during your life to do a better job of living? (CHECK ONLY ONE)

    1____ Not at all
    2____ Somewhat
    3____ A good deal

27. What are your plans for the next five to ten years? (CHECK ONLY ONE)

    1____ I expect to take life easy and enjoy myself
    2____ I expect to find some work to keep me busy
    3____ I do not expect to live another five to ten years
    4____ I don't know

CONFIDENTIAL

-5-

NOW WE WOULD LIKE TO ASK YOU·SOME QUESTIONS ABOUT YOUR HEALTH

28. How would you rate your health at the present time? (CHECK ONLY ONE)

    1_____ Excellent
    2_____ Good
    3_____ Fair
    4_____ Poor
    5_____ Very poor

29. Do you think stopping work has made your health better or worse?
    (CHECK ONLY ONE)

    1_____ Stopping work has made my health better
    2_____ Stopping work has made my health worse
    3_____ Stopping work has made no difference in my health

30. Do you have any particular physical or health problems at present?
    (CHECK ONLY ONE)

    1_____ No
    _____ Yes. If YES, what are they? _____

31. Are any of your health problems because you're getting older? (CHECK
    ONLY ONE)

    1_____ I don't have any health problems

    2_____ No, my health problems are not because I'm getting older
    3_____ Yes, my health problems are because I'm getting older

32. For what reasons have you been seen by a doctor during the past year?
    (CHECK AS MANY AS YOU NEED TO)

    1_____ I have not been seen by a doctor

    2_____ For regular examination by the company doctor
    3_____ For regular examination by my own doctor
    4_____ For illness, seen only in doctor's office
    5_____ For illness, seen at home
    6_____ For first aid or accident
    7_____ Admitted to hospital

NOW WE WOULD LIKE TO ASK YOU SOME QUESTIONS ABOUT LIFE IN GENERAL

33. All in all, how much unhappiness would you say you find in life today?
    (CHECK ONLY ONE)

    1_____ Almost none
    2_____ Some, but not very much
    3_____ A good deal

34. On the whole, how satisfied would you say you are with your way of
    life today? (CHECK ONLY ONE)

    1_____ Very satisfied
    2_____ Fairly satisfied
    3_____ Not very satisfied
    4_____ Not satisfied at all

-6-

35. How do you think of yourself as far as age goes — do you think of
     yourself as: (CHECK ONLY ONE)

     1____ Elderly
     2____ Middle-aged
     3____ Late middle-aged
     4____ Old

36. Which of these things give you the most satisfaction and comfort in
     life today? (CHECK AS MANY AS YOU NEED TO TELL ALL THE THINGS THAT
     GIVE YOU THE GREATEST COMFORT AND SATISFACTION)

     1____ Just being with my family at home
     2____ Working around the house, garden or yard
     3____ Having relatives other than my children visit me
     4____ Doing things I like to do by myself at home
     5____ My religion or church work
     6____ Spending time with close friends
     7____ Just sitting and thinking about things
     8____ Reading
     9____ My recreation outside the home
     0____ Getting out to visit relatives other than my children

37. In general, how would you say you feel most of the time, in good
     spirits or in low spirits? (CHECK ONLY ONE)

     1____ I am usually in good spirits
     2____ I am in good spirits some of the time and in low spirits
           some of the time
     3____ I am usually in low spirits

38. When you are troubled about life and its meaning, what do you most
     often do? (CHECK THE ONE YOU DO MOST OFTEN)

     1____ Think it through by myself
     2____ Talk it over with my wife (or husband)
     3____ Talk it over with a friend
     4____ Pray to God for help
     5____ Talk it over with my minister, priest or rabbi
     6____ Worry about it
     7____ Other: What?_____

39. Do you believe in a life after death (heaven)? (CHECK ONLY ONE)

     1____ No
     2____ Not sure
     3____ Yes, I'm sure of it

40. How much comfort does religion (not just going to church) give you in
     times of trouble and difficulty? (CHECK ONLY ONE)

     1____ A great deal of comfort
     2____ Some comfort
     3____ Very little comfort
     4____ None at all

41. Would you say you are a religious person, or doesn't religion mean
     very much to you? (CHECK ONLY ONE)

     1____ I'd say I am a religious person
     2____ Religion doesn't mean very much to me
     3____ Undecided

-7-

42. On this question just go down the list and check how often you do each of the following things: (PUT A CHECK IN FRONT OF EITHER "OFTEN" OR "SOMETIMES" OR "HARDLY EVER OR NEVER" FOR EVERY ITEM IN THE LIST)

HOW OFTEN DO YOU:

Feel you have lost your self respect	___OFTEN	___SOMETIMES	___HARDLY EVER OR NEVER
Worry about your health	___OFTEN	___SOMETIMES	___HARDLY EVER OR NEVER
Feel you deserve a good rest	___OFTEN	___SOMETIMES	___HARDLY EVER OR NEVER
Miss being with other people at work	___OFTEN	___SOMETIMES	___HARDLY EVER OR NEVER
Have times when you just don't know what to do to keep occupied	___OFTEN	___SOMETIMES	___HARDLY EVER OR NEVER
Worry about your family	___OFTEN	___SOMETIMES	___HARDLY EVER OR NEVER
Feel there's just no point in living	___OFTEN	___SOMETIMES	___HARDLY EVER OR NEVER
Like the feeling of not living by the clock	___OFTEN	___SOMETIMES	___HARDLY EVER OR NEVER
Miss the feeling of doing a good job	___OFTEN	___SOMETIMES	___HARDLY EVER OR NEVER
Worry about not having a job	___OFTEN	___SOMETIMES	___HARDLY EVER OR NEVER
Feel lonely	___OFTEN	___SOMETIMES	___HARDLY EVER OR NEVER
Worry about the future	___OFTEN	___SOMETIMES	___HARDLY EVER OR NEVER
Wish you could live in a warmer climate	___OFTEN	___SOMETIMES	___HARDLY EVER OR NEVER
Feel that you want to go back to work	___OFTEN	___SOMETIMES	___HARDLY EVER OR NEVER
Wish you had a hobby	___OFTEN	___SOMETIMES	___HARDLY EVER OR NEVER
Worry about money matters	___OFTEN	___SOMETIMES	___HARDLY EVER OR NEVER
Wish you had the chance to live your life over	___OFTEN	___SOMETIMES	___HARDLY EVER OR NEVER
Do the things you never had time to do while you were working	___OFTEN	___SOMETIMES	___HARDLY EVER OR NEVER
Enjoy the chance to take life easy	___OFTEN	___SOMETIMES	___HARDLY EVER OR NEVER

BE SURE YOU CHECKED SOMETHING FOR EVERY ITEM

CONFIDENTIAL

-8-

43. What changes for the WORSE have taken place in your life since you filled out our first questionnaire over a year ago? (CHECK AS MANY AS APPLY TO YOU)

1_____Change in health
2_____Change in income
3_____Change in residence
4_____Change in my family. What?_____
5_____Not working
6_____Death in my family. Who?_____
7_____Change in my outlook on life
8_____Other: What?_____

9_____No changes for the worse

44. What would you say is the MOST IMPORTANT change for the WORSE that has taken place in your life since you filled out our first questionnaire? (CHECK ONLY THE ONE MOST IMPORTANT)

1_____No important change for the worse

2_____Change in health
3_____Change in income
4_____Change in residence
5_____Change in my family. What?_____
6_____Not working
7_____Death in my family. Who?_____
8_____Change in my outlook on life
9_____Other: What?_____

45. Some people say that retirement is good for a person, some say it is bad. In general, what do you think? (CHECK ONLY ONE)

0_____Retirement is mostly good for a person
X_____Retirement is mostly bad for a person

46. Would you say that not working turned out better or worse than you expected? (CHECK ONLY ONE)

1_____Not working has turned out better
2_____Not working has turned out worse
3_____Not working has turned out about as I expected

47. Which ONE of these things would you say you've worked hardest at in your life? (CHECK ONLY ONE)

1_____Trying to get ahead in life
2_____Trying to make the future secure
3_____Trying to find happiness in life
4_____Trying to be a good citizen in the community
5_____Trying to live an upright life with nothing to regret

48. Now, how well have you lived up to what you expected of yourself in achieving this one thing you have just checked? (CHECK ONLY ONE)

1_____Very well
2_____Fairly well
3_____Not so well

CONFIDENTIAL

-9-

49. On this question just go down the list and check how often you do each of the following things: (PUT A CHECK IN FRONT OF EITHER "OFTEN" OR "SOMETIMES" OR "HARDLY EVER OR NEVER" FOR EVERY ITEM IN THE LIST)

HOW OFTEN DO YOU:

Just spend time with your family at home	___OFTEN	___SOMETIMES	___HARDLY EVER OR NEVER
See some of your children	___OFTEN	___SOMETIMES	___HARDLY EVER OR NEVER
See some of your grandchildren	___OFTEN	___SOMETIMES	___HARDLY EVER OR NEVER
Attend church	___OFTEN	___SOMETIMES	___HARDLY EVER OR NEVER
Take walks by yourself	___OFTEN	___SOMETIMES	___HARDLY EVER OR NEVER
Have relatives other than your children visit you	___OFTEN	___SOMETIMES	___HARDLY EVER OR NEVER
Read	___OFTEN	___SOMETIMES	___HARDLY EVER OR NEVER
Do things you like to do by yourself at home	___OFTEN	___SOMETIMES	___HARDLY EVER OR NEVER
Watch television	___OFTEN	___SOMETIMES	___HARDLY EVER OR NEVER
Listen to the radio	___OFTEN	___SOMETIMES	___HARDLY EVER OR NEVER
Just sit and think about things	___OFTEN	___SOMETIMES	___HARDLY EVER OR NEVER
Work around the house, garden or yard	___OFTEN	___SOMETIMES	___HARDLY EVER OR NEVER
Go outside the home for recreation	___OFTEN	___SOMETIMES	___HARDLY EVER OR NEVER
Get out to visit your relatives other than your children	___OFTEN	___SOMETIMES	___HARDLY EVER OR NEVER
Do baby sitting	___OFTEN	___SOMETIMES	___HARDLY EVER OR NEVER

BE SURE YOU CHECKED SOMETHING FOR EVERY ITEM

NOW WE WOULD LIKE TO ASK YOU SOME QUESTIONS ABOUT RETIREMENT

50. How do you feel about the pension plan of the company you used to work for? (CHECK ONLY ONE)

1____My company has no pension plan

2____It's a very good plan
3____It's a fairly good plan
4____It's not so good
5____It's no good at all

CONFIDENTIAL

-10-

51. Do you think the pension plan of the company you used to work for could be improved in any way? (CHECK ONLY ONE)

    1____ No
    ____ Yes: In what way?_____

52. Were your job activities and responsibilities the same right up until the time you left the company? (CHECK ONLY ONE)

    1____ Yes, my job was the same until I left the company
    2____ No, I was changed to an easier job for some time before I left
    3____ No, my regular job was made easier for me for some time before I left
    4____ No, my job activities and responsibilities were increased

53. Here are some statements that people answer in different ways. Read each one carefully and decide whether you tend to agree or disagree with it. If you tend to agree with the statement, check YES. If you tend to disagree, check NO. Remember, there are no right or wrong answers. But be sure to check something for each one.

	IF YOU AGREE	IF YOU DISAGREE	
I got tired of being run by an alarm clock and a time clock	___YES	___NO	___UNDECIDED
Everybody ought to stop work and take things easy when they get older	___YES	___NO	___UNDECIDED
Almost everything these days is a racket	___YES	___NO	___UNDECIDED
Just staying home drives a person nuts	___YES	___NO	___UNDECIDED
It gets harder and harder for me to keep up the pace as I get older	___YES	___NO	___UNDECIDED
These days I find myself giving up hope of trying to improve myself	___YES	___NO	___UNDECIDED
I really can't afford to be retired	___YES	___NO	___UNDECIDED
Things just keep getting worse and worse for me as I get older	___YES	___NO	___UNDECIDED
It is unfair for my employer to retire older employees	___YES	___NO	___UNDECIDED

BE SURE YOU CHECKED SOMETHING FOR EVERY ITEM

54. Do you think stopping work has made you feel in better spirits or in worse spirits? (CHECK ONLY ONE)

    1____ Stopping work has made me feel in better spirits
    2____ Stopping work has made me feel in worse spirits
    3____ Stopping work has made no difference

55. How much do you feel the "breaks" in life were against you? (CHECK ONLY ONE)

    1____ Most of the "breaks" were against me
    2____ Some, but not most of them were
    3____ Hardly any of them were against me

-11-

56. On this question just go down the list and check how often you do each of the following things: (PUT A CHECK IN FRONT OF EITHER "OFTEN" OR "SOMETIMES" OR "HARDLY EVER OR NEVER" FOR EVERY ITEM IN THE LIST)

HOW OFTEN DO YOU:

Find yourself day-dreaming about the past   ___OFTEN   ___SOMETIMES   ___HARDLY EVER OR NEVER

Find yourself being absent-minded   ___OFTEN   ___SOMETIMES   ___HARDLY EVER OR NEVER

Find yourself feeling "blue"   ___OFTEN   ___SOMETIMES   ___HARDLY EVER OR NEVER

Find yourself having thoughts about dying   ___OFTEN   ___SOMETIMES   ___HARDLY EVER OR NEVER

Have trouble in getting to sleep and staying asleep   ___OFTEN   ___SOMETIMES   ___HARDLY EVER OR NEVER

Get the feeling that your life today is not very useful   ___OFTEN   ___SOMETIMES   ___HARDLY EVER OR NEVER

Find yourself wishing you were younger   ___OFTEN   ___SOMETIMES   ___HARDLY EVER OR NEVER

Have physical aches and pains   ___OFTEN   ___SOMETIMES   ___HARDLY EVER OR NEVER

Find yourself being nervous   ___OFTEN   ___SOMETIMES   ___HARDLY EVER OR NEVER

Have headaches   ___OFTEN   ___SOMETIMES   ___HARDLY EVER OR NEVER

Have an upset stomach   ___OFTEN   ___SOMETIMES   ___HARDLY EVER OR NEVER

Feel hurt by the things that people say or do to you   ___OFTEN   ___SOMETIMES   ___HARDLY EVER OR NEVER

Get upset by the things that happen in your day to day living   ___OFTEN   ___SOMETIMES   ___HARDLY EVER OR NEVER

BE SURE YOU CHECKED SOMETHING FOR EVERY ITEM

57. Do you think that stopping work has made you less satisfied with your way of life today? (CHECK ONLY ONE)

    1____Yes
    2____No
    3____Undecided

58. Do you think that stopping work has made you feel that you find less happiness in life today? (CHECK ONLY ONE)

    1____Yes
    2____No
    3____Undecided

-12-

59. Do you think that continuing work has made you think of yourself as older or younger? (CHECK ONLY ONE)

   1____Continuing work has made me think of myself as <u>older</u>
   2____Continuing work has made me think of myself as <u>younger</u>
   3____Continuing work has made <u>no difference</u>

60. Compared to other people your age, would you say you find it harder to get used to changes, or do you find it easier to get used to changes? (CHECK ONLY ONE)

   1____I find it <u>harder</u> to get used to changes
   2____I find it <u>easier</u> to get used to changes
   3____I find it just about the same as others

61. Do you think continuing work has kept you from feeling your life today is not very useful? (CHECK ONLY ONE)

   1____Yes
   2____No
   3____Undecided

62. What changes for the <u>BETTER</u> have taken place in your life since you filled out our first questionnaire over a year ago? (CHECK <u>AS MANY AS APPLY TO YOU</u>)

   1____Change in health
   2____Change in my family. What? _____
   3____Change in income
   4____Change in residence
   5____Change in my job. What? _____
   6____Change in my outlook on life
   7____Other: What? _____

   8____No changes for the better

63. What would you say is the <u>MOST IMPORTANT</u> change for the <u>BETTER</u> that has taken place in your life since you filled out our first questionnaire? (CHECK <u>ONLY THE ONE MOST IMPORTANT</u>)

   1____No important change for the better

   2____Change in health
   3____Change in my family. What? _____
   4____Change in income
   5____Change in residence
   6____Change in my job. What? _____
   7____Change in my outlook on life
   8____Other: What? _____

64. Did anyone help you fill out this questionnaire? (CHECK ONLY ONE)

   1____No
   ____Yes. Who? _____

<u>THANK YOU FOR YOUR COOPERATION</u>

S-1 (RW) 1955

No._____

WAVE III RETIRED-WORKING QUESTIONNAIRE

WHAT THIS IS ALL ABOUT

This is the third part of the Cornell University survey of America's older citizens in which you are participating.

This is not a "test". You probably remember that there are no right or wrong answers. Just answer the questions in the way you, yourself, feel about them. GIVE YOUR OWN HONEST OPINIONS.

The information you give us will be kept strictly confidential.

Read every question carefully. Then check the answer which best gives your opinion. If you find that a question does not fit your situation, or does not give you a chance to express your opinion, first check the answer which most nearly expresses your opinion, and then please feel free to write what you think.

Sometimes the pages stick together, so be sure you have answered the questions on every page. And please be sure to answer every question. If you are not sure, guess. It is important that you answer them all.

Some of the questions will have special instructions which you should follow.

THANK YOU FOR YOUR COOPERATION.

            *   *   *   *   *   *   *

1. Our records show that you are no longer working at the company you worked for when you filled out our first questionnaire, over two years ago. How long ago did you stop working at that company? (CHECK ONLY ONE)

    (JUST PUT A CHECK MARK IN FRONT OF YOUR ANSWERS, LIKE THIS: ✓)

    1_____ Less than three months ago
    2_____ Three to six months ago
    3_____ Six months to a year ago
    4_____ A year or more ago

2. Which one of these things had the most to do with your stopping work at that company? (CHECK ONLY THE MOST IMPORTANT ONE)

    1_____ My health
    2_____ Difficulty in doing my regular work
    3_____ Not being able to do my work as well as younger people
    4_____ Wanting more leisure time
    5_____ None of these, just company policy
    6_____ Some other reason: What?_____

3. Who decided that you should stop working at that company when you did? (CHECK ONLY ONE)

    0_____ The company decided
    X_____ I decided myself

4. Do you consider yourself retired? (CHECK ONLY ONE)

    0_____ No
    X_____ Yes

-2-

5. During the time before you went back to work you may have had a chance to see for yourself just what it is like to be "retired". How much did you enjoy not working? (CHECK ONLY ONE)

    1_____I enjoyed it the whole time I was not working
    2_____I enjoyed it at first, but then I got tired of not working
    3_____I did not enjoy it at first, but then I began to enjoy it
    4_____I did not enjoy it any of the time

6. Did stopping work make you less satisfied with your way of life? (CHECK ONLY ONE)

    0_____Yes
    X_____No

7. While you were not working, was your total income from all sources enough to meet your living expenses? (CHECK ONLY ONE)

    0_____It was enough
    X_____It was not enough

8. Did stopping work make your health better or worse? (CHECK ONLY ONE)

    1_____Stopping work made my health better
    2_____Stopping work made my health worse
    3_____Stopping work made no difference in my health

9. Did stopping work make you think of yourself as older or younger? (CHECK ONLY ONE)

    1_____Stopping work made me think of myself as older
    2_____Stopping work made me think of myself as younger
    3_____Stopping work made no difference

10. Did stopping work give you the feeling that your life was not very useful? (CHECK ONLY ONE)

    0_____Yes
    X_____No

11. On this question just go down the list and check how often you did each of the following things while you were not working: (PUT A CHECK IN FRONT OF EITHER "OFTEN" OR "SOMETIMES" OR "HARDLY EVER OR NEVER" FOR EVERY ITEM IN THE LIST)

How often did you:

Miss being with other people at work	___OFTEN	___SOMETIMES	___HARDLY EVER OR NEVER
Miss the feeling of doing a good job	___OFTEN	___SOMETIMES	___HARDLY EVER OR NEVER
Feel that you wanted to go back to work	___OFTEN	___SOMETIMES	___HARDLY EVER OR NEVER
Worry about not having a job	___OFTEN	___SOMETIMES	___HARDLY EVER OR NEVER

BE SURE YOU CHECKED SOMETHING FOR EVERY ITEM

CONFIDENTIAL

12. How long after you stopped working was it until you started working again? (CHECK ONLY ONE)

      1 _____ About a week or two (or less)
      2 _____ About a month
      3 _____ About two or three months
      4 _____ More than three months

13. ON THIS QUESTION, CHECK AS MANY ANSWERS AS APPLY TO YOU. Why did you go back to work?

      1 _____ Because I could not get used to not working
      2 _____ Because I wanted more money
      3 _____ Because I needed more money
      4 _____ Because I was not keeping busy
      5 _____ Because I like to work so much I didn't want to give it up

      6 _____ Some other reason: What?_____

14. ON THIS QUESTION, CHECK ONLY THE MOST IMPORTANT ANSWER. What was the MOST IMPORTANT reason why you went back to work?

      1 _____ Because I could not get used to not working
      2 _____ Because I wanted more money
      3 _____ Because I needed more money
      4 _____ Because I was not keeping busy
      5 _____ Because I like to work so much I didn't want to give it up
      6 _____ Some other reason

15. What is your job now?_____

16. Do you have a part-time job now, or do you have a full-time job?

      0 _____ I have a part-time job
      X _____ I have a full-time job

17. Which would you say you like the best — the job you are doing now or the job you were doing when you filled out our first questionnaire over two years ago? (CHECK ONLY ONE)

      1 _____ I like the job I have now better than the one I used to have
      2 _____ I liked the job I used to have better than the one I have now
      3 _____ I like the one as much as the other

18. Is the work you are doing now the same sort of work you were doing when you filled out our first questionnaire over two years ago? (CHECK ONLY ONE)

      0 _____ Yes, it is the same sort of work
      X _____ No, it is not the same sort of work

19. Would you say the job you have now is more, or less, difficult than the one you used to have? (CHECK ONLY ONE)

      1 _____ The job I have now is more difficult
      2 _____ The job I have now is less difficult
      3 _____ The job I have now is about the same as the one I had

CONFIDENTIAL

-4-

20. Do you think going back to work has made your health better or worse? (CHECK ONLY ONE)

    1_____Going back to work has made my health better
    2_____Going back to work has made my health worse
    3_____Going back to work has made no difference in my health

21. Do you think that going back to work has made you more satisfied with your way of life? (CHECK ONLY ONE)

    1_____Yes
    2_____No
    3_____Undecided

22. Has going back to work made an important difference in your income? (CHECK ONLY ONE)

    0_____Yes
    X_____No

23. Are you glad you went back to work, or do you regret it? (CHECK ONLY ONE)

    0_____I am glad I went back to work
    X_____I regret it

24. Do you think the government is doing enough, not enough, or too much for people who have stopped working? (CHECK ONLY ONE)

    1_____The government is doing enough
    2_____Not enough
    3_____Too much
    4_____Undecided

25. Do you think the company you worked for when we first got in touch with you is doing enough, not enough, or too much for its employees who have stopped working? (CHECK ONLY ONE)

    1_____It is doing enough
    2_____Not enough
    3_____Too much
    4_____Undecided

26. Some people say that retirement is good for a person, some say it is bad. In general, who do you think? (CHECK ONLY ONE)

    0_____Retirement is mostly good for a person
    X_____Retirement is mostly bad for a person

27. If it were up to you alone, would you continue working at your present job? (CHECK ONLY ONE)

    0_____I would continue working
    X_____I would stop working

28. Have you made any plans for anything you would like to do after you stop working? (CHECK ONLY ONE)

    1_____No
    2_____Yes: What?_____

CONFIDENTIAL

-5-

29. How do the retired people you know feel about retirement?   (CHECK ONLY ONE)

    1_____ I do not know anyone who is retired
    2_____ They mostly like retirement
    3_____ They mostly dislike retirement
    4_____ I don't know

30. How do the people you know who are still working feel about retirement? (CHECK ONLY ONE)

    1_____ I do not know anyone who is still working
    2_____ They mostly think they would like retirement
    3_____ They mostly think they would dislike retirement
    4_____ I don't know

31. Do you mostly look forward to the time when you will stop working and retire, or in general do you dislike the idea? (CHECK ONLY ONE)

    1_____ I look forward to it
    2_____ I dislike the idea
    3_____ Undecided

32. ON THIS QUESTION, CHECK ONLY THE ONE MOST IMPORTANT REASON. If you are planning to retire during the next five years, why are you planning to retire?

    1_____ I do not plan to retire
    2_____ Because of my health
    3_____ Because I have difficulty in doing my job
    4_____ Because I am not able to work as well as younger men
    5_____ Because I want more leisure time
    6_____ Because my employer says I have to retire

33. ON THIS QUESTION, CHECK AS MANY ANSWERS AS YOU THINK SHOULD BE INCLUDED. Who do you think should provide for the older person who has stopped working, if he needs help in taking care of his problems?

    1_____ The federal government
    2_____ Each state government
    3_____ The local government
    4_____ Community agencies
    5_____ The company he worked for
    6_____ His union
    7_____ His family

NOW WE WOULD LIKE TO ASK YOU SOME QUESTIONS ABOUT YOUR LIFE AT PRESENT

34. Would you say you now take part in many, a few, or practically no activities such as card clubs, lodge, church groups, unions, community activities and the like? (CHECK ONLY ONE)

    1_____ I take part in many activities
    2_____ I take part in a few activities
    3_____ I take part in practically no activities

35. Do you spend most of your free time with other people, or are you usually alone? (CHECK ONLY ONE)

    1_____ I spend most of my free time with my wife (or husband) only
    2_____ I spend most of my free time with other people also
    3_____ I spend most of my free time alone

-6-

36. Do you have a hobby? (CHECK ONLY ONE)

    1_____ No
    2_____ Yes: What?_____

37. Check the one statement below that best describes your present marriag
    (CHECK ONLY ONE)

    1_____ I have never been married

    2_____ I am married, and living with my wife (or husband)
    3_____ I am married, but separated from my wife (or husband)
    4_____ I am widowed
    5_____ I am divorced

38. In your family, who is it that makes most of the important decisions?
    (CHECK ONLY ONE)

    1_____ I make most of the important decisions myself
    2_____ Someone else makes most of the important decisions
    3_____ No one person makes the decisions — we make the decisions
           together

39. How many other people live with you in the same house or apartment?

    1_____ I live alone
    2_____ I live with my wife (or husband)
    3_____ Someone else lives with me also: Who? (WRITE IN HOW MANY
                                                        OF EACH)

           HOW MANY of your daughters live with you?
           HOW MANY of your sons live with you?   _____
           HOW MANY of your daughters-in-law live with you? _____
           HOW MANY of your sons-in-law live with you?   _____
           HOW MANY of your grandchildren live with you?   _____
           HOW MANY of your other relatives live with you —
               such as parents, brothers, sisters, uncles,
               cousins, mother-in-law, and the like
           HOW MANY other people live with you — such as   _____
               roomers or friends
                                                            _____

40. How much would you like to be in touch with your children more than
    you are these days? (CHECK ONLY ONE)

    1_____ I do not have any living children

    2_____ I would like to be in touch with them a good deal more
    3_____ I would like to be in touch with them somewhat more
    4_____ I would not like to be in touch with them any more than I am
    5_____ I would like to be in touch with them less than I am

41. Have most of your friends stopped working, or are most of your friends
    still working? (CHECK ONLY ONE)

    1_____ I do not have any friends

    2_____ Most of my friends have stopped working
    3_____ Some of my friends have stopped, some of them are still workin
    4_____ Most of my friends are still working

                            CONFIDENTIAL

42. About how many really close friends do you have here in town with whom you talk over personal matters? (CHECK ONLY ONE)

    1____ Many close friends
    2____ Some close friends
    3____ Few close friends
    4____ No close friends

43. Would you say you go around with a certain bunch of close friends who visit back and forth in each other's homes? (CHECK ONLY ONE)

    0____ Yes
    X____ No

44. How many of your close friends are people from your place of work? (CHECK ONLY ONE)

    1____ All my close friends are from my place of work
    2____ Most of my close friends are from my place of work
    3____ Some of my close friends are from my place of work
    4____ None of my close friends are from my place of work

45. On this question, just go down the list and check whether in your family it is mainly the wife's job or the husband's job to do each of the following things:

	MAINLY WIFE'S JOB	MAINLY HUSBAND'S JOB	BOTH THE SAME	QUESTION DOES NOT APPLY
To decide upon the kind of car to buy	___WIFE	___HUSBAND	___BOTH	___DOESN'T APPLY
To decide how the family income should be spent	___WIFE	___HUSBAND	___BOTH	___DOESN'T APPLY
To decide how we should spend our free time	___WIFE	___HUSBAND	___BOTH	___DOESN'T APPLY
To discipline the children when they were bad	___WIFE	___HUSBAND	___BOTH	___DOESN'T APPLY

BE SURE YOU CHECKED SOMETHING FOR EVERY ITEM

46. All in all, how satisfied would you say you are with your job and your place of work today? (CHECK ONLY ONE)

    1____ Very satisifed
    2____ Fairly satisfied
    3____ Not very satisfied
    4____ Not satisfied at all

47. How much do you plan ahead the things that you will be doing next week or the week after? (CHECK ONLY ONE)

    1____ I make many plans
    2____ I make few plans
    3____ I make almost no plans

CONFIDENTIAL

-8-

48. In general, how would you say you feel most of the time, in good spirits or in low spirits? (CHECK ONLY ONE)

   1_____ I am usually in good spirits
   2_____ I am in good spirits some of the time and in low spirits some of the time
   3_____ I am usually in low spirits

49. Thinking back over your life, how easy would you say it has been for you to get used to the changes that have happened in your life? (CHECK ONLY ONE)

   1_____ It has always been <u>very easy</u> for me to get used to changes
   2_____ It has always been <u>fairly easy</u> for me to get used to changes
   3_____ It has always been <u>fairly difficult</u> for me to get used to changes
   4_____ It has always been <u>very difficult</u> for me to get used to changes

50. Do you prefer to have new things happening all the time, or do you prefer to have life go along at a steady pace? (CHECK ONLY ONE)

   0_____ I prefer to have a lot of new things happening all the time
   X_____ I prefer to have life go along at a steady pace

51. All in all, how much happiness would you say you find in life today? (CHECK ONLY ONE)

   1_____ Almost none
   2_____ Some, but not very much
   3_____ A good deal

52. On the whole, how satisfied would you say you are with your way of life today? (CHECK ONLY ONE)

   1_____ Very satisfied
   2_____ Fairly satisfied
   3_____ Not very satisfied
   4_____ Not satisfied at all

53. How do you think of yourself as far as age goes — do you think of yourself as: (CHECK ONLY ONE)

   1_____ Elderly
   2_____ Middle-aged
   3_____ Late middle-aged
   4_____ Old

54. Which <u>one</u> of these things would you say you've worked hardest at in your <u>life</u>? (CHECK ONLY ONE)

   1_____ Trying to live my own life according to the dictates of my own conscience
   2_____ Trying to be a friend to others and their friend in turn
   3_____ Trying to earn a good living and get ahead in life

55. Now, how well have you lived up to what you expected of yourself in achieving this one thing you have just checked? (CHECK ONLY ONE)

   1_____ Very well
   2_____ Fairly well
   3_____ Not so well

CONFIDENTIAL

56. Here are some statements that people answer in different ways. Read
each one carefully and decide whether you tend to agree or disagree with
it. If you tend to agree with the statement, check YES. If you tend to
disagree, check NO. Be sure to check something for each one.

	IF YOU AGREE	IF YOU DISAGREE	
I have a pretty good idea of what my life would be like if I stopped working	___YES	___NO	___UNDECIDED
Older people should stop working and give younger people a chance	___YES	___NO	___UNDECIDED
Almost everything these days is a racket	___YES	___NO	___UNDECIDED
In my opinion, a person's job is what gives meaning to life	___YES	___NO	___UNDECIDED
Obedience to parents is about the most important thing for children to learn	___YES	___NO	___UNDECIDED
Troubles and difficulties make me unhappy	___YES	___NO	___UNDECIDED
Things just keep getting worse and worse for me as I get older	___YES	___NO	___UNDECIDED
If you don't watch yourself, people will take advantage of you	___YES	___NO	___UNDECIDED
Parents can always learn something by listening to children's ideas	___YES	___NO	___UNDECIDED
These days I find myself giving up hope of trying to improve myself	___YES	___NO	___UNDECIDED
These days I get the feeling that my health is gradually getting worse	___YES	___NO	___UNDECIDED
No one is going to care much what happens to you, when you get right down to it	___YES	___NO	___UNDECIDED
Every member of the family, except infants, should have an equal say in making important decisions	___YES	___NO	___UNDECIDED
I often think about my work when I am away from it	___YES	___NO	___UNDECIDED
These days I get the feeling that I'm just not a part of things	___YES	___NO	___UNDECIDED
When you get right down to it, a job is nothing more than just a way to make a living	___YES	___NO	___UNDECIDED

BE SURE YOU CHECKED SOMETHING FOR EVERY ITEM

CONFIDENTIAL

-10-

JUST CHECK WHETHER YOU AGREE OR DISAGREE WITH EACH ONE:

	IF YOU AGREE	IF YOU DISAGREE	

It gets harder and harder for me to keep up the pace as I get older

___YES ___NO ___UNDECIDED

A life filled with problems to solve is better than a life without problems

___YES ___NO ___UNDECIDED

Everyone would be better off today if there were not so many changes taking place all the time

___YES ___NO ___UNDECIDED

If they can afford it, when people get older they ought to stop work and take things easy

___YES ___NO ___UNDECIDED

BE SURE YOU CHECKED SOMETHING FOR EVERY ITEM

57. About how much does your total income from all sources amount to a MONTH? (CHECK ONLY ONE)

1 ___ Less than $50 a month
2 ___ More than $50 but less than $100 a month
3 ___ More than $100 but less than $150 a month
4 ___ More than $150 but less than $200 a month
5 ___ More than $200 but less than $250 a month
6 ___ More than $250 but less than $300 a month
7 ___ More than $300 but less than $400 a month
8 ___ More than $400 but less than $600 a month
9 ___ More than $600 a month

58. Do you consider your present income enough to meet your living expenses (CHECK ONLY ONE)

0 ___ It is enough
X ___ It is not enough

59. Is your standard of living better today or was it better during most of your lifetime? (CHECK ONLY ONE)

1 ___ My standard of living is better today
2 ___ My standard of living was better during most of my lifetime
3 ___ My standard of living has not changed

60. Does your present income keep you from doing any of the things you would like to do? (CHECK ONLY ONE)

1 ___ No
2 ___ Yes: What? _____

61. How many people — counting yourself — are supported mostly by your present income? (CHECK ONLY ONE)

1 ___ Myself only
2 ___ Two people, counting myself
3 ___ Three people, counting myself
4 ___ Four people, counting myself
5 ___ Five people, counting myself
6 ___ Six people, counting myself
7 ___ More than six people, counting myself

CONFIDENTIAL

NOW WE WOULD LIKE TO ASK YOU SOME QUESTIONS ABOUT YOUR HEALTH

62. How would you rate your health at the present time? (CHECK ONLY ONE)

     1_____Excellent
     2_____Good
     3_____Fair
     4_____Poor
     5_____Very poor

63. Do you have any particular physical or health problems at present?
     (CHECK ONLY ONE)

     1_____No
     2_____Yes: What?_____

64. Does your health or physical condition keep you from doing any of the
     things you would like to do? (CHECK ONLY ONE)

     1_____No
     2_____Yes: What?_____

65. ON THIS QUESTION, CHECK AS MANY ANSWERS AS YOU NEED TO. For what
     reasons have you been seen by a doctor during the past year?

     1_____I have not been seen by a doctor

     2_____For regular examination by the company doctor
     3_____For regular examination by my own doctor
     4_____For illness, seen only in doctor's office
     5_____For illness, seen at home
     6_____For first aid or an accident
     7_____Admitted to hospital

66. ON THIS QUESTION, CHECK ONLY ONE ANSWER. If you have been to a doctor
     in recent years, what did he tell you?

     1_____I have not been to a doctor in recent years

     2_____He said I was in good health and physical condition
     3_____He did not recommend medicine or treatment, but said I should
           "watch my health"
     4_____He said I should have medicine or treatment, but that I'd be
           all right after a while
     5_____He said I could expect to take medicine or have treatment the
           rest of my life
     6_____Something else: What?_____

NOW WE WOULD LIKE TO ASK YOU SOME QUESTIONS ABOUT LIFE IN GENERAL

67. Some people say that most people can be trusted. Others say you can't
     be too careful in your dealings with people. How do you feel about
     it? (CHECK ONLY ONE)

     0_____Most people can be trusted
     X_____You can't be too careful in your dealings with people

68. Would you say that most people are more inclined to help others, or more inclined to look out for themselves? (CHECK ONLY ONE)

    0_____Most people are inclined to help others

    X_____Most people are inclined to look out for themselves

69. If you had your choice, which of the following would you <u>most</u> like to be? (CHECK ONLY ONE)

    1_____Independent

    2_____Successful

    3_____Well-liked

70. On this question just go down the list and check how often you do each of the following things: (PUT A CHECK IN FRONT OF EITHER "OFTEN" OR "SOMETIMES" OR "HARDLY EVER OR NEVER" FOR EVERY ITEM IN THE LIST)

HOW OFTEN DO YOU:

Have times when you
just don't know what
to do to keep occupied ___OFTEN ___SOMETIMES ___HARDLY EVER OR NEVE

Feel lonely ___OFTEN ___SOMETIMES ___HARDLY EVER OR NEVE

Find yourself feeling
"blue" ___OFTEN ___SOMETIMES ___HARDLY EVER OR NEVE

Get the feeling that
your life today is not
very useful ___OFTEN ___SOMETIMES ___HARDLY EVER OR NEVE

Get upset by the things
that happen in your day
to day living ___OFTEN ___SOMETIMES ___HARDLY EVER OR NEVE

Wish you had the chance
to live your life over ___OFTEN ___SOMETIMES ___HARDLY EVER OR NEVE

Find yourself wishing
you were younger ___OFTEN ___SOMETIMES ___HARDLY EVER OR NEVE

Worry about money
matters ___OFTEN ___SOMETIMES ___HARDLY EVER OR NEVE

See some of your
children ___OFTEN ___SOMETIMES ___HARDLY EVER OR NEVE

See some of your
grandchildren ___OFTEN ___SOMETIMES ___HARDLY EVER OR NEVE

See some of your
other relatives ___OFTEN ___SOMETIMES ___HARDLY EVER OR NEVER

BE SURE YOU CHECKED SOMETHING FOR EVERY ITEM

71. ON THIS QUESTION, CHECK AS MANY ANSWERS AS YOU NEED TO TELL ALL THE
     THINGS THAT GIVE YOU THE GREATEST COMFORT AND SATISFACTION IN LIFE.
     Which ones give you the most comfort and satisfaction in life today?

     1____ Just being with my family at home
     2____ Working around the house, garden, or yard
     3____ Having relatives other than my children visit me
     4____ Doing things I like to do by myself
     5____ My religion or church work
     6____ Spending time with close friends
     7____ Just sitting and thinking about things
     8____ Reading
     9____ My recreation outside the home
     0____ Getting out to visit relatives other than my children
     X____ My work

72. ON THIS QUESTION, CHECK AS MANY ANSWERS AS APPLY TO YOU. What changes
     for the WORSE have taken place in your life since you filled out our
     questionnaires in 1954?

     Changes for the WORSE:

     1____ Change in my health
     2____ Change in my job
     3____ Change in residence
     4____ Change in my family
     5____ Change in income
     6____ Death in my family
     7____ Change in my outlook on life
     8____ Other changes for the worse: What?_____

     9____ No changes for the worse

73. Now, what changes for the BETTER have taken place in your life since
     you filled out our questionnaire in 1954? (CHECK AS MANY ANSWERS AS
     APPLY TO YOU)

     Changes for the BETTER:

     1____ Change in my health
     2____ Change in my job
     3____ Change in residence
     4____ Change in my family
     5____ Change in income
     6____ Change in my outlook on life
     7____ Other changes for the better: What?_____

     8____ No changes for the better

74. When were you born? Month_____Day_____Year_____

75. Sex:

     0____ Male
     X____ Female

76. In what city and state were you born?_____
     (If not born in the United States, which country?)

CONFIDENTIAL

M2 - 1955

-14-

FOLLOW-UP HEALTH QUESTIONNAIRE

These are questions about your health. We would like to have you answer them in terms of WHAT HAS HAPPENED TO YOUR HEALTH DURING THE PAST YEAR, or since you last filled out a questionnaire for this Study.

DURING THE PAST YEAR:

1. Has your eyesight changed so as to handicap you?......... ___Yes ___NO
   If YES, has the change been corrected to your satisfaction by glasses?..................................... ___YES ___NO

2. Has your hearing changed so as to handicap you?.......... ___YES ___NO
   If YES, has the change been corrected to your satisfaction by a hearing aid?........................... ___YES ___NO

3. Have your teeth or dentures caused trouble?.............. ___YES ___NO
   If YES, has the trouble been corrected to your satisfaction?... ___YES ___NO

4. Have you been troubled by frequent hoarseness?........... ___YES ___NO

5. Have you had a cough most of the time?................... ___YES ___NO

6. Have you often had spells of severe dizziness?........... ___YES ___NO

7. Have you often been troubled by your heart beating fast?. ___YES ___NO

8. Have you often had some physical exercise, such as walking?... ___YES ___NO

9. Has shortness of breath cut down your usual walking or stair climbing?...................................... ___YES ___NO

10. Has your usual walking or stair climbing caused pain in your chest?.................................... ___YES ___NO

11. Has your usual walking or stair climbing caused cramps in your legs?.. ___YES ___NO

12. Have you often lost your appetite?...................... ___YES ___NO

13. Have you often had difficulty in falling asleep or staying asleep?.. ___YES ___NO

14. Have you often suffered from severe or "sick" headaches (migraine)?.. ___YES ___NO

15. Have troubles with your digestion caused you to see your doctor?... ___YES ___NO

16. Have you often been troubled by your hands trembling?.... ___YES ___NO

17. Have you often had small accidents or injuries?......... ___YES ___NO

18. Have you had to stay in bed more than 3 days due to illness, injury or operation?........................... ___YES ___NO
    If YES, name the condition which kept you in bed:
    _____

19. Have you had any serious illness?....................... ___YES ___NO
    If YES, name the illness:
    _____

DURING THE PAST YEAR:

20. Have you been told that you are looking well?........... ___YES ___NO

21. Have you had new trouble with your bowels, or seen
    blood on your stool or on the toilet paper?............. ___YES ___NO

22. Has pressure or pain in the head often made your
    life miserable?....................................... ___YES ___NO

23. Have you often sighed without being able to control it?. ___YES ___NO

24. Have you enjoyed meeting people and making new friends?. ___YES ___NO

25. Have you often had a nightmare?......................... ___YES ___NO

26. Have you often started the day feeling full of energy?.. ___YES ___NO

27. Have strange people or places made you afraid?.......... ___YES ___NO

28. Has it usually been easy for you to make up your mind?.. ___YES ___NO

29. Have you usually awakened tired and exhausted?.......... ___YES ___NO

30. Have you wanted or taken any treatment because of
    trouble in passing urine?............................. ___YES ___NO

31. Have you frequently felt unhappy and depressed?......... ___YES ___NO

32. Have you enjoyed doing things you have never done
    before?... ___YES ___NO

33. Have you had a nervous breakdown?....................... ___YES ___NO

34. Have you thought seriously of suicide?.................. ___YES ___NO

35. Have you enjoyed being by yourself?..................... ___YES ___NO

36. Have you enjoyed being with other people?.............. ___YES ___NO

37. Do you think your health is better now than it was
    when you were 50 years old?........................... ___YES ___NO

38. Have you been refused employment because of your health? ___YES ___NO

39. Have you been refused employment because of your age?... ___YES ___NO

40. Have you been handicapped by arthritis of any part
    of your body?... ___YES ___NO

41. Have you been troubled with any weakness or paralysis?.. ___YES ___NO

42. Has your weight changed?................................ ___YES ___NO
    Pounds gained:_____ Pounds lost:_____

43. Have you gone on a special diet prescribed by your
    doctor?... ___YES ___NO

44. Has your doctor prescribed any medicine for you to take? ___YES ___NO

45. Have hormones been prescribed for you by your doctor?... ___YES ___NO

CONFIDENTIAL

-16-

RECORD VERIFICATION FORM

Just for our records, on this question please check whether you were working or not working <u>most</u> of the time during each period we have listed. For example, if you <u>were</u> working most of the time between January and July, 1952, your answer would be checked like this:

January through June, 1952   ✓ Working   ___Not Working

Just check what you were doing during <u>most</u> of the time in each period.

In the period:	Most of the time I was:	
July through December, 1952	___Working	___Not Working
January through June, 1953	___Working	___Not Working
July through December, 1953	___Working	___Not Working
January through June, 1954	___Working	___Not Working
July through December, 1954	___Working	___Not Working
January through June, 1955	___Working	___Not Working
July through December, 1955	___Working	___Not Working

We would like to make sure we have the correct name and address of someone who will always know where you are in case you move. Would you please give us the name and address of a relative or close friend who would always know about you and would know your address? Do <u>not</u> give the name of your wife (or husband) whose address would be the same as yours. (The best person to whom you might refer us would be one of your children, if you have any living children.)

Name and address of someone who knows about me and who will always know my address:

_____

_____

_____

This person whose name and address I have just given is:

_____A friend of mine
_____One of my children
_____My brother
_____My sister
_____Some other relative of mine

BE SURE NONE OF THE PAGES HAVE STUCK TOGETHER AND THAT YOU HAVE ANSWERED ALL THE QUESTIONS.   THANK YOU FOR YOUR COOPERATION.

CONFIDENTIAL

S-1 (R) 1957

WAVE IV RETIRED QUESTIONNAIRE

WHAT THIS IS ALL ABOUT

This is the fourth part of the Cornell University survey of America's older citizens in which you are participating.

This is not a "test". You probably remember that there are no right or wrong answers. Just answer the questions in the way you, yourself, feel about them. GIVE YOUR OWN HONEST OPINIONS.

The information you give us will be kept strictly confidential.

Read every question carefully. Then check the answer which best gives your opinion. If you find that a question does not fit your situation, or does not give you a chance to express your opinion, first check the answer which most nearly expresses your opinion, and then please feel free to write what you think.

Sometimes the pages stick together, so be sure you have answered the questions on every page. And please be sure to answer every question. If you are not sure, guess. It is important that you answer them all.

Some of the questions will have special instructions which you should follow.

THANK YOU FOR YOUR COOPERATION.

CONFIDENTIAL

-1-

1. Our records show that you are not working now. Which things about not
   working do you like and which things do you dislike? (JUST GO DOWN THE
   LIST AND CHECK WHETHER YOU LIKE OR DISLIKE EACH OF THE FOLLOWING ITEMS)

   (JUST PUT A CHECK MARK IN FRONT OF YOUR ANSWERS, LIKE THIS: ✔)

	(5)	(6)	(7)	(8)

   Do you like or dislike:

   Having a lot of free time   ___LIKE   ___DISLIKE   ___DOESN'T APPLY

   Not having a routine to follow   ___LIKE   ___DISLIKE   ___DOESN'T APPLY

   Being at home a lot of the time   ___LIKE   ___DISLIKE   ___DOESN'T APPLY

   Something else about not working I like: What?_____

   Something else about not working I dislike: What?_____

2. Some people say that retirement is good for a person, some say it is bad.
   In general, what do you think? (CHECK ONLY ONE)

   0____Retirement is mostly good for a person
   X____Retirement is mostly bad for a person

3. How do the people you know who are still working feel about retirement?
   (CHECK ONLY ONE)

   1____I do not know anyone who is still working
   2____They mostly think they would like retirement
   3____They mostly think they would dislike retirement
   4____I don't know

4. How do the retired people you know feel about retirement? (CHECK ONLY
   ONE)

   6____I do not know anyone who has retired
   7____They mostly like retirement
   8____They mostly dislike retirement
   9____I don't know

5. Do you think the government is doing enough, not enough or too much for
   people who have stopped working? (CHECK ONLY ONE)

   1____The government is doing enough
   2____Not enough
   3____Too much
   4____Undecided

6. Do you think the company you worked for when we first got in touch with
   you is doing enough, not enough, or too much for its employees who have
   stopped working? (CHECK ONLY ONE)

   6____It is doing enough
   7____Not enough
   8____Too much
   9____I don't know

-2-

1. Do you consider yourself retired?   (CHECK ONLY ONE)

        0 _____ No
        X _____ Yes

2. Which one of these things had the most to do with your stopping work?
    (CHECK ONLY THE MOST IMPORTANT ONE)

        1 _____ My health
        2 _____ Difficulty in doing my regular work
        3 _____ Not being able to do my work as well as younger people
        4 _____ Wanting more leisure time

        5 _____ None of these, just company policy
        6 _____ Some other reason: What?_____

3. Who decided that you should stop work when you did?   (CHECK ONLY ONE)

        0 _____ The company decided
        X _____ I decided myself

4. It takes some people a little while to get used to not working. About
    how long would you say it took you to become used to not working?
    (CHECK ONLY ONE)

        1 _____ I am still not used to it

        2 _____ It took me a week or two (or less)
        3 _____ It took me about a month
        4 _____ It took me two or three months
        5 _____ It took me more than three months

5. Are you looking for work?   (CHECK ONLY ONE)

        1 _____ No
        2 _____ Yes, I am looking for part-time work
        3 _____ Yes, I am looking for full-time work

6. Do you think stopping work has made your health better or worse?
    (CHECK ONLY ONE)

        1 _____ Stopping work has made my health better
        2 _____ Stopping work has made my health worse
        3 _____ Stopping work has made no difference in my health

7. Do you think stopping work has made you less satisfied with your way
    of life today?   (CHECK ONLY ONE)

        1 _____ Yes
        2 _____ No
        3 _____ Undecided

8. Do you think that stopping work has made you think of yourself as older
    or younger?   (CHECK ONLY ONE)

        1 _____ Stopping work has made me think of myself as older
        2 _____ Stopping work has made me think of myself as younger
        3 _____ Stopping work has made no difference

9. Do you think that stopping work has given you the feeling that your life
    today is not very useful?   (CHECK ONLY ONE)

        1 _____ Yes
        2 _____ No
        3 _____ Undecided

-3-

As people grow older they sometimes see less of their relatives, although this is not always the case. We are interested in knowing how
often you are in touch with your relatives.

1. ON THIS QUESTION, CHECK AS MANY ANSWERS AS APPLY TO YOU. When your
family has get-togethers, who attends?

    1_____In my family we don't have get-togethers
    2_____My children attend family get-togethers
    3_____My brothers attend family get-togethers
    4_____My sisters attend family get-togethers
    5_____My grandchildren attend family get-togethers
    6_____My nieces attend family get-togethers
    7_____My nephews attend family get-togethers
    8_____My cousins attend family get-togethers

2. How many living children do you have? (WRITE IN HOW MANY)

    I have _____ living children

3. ON THIS QUESTION, CHECK ONLY ONE ANSWER. How many of your children
live close enough so that you can see them whenever you want to?

    1_____I do not have any living children
    2_____All of my children live close enough for me to see them
         whenever I want to
    3_____Some of my children live close enough for me to see them
         whenever I want to
    4_____None of my children live close enough for me to see them
         whenever I want to

4. Do you have any children whom you do not see often? (CHECK ONLY ONE)

    6_____I do not have any living children
    7_____I see all of my children often
    8_____A few of my children I do not see often
    9_____Most of my children I do not see often
    0_____I do not see any of my children often
    X_____Some I see often, some I do not

5. How many living grandchildren do you have (WRITE IN HOW MANY)

    I have _____ living grandchildren

6. ON THIS QUESTION CHECK ONLY ONE ANSWER. How many of your grandchildren
live close enough so that you can see them whenever you want to?

    1_____I do not have any living grandchildren
    2_____All of my grandchildren live close enough for me to see
         them whenever I want to
    3_____Some of my grandchildren live close enough for me to see
         them whenever I want to
    4_____None of my grandchildren live close enough for me to see
         them whenever I want to

-4-

1. How many living brothers do you have? (WRITE IN HOW MANY)

    I have _____ living brothers

2. ON THIS QUESTION, CHECK ONLY ONE ANSWER. How many of your brothers live
    close enough so that you can see them whenever you want to?

    1_____I do not have any living brothers

    2_____All of my brothers live close enough for me to see them
            whenever I want to
    3_____Some of my brothers live close enough for me to see them
            whenever I want to
    4_____None of my brothers live close enough for me to see them
            whenever I want to

3. How many living sisters do you have? (WRITE IN HOW MANY)

    I have _____ living sisters

4. ON THIS QUESTION, CHECK ONLY ONE ANSWER. How many of your sisters live
    close enough so that you can see them whenever you want to?

    6_____I do not have any living sisters

    7_____All of my sisters live close enough for me to see them
            whenever I want to
    8_____Some of my sisters live close enough for me to see them
            whenever I want to
    9_____None of my sisters live close enough for me to see them
            whenever I want to

5. On this question, just go down the list and check how often you see SOME
    of the following relatives: (PUT A CHECK IN FRONT OF EITHER "OFTEN" OR
    "SOMETIMES" OR "HARDLY EVER OR NEVER" FOR EACH ITEM IN THE LIST)

    HOW OFTEN DO YOU SEE:

	(1)	(2)	(3)	(4)
Some of your children	___OFTEN	___SOMETIMES	___HARDLY EVER OR NEVER	
Some of your brothers	___OFTEN	___SOMETIMES	___HARDLY EVER OR NEVER	
Some of your sisters	___OFTEN	___SOMETIMES	___HARDLY EVER OR NEVER	
Some of your grand-children	___OFTEN	___SOMETIMES	___HARDLY EVER OR NEVER	
Some of your nieces	___OFTEN	___SOMETIMES	___HARDLY EVER OR NEVER	
Some of your nephews	___OFTEN	___SOMETIMES	___HARDLY EVER OR NEVER	
Some of your cousins	___OFTEN	___SOMETIMES	___HARDLY EVER OR NEVER	

-5-

1. Check the one statement below that best describes your present marriage. (CHECK ONLY ONE)

    1_____ I have never been married

    2_____ I am married and living with my wife (or husband)
    3_____ I am married, but separated from my wife (or husband)
    4_____ I am widowed
    5_____ I am divorced

2. How often does your immediate family get together for a meal? (CHECK ONLY ONE)

    1_____ My immediate family never has such get-togethers

    2_____ We often get together
    3_____ We sometimes get together
    4_____ We seldom get together

3. How much do you enjoy these immediate family get-togethers (CHECK ONLY ONE)

    6_____ My immediate family does not have such get-togethers

    7_____ I enjoy them a great deal
    8_____ I enjoy them somewhat
    9_____ I enjoy them very little
    0_____ I do not enjoy them at all

4. How much would you like to be in touch with your children more than you are these days? (CHECK ONLY ONE)

    7_____ I do not have any living children

    8_____ I would like to be in touch with them a good deal more
    9_____ I would like to be in touch with them somewhat more
    0_____ I would not like to be in touch with them any more than I am

5. On this question, just go down the list and check how often you telephone SOME of your relatives: (PUT A CHECK IN FRON OF EITHER "OFTEN" OR "SOMETIMES" OR "HARDLY EVER OR NEVER" FOR EACH ITEM IN THE LIST)

HOW OFTEN DO YOU TELEPHONE:

	(5)	(6)	(7)	(8)
Some of your children	OFTEN	SOMETIMES	HARDLY EVER OR NEVER	
Some of your brothers	OFTEN	SOMETIMES	HARDLY EVER OR NEVER	
Some of your sisters	OFTEN	SOMETIMES	HARDLY EVER OR NEVER	
Some of your grand-children	OFTEN	SOMETIMES	HARDLY EVER OR NEVER	
Some of your nieces	OFTEN	SOMETIMES	HARDLY EVER OR NEVER	
Some of your nephews	OFTEN	SOMETIMES	HARDLY EVER OR NEVER	
Some of your cousins	OFTEN	SOMETIMES	HARDLY EVER OR NEVER	

CONFIDENTIAL

-6-

1. On this question, just go down the list and check how often you <u>write</u>
SOME of your relatives: (PUT A CHECK IN FRONT OF EITHER "OFTEN" OR
"SOMETIMES" OR "HARDLY EVER OR NEVER" FOR EACH ITEM IN THE LIST)

HOW OFTEN DO YOU WRITE TO:

	(9)	(0)	(X)	(Y)
Some of your children	___OFTEN	___SOMETIMES	___HARDLY EVER OR NEVER	
Some of your brothers	___OFTEN	___SOMETIMES	___HARDLY EVER OR NEVER	
Some of your sisters	___OFTEN	___SOMETIMES	___HARDLY EVER OR NEVER	
Some of your grand-children	___OFTEN	___SOMETIMES	___HARDLY EVER OR NEVER	
Some of your nieces	___OFTEN	___SOMETIMES	___HARDLY EVER OR NEVER	
Some of your nephews	___OFTEN	___SOMETIMES	___HARDLY EVER OR NEVER	
Some of your cousins	___OFTEN	___SOMETIMES	___HARDLY EVER OR NEVER	

2. ON THIS QUESTION, CHECK AS MANY ANSWERS AS APPLY TO YOU. Do your family
and relatives, either yours or your wife's, ever have any <u>large</u> family
gatherings, when a lot of you get together at one time?

1_____ We have no such large family gatherings

2_____ We have such gatherings on national holidays such as
Thanksgiving and Labor Day

3_____ We have such gatherings on religious holidays such as
Christmas and Easter

4_____ We also have such gatherings on other occasions. When?_____

3. How much do you enjoy these large family get-togethers?
(CHECK ONLY ONE)

6_____ We do not have such get-togethers

7_____ I enjoy them a great deal

8_____ I enjoy them somewhat

9_____ I enjoy them very little

0_____ I do not enjoy them at all

4. How much should parents be concerned with their grown-up children's
affairs? (CHECK ONLY ONE)

1_____ They should not be concerned at all

2_____ They should be concerned a little

3_____ They should be concerned some

4_____ They should be concerned a great deal

CONFIDENTIAL

-7-

1. How much should children be concerned with their parents' affairs?
(CHECK ONLY ONE)

   6_____They should not be concerned at all
   7_____They should be concerned a little
   8_____They should be concerned some
   9_____They should be concerned a great deal

2. Here are some statements that people answer in different ways. Read
each one carefully and decide whether you tend to agree or disagree with
it. If you tend to agree with the statement, check AGREE. If you tend
to disagree, check DISAGREE. Be sure to check something for each one.

	If you Agree (1)	If you Disagree (2)	(3)	(4
When children are trying to make their own way in the world they should not have to help support their parents	___AGREE	___DISAGREE	___UNDECIDED	
When children have a job and are settled they should help out if their parents need it	___AGREE	___DISAGREE	___UNDECIDED	
Even when children have families of their own they should help out if their parents need it	___AGREE	___DISAGREE	___UNDECIDED	
Children who move up in the world tend to neglect their parents	___AGREE	___DISAGREE	___UNDECIDED	
When parents get older their children should help support them	___AGREE	___DISAGREE	___UNDECIDED	
After children have left home they should keep in close contact with their parents	___AGREE	___DISAGREE	___UNDECIDED	
Even when children have families of their own they should keep in close contact with their parents	___AGREE	___DISAGREE	___UNDECIDED	
No one is going to care much what happens to you, when you get right down to it	___AGREE	___DISAGREE	___UNDECIDED	

3. Would you say that you and your children form a close family group?
(CHECK ONLY ONE)

   1_____I do not have any children

   2_____We are very close
   3_____We are somewhat close
   4_____We are not a close family group

4. Would you say that you and your brothers and sisters form a close family
group? (CHECK ONLY ONE)

   6_____I do not have any brothers and sisters

   7_____We are very close
   8_____We are somewhat close
   9_____We are not a close family group

-8-

1. Here are some statements that people answer in different ways. Read each one carefully and decide whether you tend to agree or disagree with it. If you tend to agree with the statement, check AGREE. If you tend to disagree, check DISAGREE. Be sure to check something for each one.

	If you Agree (1)	If you Disagree (2)	(3)	(4)
Parents are the ones who suffer most when children move away	___AGREE	___DISAGREE	___UNDECIDED	
Children who move far away are not being fair to their parents	___AGREE	___DISAGREE	___UNDECIDED	
It is better to get a steady job than always try to get ahead	___AGREE	___DISAGREE	___UNDECIDED	
When children move away they get different ideas and lose respect for their parents	___AGREE	___DISAGREE	___UNDECIDED	
When children move too far away family ties become broken	___AGREE	___DISAGREE	___UNDECIDED	
When children move far away they tend to neglect financial responsibilities to their parents	___AGREE	___DISAGREE	___UNDECIDED	
When your children go out on their own you have to turn to your brothers and sisters if you are going to have any family ties	___AGREE	___DISAGREE	___UNDECIDED	

2. ON THIS QUESTION, CHECK ONLY ONE ANSWER. The way life is today my children have less respect for me than they should.

    1 ____ I do not have any children

    2 ____ I agree: they do have less respect than they should
    3 ____ I disagree: they respect me as much as they should

3. If parents need financial assistance, how much should children be expected to help? (CHECK ONLY ONE)

    1 ____ They should be expected to help a great deal
    2 ____ They should be expected to help some
    3 ____ They should be expected to help a little
    4 ____ They should not be expected to help

4. What do you think is the most important thing for children to consider when choosing their life work? (CHECK ONLY ONE)

    0 ____ Getting a job that keeps them near their family
    X ____ Getting ahead in life no matter where it takes them

CONFIDENTIAL

-9-

1. (ON THIS QUESTION, CHECK AS MANY ANSWERS AS YOU THINK SHOULD BE INCLUDED)
When children grow up they should:

1_____Help their parents
2_____Visit their parents frequently
3_____Write their parents often
4_____Ask their parents to visit them often
5_____Live close to their parents
6_____Take care of their parents when they are ill
7_____None of the above are important

2. How willing are your children to make sacrifices for you? (CHECK ONLY ONE)

6_____I do not have any children

7_____My children are very willing to make sacrifices for me
8_____My children are somewhat willing to make sacrifices for me
9_____My children are not willing to make sacrifices for me

3. Here are a list of ways in which children may help their parents (JUST GO DOWN THE LIST AND CHECK THE THINGS THAT YOUR CHILDREN DO FOR YOU)

1_____I do not have any children

2_____Help when someone is ill
3_____Give advice on business or money matters
4_____Give valuable gifts
5_____Give financial help
6_____Provide a home
7_____None of the above

4. Here are a list of ways in which parents may help their children. How many do you do for your children? (JUST GO DOWN THE LIST AND CHECK THE THINGS THAT YOU DO FOR YOUR CHILDREN)

1_____I do not have any children

2_____Help when someone is ill
3_____Give advice on business or money matters
4_____Give valuable gifts
5_____Give financial help
6_____Provide a home for your grown-up children
7_____Baby-sitting and child care
8_____None of the above

5. ON THIS QUESTION, CHECK ONLY ONE ANSWER. Some people think that the major responsibility children have to their parents is financial; others feel that ties of affection are more important. How do you feel?

1_____I feel that financial help from children is more important than ties of affection
2_____I feel that ties of affection are more important than financial help
3_____I feel that they are equally important.

6. If you had a son or daughter graduating from high school would you prefer that he or she go on to college, or would you prefer that he or she take a good job? (CHECK ONLY ONE)

0_____I would prefer my children to go on to college
X_____I would prefer my children to take a good job

APPENDIX II   [271]

CONFIDENTIAL

-10-

1. Here are some statements that people answer in different ways. Read
    each one carefully and decide whether you tend to agree or disagree with
    it. If you tend to agree with the statement, check AGREE. If you tend
    to disagree, check DISAGREE. Be sure to check something for each one.

	If you Agree (9)	If you Disagree (0)	(X)	(Y)
Children should not allow getting ahead in the world to interfere with their responsibilities to their parents	___AGREE	___DISAGREE	___UNDECIDED	
When parents get older and need help they should be asked to move in with their married children	___AGREE	___DISAGREE	___UNDECIDED	
When children have become adults it is still nice to have them live at home with their parents	___AGREE	___DISAGREE	___UNDECIDED	
Even when children are married it is nice to have them living with their parents	___AGREE	___DISAGREE	___UNDECIDED	
Getting ahead in the world can be a bad thing if it keeps your family from being close	___AGREE	___DISAGREE	___UNDECIDED	
Children should not allow better financial opportunities else-where to take them away from their parents	___AGREE	___DISAGREE	___UNDECIDED	

2. How many of your children have offered you financial help? (CHECK ONLY
    ONE)

    1_____ I do not have any children

    2_____ All of them have offered financial help
    3_____ Some of them have offered financial help
    4_____ None of them have ever offered help
    5_____ I have never needed financial help

3. Would you say that your children have been more successful in earning a
    living and getting ahead in life than you have been? (CHECK ONLY ONE)

    1_____ I do not have any children

    2_____ All of my children have been more successful
    3_____ Most of my children have been more successful
    4_____ Some of my children have been more successful
    5_____ None of my children have been more successful

4. How often have you asked your children to give you financial help?
    (CHECK ONLY ONE)

    7_____ I do not have any children

    8_____ I have often asked for financial help
    9_____ I have sometimes asked for financial help
    0_____ I have never asked for financial help
    X_____ I have never needed financial help

-11-

1. Would you say that, for the most part, you have not worried about your grown-up children's affairs? (CHECK ONLY ONE)

   1_____I do not have any children

   2_____I have not worried
   3_____I have worried
   4_____Undecided

2. Would you say that, for the most part, your children have not mixed in your affairs? (CHECK ONLY ONE)

   6_____I do not have any children

   7_____My children have mixed in my affairs
   8_____My children have not mixed in my affairs
   9_____Undecided

3. Have your children kept in close contact with you since leaving home? (CHECK ONLY ONE)

   1_____I do not have any children
   2_____My children have not left home

   3_____All of my children have kept in close contact with me
   4_____Some of my children have kept in close contact with me
   5_____None of my children have kept in close contact with me

4. Have your children who have families of their own kept in close contact with you? (CHECK ONLY ONE)

   7_____I do not have any children
   8_____None of my children have families of their own

   9_____All have kept in close contact with me
   0_____Some have kept in close contact with me
   X_____None have kept in close contact with me

5. Have you kept in touch with your brothers and/or sisters since leaving home? (CHECK ONLY ONE)

   1_____I don't have any brothers and sisters

   2_____I have kept in touch with all of my brothers and/or sisters
   3_____I have kept in touch with some of my brothers and/or sisters
   4_____I have kept in touch with none of my brothers and/or sisters

6. The way life is today children have less respect for their parents than they should. (CHECK ONLY ONE)

   5_____I agree: they do have less respect than they should
   6_____I disagree: they do not have less respect than they should
   7_____Undecided

-12-

NOW WE WOULD LIKE TO ASK YOU SOME QUESTIONS ABOUT YOUR LIFE AT PRESENT

1. How many other people live with you in the same house or apartment?

    1_____ I live alone
    2_____ I live with my wife (or husband)
    3_____ Someone else lives with me also: Who? (WRITE IN HOW MANY OF
           EACH)
           HOW MANY of your daughters live with you?
           HOW MANY of your sons live with you?
           HOW MANY of your daughters-in-law live with you?   _____
           HOW MANY of your sons-in-law live with you?   _____
           HOW MANY of your grandchildren live with you?   _____
           HOW MANY of your other relatives live with you
             - such as parents, brothers, sisters, uncles,
               cousins, mother-in-law, and the like   _____
           HOW MANY other people live with you — such as
               roomers or friends   _____

2. In your family, who is it that makes most of the important decisions?
    (CHECK ONLY ONE)

    1_____ I make most of the important decisions myself
    2_____ Someone else makes most of the important decisions
    3_____ No one person makes the decisions — we make the decisions
           together

3. Do you spend most of your free time with other people, or are you
    usually alone? (CHECK ONLY ONE)

    5_____ I spend most of my free time with my wife (or husband) only
    6_____ I spend most of my free time with other people also
    7_____ I spend most of my free time alone

4. Would you say that you take part in many, a few, or practically no
    activities such as card clubs, lodge, church groups, unions, community
    activities and the like? (CHECK ONLY ONE)

    9_____ I take part in many activities
    0_____ I take part in a few activities
    X_____ I take part in practically no activities

5. Do you have a hobby? (CHECK ONLY ONE)

    0_____ No
    X_____ Yes: What is it?_____

6. Have most of your friends stopped working, or are most of your friends
    still working? (CHECK ONLY ONE)

    1_____ I do not have any friends

    2_____ Most of my friends have stopped working
    3_____ Some of my friends have stopped, some of them are still working
    4_____ Most of my friends are still working

7. About how many really close friends do you have here in town with whom
    you talk over personal matters? (CHECK ONLY ONE)

    6_____ Many close friends
    7_____ Some close friends
    8_____ Few close friends
    9_____ No close friends

-13-

1. Would you say you go around with a certain bunch of close friends who
    visit back and forth in each others homes? (CHECK ONLY ONE)

        0_____ Yes
        X_____ No

2. Do you prefer to have new things happening all the time, or do you prefer
    to have life go along at a steady pace? (CHECK ONLY ONE)

        0_____ I prefer to have a lot of new things happening all the time
        X_____ I prefer to have life go along at a steady pace

3. How much do you plan ahead the things that you will be doing next week
    or the week after? (CHECK ONLY ONE)

        1_____ I make many plans
        2_____ I make few plans
        3_____ I make almost no plans

4. Before you stopped working did you make any plans for anything you ex-
    pected or hoped to do when you stopped working? (CHECK ONLY ONE)

        1_____ No, I did not make any plans for when I no longer would be
                working
        2_____ Yes, I made plans: What?_____

5. Has it been possible for you to carry out the plans that you made before
    you stopped working? (CHECK ONLY ONE)

        1_____ I did not make any plans for when I would no longer be working

        2_____ It has not been possible for me to carry out my plans, but I
                expect to do so
        3_____ It has not been possible, and I do not expect to do so
        4_____ Yes, it has been possible for me to carry out the plans that I
                made before stopping work

6. In general, how would you say you feel most of the time, in good spirits
    or in low spirits? (CHECK ONLY ONE)

        1_____ I am usually in good spirits
        2_____ I am in good spirits some of the time and in low spirits some
                of the time
        3_____ I am usually in low spirits

7. Thinking back over your life, how easy would you say it has been for you
    to get used to the changes that have happened in your life? (CHECK ONLY
    ONE)

        1_____ It has always been very easy for me to get used to changes
        2_____ It has always been fairly easy for me to get used to changes
        3_____ It has always been fairly difficult for me to get used to
                changes
        4_____ It has always been very difficult for me to get used to changes

8. If you were just starting out in your work, which would you prefer:
    (CHECK ONLY ONE)

        0_____ I would prefer a job which might have a future although it
                is not so secure
        X_____ I would prefer a job that is steady although it might not
                have a future

CONFIDENTIAL

-14-

1. Here are some statements that people answer in different ways. Read
    each one carefully and decide whether you tend to agree or disagree with
    it. If you tend to agree with the statement, check YES. If you tend to
    disagree, check NO. Be sure to check something for each one.

	If you Agree (1)	If you Disagree (2)	(3)	(4)
Older people should stop working and give younger people a chance	___YES	___NO	___UNDECIDED	
Almost everything these days is a racket	___YES	___NO	___UNDECIDED	
In my opinion, a person's job is what gives meaning to life	___YES	___NO	___UNDECIDED	
Things just keep getting worse and worse for me as I get older	___YES	___NO	___UNDECIDED	
If you don't watch yourself, people will take advantage of you	___YES	___NO	___UNDECIDED	
These days I find myself giving up hope of trying to improve myself	___YES	___NO	___UNDECIDED	
These days I get the feeling that my health is gradually getting worse	___YES	___NO	___UNDECIDED	
I had a pretty good idea of what my life would be like in retirement even before I stopped working	___YES	___NO	___UNDECIDED	
These days I get the feeling that I'm just not a part of things	___YES	___NO	___UNDECIDED	
When you get right down to it, a job is just a way of making a living	___YES	___NO	___UNDECIDED	
It gets harder and harder for me to keep up the pace as I get older	___YES	___NO	___UNDECIDED	
If they can afford it, when people get older they ought to stop work and take things easy	___YES	___NO	___UNDECIDED	

BE SURE YOU CHECKED SOMETHING FOR EVERY ITEM

2. All in all, how much happiness would you say you find in life today?
    (CHECK ONLY ONE)

    1_____Almost none
    2_____Some, but not very much
    3_____A good deal

2. How do you think of yourself as far as age goes — do you think of
    yourself as: (CHECK ONLY ONE)

    1_____Elderly
    2_____Middle-aged
    3_____Late middle-aged
    4_____Old

CONFIDENTIAL

-15-

1. On the whole, how satisfied would you say you are with your way of life today? (CHECK ONLY ONE)

   1____Very satisfied
   2____Fairly satisfied
   3____Not very satisfied
   4____Not satisfied at all

2. If you were just starting out in your work which would you prefer: (CHECK ONLY ONE)

   0____I would prefer a job which pays well although not so secure
   X____I would prefer a job that is steady although not paying well

3. Some people say that most people can be trusted. Others say you can't be too careful in your dealings with people. How do you feel about it? (CHECK ONLY ONE)

   0____Most people can be trusted
   X____You can't be too careful in your dealings with people

4. Would you say that most people are more inclined to help others, or more inclined to look out for themselves? (CHECK ONLY ONE)

   0____Most people are inclined to help others
   X____Most people are inclined to look out for themselves

5. If you had your choice, which of the following would you most like to be (CHECK ONLY ONE)

   1____Independent
   2____Successful
   3____Well-liked

6. ON THIS QUESTION, CHECK ONLY ONE ANSWER. About how much does your total income from all sources amount to a MONTH? (CHECK ONLY ONE)

   1____Less than $50 a month
   2____More than $50 but less than $100 a month
   3____More than $100 but less than $150 a month
   4____More than $150 but less than $200 a month
   5____More than $200 but less than $250 a month
   6____More than $250 but less than $300 a month
   7____More than $300 a month
   0____I don't know

7. ON THIS QUESTION, CHECK ONLY ONE ANSWER. Do your annuities, bonds, investments and savings amount to:

   1____Less than $2,500
   2____More than $2,500 but less than $10,000
   3____More than $10,000 but less than $30,000
   4____More than $30,000 but less than $50,000
   5____More than $50,000

   6____I do not have any annuities, bonds, investments and savings

8. Is your standard of living better today or was it better during most of your lifetime? (CHECK ONLY ONE)

   1____My standard of living is better today
   2____My standard of living was better during most of my lifetime
   3____My standard of living has not changed

CONFIDENTIAL

-16-

1. ON THIS QUESTION, CHECK AS MANY ANSWERS AS YOU NEED TO. Where does your income come from now?

    1_____ Other members of my family
    2_____ Social Security
    3_____ Pension from my former employer
    4_____ Old Age Assistance (Public or Private Welfare)
    5_____ Savings
    6_____ Bonds and investments
    7_____ Income from property
    8_____ Insurance annuities
    9_____ Other: What?_____

2. Do you consider your present income enough to meet your living expenses? (CHECK ONLY ONE)

    0_____ It is enough
    X_____ It is not enough

3. ON THIS QUESTION, CHECK AS MANY ANSWERS AS YOU THINK SHOULD BE INCLUDED. Who do you think should provide for the older person who has stopped working, if he needs help in taking care of his problems?

    1_____ The federal government
    2_____ Each state government
    3_____ The local government
    4_____ Community agencies
    5_____ The company he worked for
    6_____ His union
    7_____ His family

4. Where does your income go — that is, how much of your income is spent for the major expenditures of food, housing (including utilities), and medical care (medical, dental, drugs)? (CHECK ONLY ONE)

    1_____ Almost all of my income is used for food, housing, and medical care
    2_____ About three-fourths of my income is used for food, housing, and medical care
    3_____ About half of my income is used for food, housing, and medical care
    4_____ Less than half of my income is used for food, housing, and medical care

5. Which of the above items requires the largest part of your income? (CHECK ONLY ONE)

    6_____ Food
    7_____ Housing
    8_____ Health

6. How would you rate your health at the present time? (CHECK ONLY ONE)

    1_____ Excellent
    2_____ Good
    3_____ Fair
    4_____ Poor
    5_____ Very poor

-17-

1. Do you have any particular physical or health problems at present?
   (CHECK ONLY ONE)

   0____ No
   X____ Yes: What?_____

2. ON THIS QUESTION, CHECK AS MANY ANSWERS AS YOU NEED TO. For what reaso
   have you been seen by a doctor during the past year?

   1____ I have not been seen by a doctor

   2____ For regular examination by the company doctor
   3____ For regular examination by my own doctor
   4____ For illness, seen only in doctor's office
   5____ For illness, seen at home
   6____ For first aid or an accident
   7____ Admitted to hospital

3. On this question, just go down the list and check how often you do each
   of the following things: (PUT A CHECK IN FRONT OF EITHER "OFTEN" OR
   "SOMETIMES" OR "HARDLY EVER OR NEVER" FOR EVERY ITEM IN THE LIST)

   HOW OFTEN DO YOU: (5)   (6)   (7)   (

Miss being with other people at work	___OFTEN	___SOMETIMES	___HARDLY EVER OR NEVER
Have times when you just don't know what to do to keep occupied	___OFTEN	___SOMETIMES	___HARDLY EVER OR NEVER
Miss the feeling of doing a good job	___OFTEN	___SOMETIMES	___HARDLY EVER OR NEVER
Feel lonely	___OFTEN	___SOMETIMES	___HARDLY EVER OR NEVER
Feel that you want to go back to work	___OFTEN	___SOMETIMES	___HARDLY EVER OR NEVER
Find yourself feeling "blue"	___OFTEN	___SOMETIMES	___HARDLY EVER OR NEVER
Worry about not having a job	___OFTEN	___SOMETIMES	___HARDLY EVER OR NEVER
Get the feeling that your life today is not very useful	___OFTEN	___SOMETIMES	___HARDLY EVER OR NEVER
Worry about money matters	___OFTEN	___SOMETIMES	___HARDLY EVER OR NEVER
Get upset by the things that happen in your day to day living	___OFTEN	___SOMETIMES	___HARDLY EVER OR NEVER
Find yourself wishing you were younger	___OFTEN	___SOMETIMES	___HARDLY EVER OR NEVER

BE SURE YOU CHECKED SOMETHING FOR EVERY ITEM

CONFIDENTIAL

-18-

1. Who do you think should provide for the older person who has stopped
   working if he needs help in meeting his medical expenses? (ON THIS
   QUESTION, CHECK AS MANY ANSWERS AS YOU THINK SHOULD BE INCLUDED)

   1_____ The federal government
   2_____ Each state government
   3_____ The local government
   4_____ Community agencies
   5_____ The company he worked for
   6_____ His union
   7_____ His family

2. Do you think that most retired people are able to take care of their
   medical expenses themselves? (CHECK ONLY ONE)

   0_____ Most retired people are able to take care of their own
          medical expenses
   X_____ Most retired people need help in taking care of their
          medical expenses

3. Now that you have stopped working, what do you consider the most important problem you have to face? (CHECK ONLY THE MOST IMPORTANT ONE)

   1_____ Health problems
   2_____ How to keep busy
   3_____ Financial problems
   4_____ Just being at home
   5_____ Loneliness
   6_____ Other: What?_____

4. ON THIS QUESTION, CHECK AS MANY ANSWERS AS YOU NEED TO TELL ALL THE
   THINGS THAT GIVE YOU THE GREATEST COMFORT AND SATISFACTION IN LIFE.
   Which ones give you the most comfort and satisfaction in life today?

   1_____ Just being with my family at home
   2_____ Working around the house, garden or yard
   3_____ Having relatives other than my children visit me
   4_____ Doing things I like to do by myself
   5_____ My religion or church work
   6_____ Spending time with close friends
   7_____ Just sitting and thinking about things
   8_____ Reading
   9_____ My recreation outside the home
   0_____ Getting out to visit relatives other than my children

5. In what way have your feelings toward religion changed, if at all, during
   the last few years? (CHECK ONLY ONE)

   1_____ I personally value religion more than I used to
   2_____ I personally value religion less than I used to
   3_____ My feelings toward religion have not changed

6. Would you say you are a religious person, or doesn't religion mean very
   much to you? (CHECK ONLY ONE)

   1_____ I'd say I am a religious person
   2_____ Religion doesn't mean very much to me
   3_____ Undecided

CONFIDENTIAL

-19-

1. Some people believe that satisfaction in life is the result of religiou
    faith; others believe that satisfaction in life is the result of your
    own efforts. Which do you most nearly agree with? (CHECK ONLY ONE)

       0_____ Satisfaction in life is the result of religious faith
       X_____ Satisfaction in life is the result of your own efforts

2. ON THIS QUESTION, CHECK AS MANY ANSWERS AS APPLY TO YOU. What changes
    for the WORSE have taken place in your life since you filled out our
    previous questionnaire?

       Changes for the WORSE

       1_____ Change in my health
       2_____ Not working
       3_____ Change in residence
       4_____ Change in my family
       5_____ Change in income
       6_____ Death in my family
       7_____ Change in my outlook on life
       8_____ Other changes for the worse: What?_____

       9_____ No changes for the worse

3. Now, what changes for the BETTER have taken place in your life since yo
    filled out our previous questionnaire? (CHECK AS MANY ANSWERS AS APPLY
    TO YOU)

       Changes for the BETTER

       1_____ Change in my health
       2_____ Not working
       3_____ Change in residence
       4_____ Change in my family
       5_____ Change in income
       6_____ Change in my outlook on life
       7_____ Other changes for the better: What?_____

       8_____ No changes for the better

4. When were you born? Month_____ Day_____ Year_____

5. Sex:

       0_____ Male
       X_____ Female

6. In what city and state were you born?_____
       (If not born in the United States, which country?)

              HAVE YOU ANSWERED EVERY PAGE?
              HAVE YOU CHECKED SOMETHING FOR EACH QUESTION?

              NOW PLEASE TURN TO THE HEALTH QUESTIONNAIRE ON THE NEXT PAGE

M2-1957

FOLLOW-UP HEALTH QUESTIONNAIRE

These are questions about your health. We would like to have you answer them in terms of WHAT HAS HAPPEND TO YOUR HEALTH DURING THE PAST YEAR, or since you last filled out a questionnaire for this study.

DURING THE PAST YEAR:

1. Has your eyesight changed so as to handicap you?......... ___YES ___NO
    If YES, has the change been corrected to your satis-
    faction by glasses?..................................... ___YES ___NO

2. Has your hearing changed so as to handicap you?.......... ___YES ___NO
    If YES, has the change been corrected to your satis-
    faction by a hearing aid?.............................. ___YES ___NO

3. Have your teeth or dentures caused trouble?.............. ___YES ___NO
    If YES, has the trouble been corrected to your
    satisfaction?.. ___YES ___NO

4. Have you been troubled by frequent hoarseness?........... ___YES ___NO

5. Have you had a cough most of the time?................... ___YES ___NO

6. Have you often had spells of severe dizziness?.......... ___YES ___NO

7. Have you often been troubled by your heart beating fast?. ___YES ___NO

8. Have you often had some physical exercise, such as
    walking?... ___YES ___NO

9. Has shortness of breath cut down your usual walking or
    stair climbing?.. ___YES ___NO

10. Has your usual walking or stair climbing caused pain
    in your chest?... ___YES ___NO

11. Has your usual walking or stair climbing caused
    cramps in your legs?................................... ___YES ___NO

12. Have you often lost your appetite?...................... ___YES ___NO

13. Have you often had difficulty in falling asleep or
    staying asleep?.. ___YES ___NO

14. Have you often suffered from severe or "sick" headaches
    (migraine)?... ___YES ___NO

15. Have troubles with your digestion caused you to see
    your doctor?.. ___YES ___NO

16. Have you often been troubled by your hands trembling?.... ___YES ___NO

17. Have you often had small accidents or injuries?......... ___YES ___NO

18. Have you had to stay in bed more than 3 days due to
    illness, injury or operation?.......................... ___YES ___NO
    If YES, name the condition which kept you in bed:
    _____

19. Have you had any serious illness?...................... ___YES ___NO
    If YES, name the illness:
    _____

DURING THE PAST YEAR:

20. Have you been told that you are looking well?............ ___YES   ___N

21. Have you had new trouble with your bowels, or seen
    blood on your stool or on the toilet paper?.............. ___YES   ___N

22. Has pressure or pain in the head often made your life
    miserable?... ___YES   ___N

23. Have you often sighed without being able to control it?.. ___YES   ___N

24. Have you enjoyed meeting people and making new friends?.. ___YES   ___N

25. Have you often had a nightmare?......................... ___YES   ___N

26. Have you often started the day feeling full of energy?... ___YES   ___NC

27. Have strange people or places made you afraid?.......... ___YES   ___N

28. Has it usually been easy for you to make up your mind?... ___YES   ___NC

29. Have you usually awakened tired and exhausted?........... ___YES   ___NC

30. Have you wanted or taken any treatment because of
    trouble in passing urine?.............................. ___YES   ___NC

31. Have you frequently felt unhappy and depressed?.......... ___YES   ___NC

32. Have you enjoyed doing things you have never done before? ___YES   ___NC

33. Have you had a nervous breakdown?....................... ___YES   ___NO

34. Have you thought seriously of suicide?................... ___YES   ___NO

35. Have you enjoyed being by yourself?...................... ___YES   ___NO

36. Have you enjoyed being with other people?............... ___YES   ___NO

37. Do you think your health is better now than it was when
    you were 50 years old?................................. ___YES   ___NO

38. Have you been refused employment because of your health?. ___YES   ___NO

39. Have you been refused employment because of your age?.... ___YES   ___NO

40. Have you been handicapped by arthritis of any part of
    your body?... ___YES   ___NO

41. Have you been troubled with any weakness or paralysis?... ___YES   ___NO

42. Has your weight changed?................................. ___YES   ___NO
    If YES, fill in one of these spaces:
                     Pounds gained:____ Pounds lost: ____

43. Have you gone on a special diet prescribed by your
    doctor?.. ___YES   ___NO

44. Has your doctor prescribed any medicine for you to take?. ___YES   ___NO

45. Have hormones been prescribed for you by your doctor?.... ___YES   ___NO

THANK YOU FOR YOUR COOPERATION

S-1 (R) 1958   No._____X

WAVE V RETIRED QUESTIONNAIRE

WHAT THIS IS ALL ABOUT

This is the fifth and last part of the Cornell University survey of
America's older citizens in which you are participating.

This is not a "test." You probably remember that there are no right or
wrong answers. Just answer the questions in the way you, yourself, feel
about them. GIVE YOUR OWN HONEST OPINIONS.

The information you give us will be kept strictly confidential.

Read every question carefully. Then check the answer which best gives
your opinion. If you find that a question does not fit your situation,
or does not give you a chance to express your opinion, first check the
answer which most nearly expresses your opinion, and then please feel
free to write what you think.

Sometimes the pages stick together, so be sure you have answered the
questions on every page. And please be sure to answer every question.
If you are not sure, guess. It is important that you answer them all.

Some of the questions will have special instructions which you should
follow.

THANK YOU FOR YOUR COOPERATION.

-1-

1. Our records show that you are not working now. Which things about not
    working do you like and which things do you dislike? (JUST GO DOWN
    THE LIST AND CHECK WHETHER YOU LIKE OR DISLIKE EACH OF THE FOLLOWING
    ITEMS)

    (JUST PUT A CHECK MARK IN FRONT OF YOUR ANSWERS, LIKE THIS: ✓)
                                         (5)   (6)   (7)   (
    Do you like or dislike:

    Having a lot of free time   ___LIKE ___DISLIKE ___DOESN'T APPLY

    Not having a routine to follow   ___LIKE ___DISLIKE ___DOESN'T APPLY

    Being at home a lot of the time   ___LIKE ___DISLIKE ___DOESN'T APPLY

    Something else about not working I like: What? _____

    _____

    Something else about not working I dislike: What? _____

    _____

2. Some people say that retirement is good for a person, some say it is bad.
    In general, what do you think? (CHECK ONLY ONE)

        0_____Retirement is mostly good for a person
        X_____Retirement is mostly bad for a person

3. How do the people you know who are still working feel about retirement?
    (CHECK ONLY ONE)

        1_____I do not know anyone who is still working

        2_____They mostly think they would like retirement
        3_____They mostly think they would dislike retirement
        4_____I don't know

4. How do the retired people you know feel about retirement? (CHECK ONLY
    ONE)

        6_____I do not know anyone who has retired

        7_____They mostly like retirement
        8_____They mostly dislike retirement
        9_____I don't know

5. Do you think the government is doing enough, not enough, or too much
    for people who have stopped working? (CHECK ONLY ONE)

        1_____The government is doing enough
        2_____Not enough
        3_____Too much
        4_____Undecided

6. Do you think the company you worked for when we first got in touch with
    you is doing enough, not enough, or too much for its employees who have
    stopped working? (CHECK ONLY ONE)

        6_____It is doing enough
        7_____Not enough
        8_____Too much
        9_____I don't know

1. Do you consider yourself retired?   (CHECK ONLY ONE)

    0_____No
    X_____Yes

2. Which one of these things had the most to do with your stopping work?
    (CHECK ONLY THE MOST IMPORTANT ONE)

    1_____My health
    2_____Difficulty in doing my regular work
    3_____Not being able to do my work as well as younger people
    4_____Wanting more leisure time

    5_____None of these, just company policy
    6_____Some other reason: What? _____

3. Who decided that you should stop work when you did?   (CHECK ONLY ONE)

    0_____The company decided
    X_____I decided myself

4. ON THIS QUESTION, CHECK AS MANY ANSWERS AS APPLY TO YOU. Did you
    receive any professional advice or counseling about retirement before
    you stopped working?

    1_____No, I did not receive professional advice or counseling

    2_____Yes, from the company where I worked
    3_____Yes, from my union
    4_____Yes, from someone else. Who? _____

5. If you received advice or counseling about retirement, what was it you
    received advice about?   (CHECK AS MANY ANSWERS AS APPLY TO YOU)

    6_____I did not receive advice or counseling

    7_____I received advice about my pension
    8_____I received advice about social security
    9_____I received advice about health problems
    0_____I received advice about how to keep busy in retirement
    X_____I received advice about something else: What? _____

6. Did the advice or counseling you received help you when you retired?
    (CHECK ONLY ONE)

    1_____I did not receive advice or counseling

    2_____It helped me a great deal
    3_____It helped somewhat
    4_____It did not help

7. What kind of information about retirement do you think it would be most
    helpful to have before a person retires?   (CHECK AS MANY ANSWERS AS
    APPLY TO YOU)

    1_____Information about retirement income
    2_____Information about health problems
    3_____Information about how to keep busy in retirement
    4_____Something else: What? _____

-3-

1. Now that you have stopped working, what do you consider the most important problem you have to face? (CHECK ONLY THE MOST IMPORTANT ONE)

    1_____ Health problems
    2_____ How to keep busy
    3_____ Financial problems
    4_____ Just being at home
    5_____ Loneliness
    6_____ Other: What? _____

    7_____ I have no important problems

2. It takes some people a little while to get used to not working. About how long would you say it took you to become used to not working? (CHECK ONLY ONE)

    1_____ I am still not used to it

    2_____ It took me a week or two (or less)
    3_____ It took me about a month
    4_____ It took me two or three months
    5_____ It took me more than three months

3. Are you looking for work? (CHECK ONLY ONE)

    1_____ No
    2_____ Yes, I am looking for part-time work
    3_____ Yes, I am looking for full-time work

4. How many times have you changed your residence since you retired? (CHECK ONLY ONE)

    1_____ I have not moved since I retired

    2_____ Once
    3_____ Twice
    4_____ More than twice

5. ON THIS QUESTION, CHECK AS MANY ANSWERS AS APPLY TO YOU. Where have you moved since you retired?

    1_____ I have not moved since I retired

    2_____ To a different house (or apartment) in the same city
    3_____ To the country
    4_____ To a different place in the same State
    5_____ To a different State: Where? _____

6. If you have moved since you retired, why did you move? (CHECK AS MANY ANSWERS AS APPLY TO YOU)

    1_____ I have not moved since I retired

    2_____ I moved for financial reasons
    3_____ I moved because of my health
    4_____ I moved to be closer to my children
    5_____ I moved to a nicer climate
    6_____ I moved for some other reason: What? _____

As people grow older they sometimes see less of their relatives, although this is not always the case. We are interested in knowing how often you are in touch with your relatives.

1. On this question, just go down the list and check how often you see SOME of the following relatives: (PUT A CHECK IN FRONT OF EITHER "OFTEN" OR "SOMETIMES" OR "HARDLY EVER OR NEVER" FOR EACH ITEM IN THE LIST)

HOW OFTEN DO YOU SEE:

	(1)	(2)	(3)	(4)
Some of your children	___OFTEN	___SOMETIMES	___HARDLY EVER OR NEVER	
Some of your brothers	___OFTEN	___SOMETIMES	___HARDLY EVER OR NEVER	
Some of your sisters	___OFTEN	___SOMETIMES	___HARDLY EVER OR NEVER	
Some of your grand-children	___OFTEN	___SOMETIMES	___HARDLY EVER OR NEVER	
Some of your nieces	___OFTEN	___SOMETIMES	___HARDLY EVER OR NEVER	
Some of your nephews	___OFTEN	___SOMETIMES	___HARDLY EVER OR NEVER	
Some of your cousins	___OFTEN	___SOMETIMES	___HARDLY EVER OR NEVER	

2. ON THIS QUESTION, CHECK ONLY ONE ANSWER. How many of your children live close enough so that you can see them whenever you want to?

    1_____ I do not have any living children

    2_____ All of my children live close enough for me to see them whenever I want to
    3_____ Some of my children live close enough for me to see them whenever I want to
    4_____ None of my children live close enough for me to see them whenever I want to

3. Do you have any children whom you do not see often? (CHECK ONLY ONE)

    6_____ I do not have any living children

    7_____ I see all of my children often
    8_____ A few of my children I do not see often
    9_____ Most of my children I do not see often
    0_____ I do not see any of my children often
    X_____ Some I see often, some I do not

4. Have you kept in touch with your brothers and/or sisters since leaving home? (CHECK ONLY ONE)

    1_____ I don't have any brothers and sisters

    2_____ I have kept in touch with all of my brothers and/or sisters
    3_____ I have kept in touch with some of my brothers and/or sisters
    4_____ I have kept in touch with none of my brothers and/or sisters

-5-

1. Check the one statement below that best describes your present marriage (CHECK ONLY ONE)

    1_____I have never been married

    2_____I am married and living with my wife (or husband)
    3_____I am married, but separated from my wife (or husband)
    4_____I am widowed
    5_____I am divorced

2. How often does your immediate family get together for a meal? (CHECK ONLY ONE)

    1_____My immediate family never has such get-togethers

    2_____We often get together
    3_____We sometimes get together
    4_____We seldom get together

3. How much do you enjoy these immediate family get-togethers? (CHECK ONL ONE)

    6_____My immediate family does not have such get-togethers

    7_____I enjoy them a great deal
    8_____I enjoy them somewhat
    9_____I enjoy them very little
    0_____I do not enjoy them at all

4. How much would you like to be in touch with your children more than you are these days? (CHECK ONLY ONE)

    7_____I do not have any living children

    8_____I would like to be in touch with them a good deal more
    9_____I would like to be in touch with them somewhat more
    0_____I would not like to be in touch with them any more than I am

5. ON THIS QUESTION, CHECK AS MANY ANSWERS AS APPLY TO YOU. Do your family and relatives, either yours or your wife's, ever have any large family gatherings, when a lot of you get together at one time?

    1_____We have no such large family gatherings

    2_____We have such gatherings on national holidays such as Thanksgiving and Labor Day
    3_____We have such gatherings on religious holidays such as Christmas and Easter
    4_____We also have such gatherings on other occasions. When? _____
_____

6. How much do you enjoy these large family get-togethers? (CHECK ONLY ONE)

    6_____We do not have such get-togethers

    7_____I enjoy them a great deal
    8_____I enjoy them somewhat
    9_____I enjoy them very little
    0_____I do not enjoy them at all

1. Would you say that you and your children form a close family group?
    (CHECK ONLY ONE)

    1_____ I do not have any children

    2_____ We are very close
    3_____ We are somewhat close
    4_____ We are not a close family group

2. Would you say that you and your brothers and sisters form a close
    family group? (CHECK ONLY ONE)

    6_____ I do not have any brothers and sisters

    7_____ We are very close
    8_____ We are someowhat close
    9_____ We are not a close family group

3. The way life is today my children have less respect for me than they
    should. (CHECK ONLY ONE)

    1_____ I do not have any children

    2_____ I agree: they do have less respect than they should
    3_____ I disagree: they respect me as much as they should

4. Would you say that your children have been more successful in earning
    a living and getting ahead in life than you have been? (CHECK ONLY ONE)

    1_____ I do not have any children

    2_____ All of my children have been more successful
    3_____ Most of my children have been more successful
    4_____ Some of my children have been more successful
    5_____ None of my children have been more successful

5. Have some of your children been more successful than others in earning
    a living and getting ahead in life? (CHECK ONLY ONE)

    1_____ I do not have any children
    2_____ I have only one child

    3_____ One of my children has been more successful than the others
    4_____ Some of my children have been more successful
    5_____ All of my children have been equally successful

6. How willing are your children to make sacrifices for you? (CHECK ONLY
    ONE)

    6_____ I do not have any children

    7_____ My children are very willing to make sacrifices for me
    8_____ My children are somewhat willing to make sacrifices for me
    9_____ My children are not willing to make sacrifices for me

7. Are any of your children more willing than the others to make sacrifices
    for you? (CHECK ONLY ONE)

    1_____ I do not have any children
    2_____ I have only one child

    3_____ Yes, one child is more willing than the others to make
            sacrifices for me
    4_____ Yes, some of my children are more willing than the others
    5_____ They are all equally willing to make sacrifices

1. If you were just starting out in your work, which would you prefer:
    (CHECK ONLY ONE)

    0_____I would prefer a job which might have a future although it
          is not so secure
    X_____I would prefer a job which is steady although it might not
          have a future

2. How many of your children have offered you financial help?   (CHECK ONLY
    ONE)

    1_____I do not have any children

    2_____All of them have offered financial help
    3_____Some of them have offered financial help
    4_____None of them have ever offered help
    5_____I have never needed financial help

3. How often have you asked your children to give you financial help?
    (CHECK ONLY ONE)

    7_____I do not have any children

    8_____I have often asked for financial help
    9_____I have sometimes asked for financial help
    0_____I have never asked for financial help
    X_____I have never needed financial help

4. Here are a list of ways in which children may help their parents.   (JUST
    GO DOWN THE LIST AND CHECK THE THINGS THAT YOUR CHILDREN DO FOR YOU)

    1_____I do not have any children

    2_____Take care of parents when they are ill
    3_____Give advice on business or money matters
    4_____Visit parents frequently
    5_____Write parents often
    6_____Ask parents to visit them often
    7_____Live close to their parents
    8_____Give financial help
    9_____Provide a home for their parents
    0_____None of the above

5. Here are a list of ways in which parents may help their children. How
    many do you do for your children? (JUST GO DOWN THE LIST AND CHECK THE
    THINGS THAT YOU DO FOR YOUR CHILDREN)

    1_____I do not have any children

    2_____Take care of children or their family when someone is ill
    3_____Give advice on business or money matters
    4_____Visit children frequently
    5_____Write children often
    6_____Ask children to visit often
    7_____Live close to children
    8_____Give financial help
    9_____Provide a home for grown-up children
    0_____Baby-sitting and child care
    X_____None of the above

1. How much have you helped your grown-up children in their personal affairs? (CHECK ONLY ONE)

     1_____I do not have any children

     2_____I have helped my children a great deal
     3_____I have helped my children somewhat
     4_____I have helped my children a little
     5_____I have not helped my children at all

2. How much have your children helped you in your personal affairs? (CHECK ONLY ONE)

     1_____I do not have any children

     2_____My children have helped me a great deal
     3_____My children have helped me somewhat
     4_____My children have helped me a little
     5_____My children have not helped me at all

3. Have your children kept in close contact with you since leaving home? (CHECK ONLY ONE)

     1_____I do not have any children
     2_____My children have not left home

     3_____All of my children have kept in close contact with me
     4_____Some of my children have kept in close contact with me
     5_____None of my children have kept in close contact with me

4. Have your children who have families of their own kept in close contact with you? (CHECK ONLY ONE)

     7_____I do not have any children
     8_____None of my children have families of their own

     9_____All have kept in close contact with me
     0_____Some have kept in close contact with me
     X_____None have kept in close contact with me

5. The way life is today children have less respect for their parents than they should. (CHECK ONLY ONE)

     5_____I agree: they do have less respect than they should
     6_____I disagree: they do not have less respect than they should
     7_____Undecided

6. ON THIS QUESTION CHECK ONLY ONE ANSWER. Some people think that the major responsibility children have to their parents is financial; others feel that ties of affection are more important. How do you feel?

     1_____I feel that financial help from children is more important than ties of affection
     2_____I feel that ties of affection are more important than financial help
     3_____I feel that they are equally important

1. Here are some statements that people answer in different ways. Read each one carefully and decide whether you tend to agree or disagree with it. If you tend to agree with the statement, check AGREE. If you tend to disagree, check DISAGREE. Be sure to check something for each one.

	If you Agree (1)	If you Disagree (2)	(3)
When children have a job and are settled they should help out if their parents need it	___AGREE	___DISAGREE	___UNDECI▮
Even when children have families of their own they should help out if their parents need it	___AGREE	___DISAGREE	___UNDECIL
Children who move up in the world tend to neglect their parents	___AGREE	___DISAGREE	___UNDECID▮
When parents get older their children should help support them	___AGREE	___DISAGREE	___UNDECID▮
No one is going to care much what happens to you, when you get right down to it	___AGREE	___DISAGREE	___UNDECID▮
Children who move far away are not being fair to their parents	___AGREE	___DISAGREE	___UNDECID▮
When children move away they get different ideas and lose respect for their parents	___AGREE	___DISAGREE	___UNDECID▮
When children move too far away family ties become broken	___AGREE	___DISAGREE	___UNDECID▮
When children move far away they tend to neglect financial responsibilities to their parents	___AGREE	___DISAGREE	___UNDECIDE▮
When your children go out on their own you have to turn to your brothers and sisters if you are going to have any family ties	___AGREE	___DISAGREE	___UNDECIDE▮
Children should not allow getting ahead in the world to interfere with their responsibilities to their parents	___AGREE	___DISAGREE	___UNDECIDE▮
Getting ahead in the world can be a bad thing if it keeps your family from being close	___AGREE	___DISAGREE	___UNDECIDE▮
Children should not allow better financial opportunities elsewhere to take them away from their parents	___AGREE	___DISAGREE	___UNDECIDE▮

BE SURE YOU CHECKED SOMETHING FOR EVERY ITEM

1. ON THIS QUESTION CHECK AS MANY ANSWERS AS YOU THINK SHOULD BE INCLUDED.
    When children grow up, they should:

    1_____ Take care of parents when they are ill
    2_____ Give advice on business or money matters
    3_____ Visit parents frequently
    4_____ Write parents often
    5_____ Ask parents to visit them often
    6_____ Live close to their parents
    7_____ Give parents financial help
    8_____ Provide a home for their parents
    9_____ None of the above

    NOW WE WOULD LIKE TO ASK YOU SOME QUESTIONS ABOUT YOUR LIFE AT PRESENT

2. How many other people live with you in the same house or apartment?

    1_____ I live alone
    2_____ I live with my wife (or husband)
    3_____ Someone else lives with me also: How many others?_____
           (CHECK WHO LIVES WITH YOU--CHECK ALL THAT APPLY)

        4_____ Child (or children) without a family of their own
               live with me
        5_____ Child (or children) and their family live with me
        6_____ Grandchild (or grandchildren) live with me
        7_____ Other relatives--such as parents, brothers, sisters,
               uncles, cousins, mother-in-law, and the like
        8_____ Other people who are not relatives live with me

3. Most parents try to treat all their children alike. However, it is a
    very human experience to feel closer to some children than to others.
    Would you say that you feel closer to some of your children than to
    the others? (CHECK ONLY ONE)

    1_____ I do not have any children
    2_____ I have only one child

    3_____ I feel closer to one of my sons. Why?_____
    4_____ I feel closer to one of my daughters. Why?_____
    5_____ I feel closer to some of my children. Why?_____
    6_____ I feel about the same towards all of my children

4. Is there a tendency for some members of your family to keep their plans
    and problems to themselves, or are all personal matters discussed
    freely within the family? (CHECK ONLY ONE)

    1_____ All personal matters are discussed freely with family members
    2_____ Some personal matters are discussed with family members
    3_____ Hardly any personal matters are discussed with family members
    4_____ Personal matters are never discussed with other family members

5. How often do the members of your family criticize each other?
    (CHECK ONLY ONE)

    1_____ We often criticize each other
    2_____ We sometimes criticize each other
    3_____ We seldom criticize each other
    4_____ We never criticize each other

1. Do the members of your family agree on what is most important in life? (CHECK ONLY ONE)

    1_____We agree completely on what is most important in life
    2_____We agree very closely on what is most important
    3_____We agree fairly well on what is most important

    4_____No, we disagree somewhat on what is most important
    5_____No, we disagree very much on what is most important

2. In your family, who is it that makes most of the important decisions? (CHECK ONLY ONE)

    1_____I make most of the important decisions myself
    2_____Someone else makes most of the important decisions
    3_____No one person makes the decisions--we make the decisions
          together

3. Do you spend most of your free time with other people, or are you usually alone? (CHECK ONLY ONE)

    5_____I spend most of my free time with my wife (or husband) only
    6_____I spend most of my free time with other people also
    7_____I spend most of my free time alone

4. Would you say that you take part in many, a few, or practically no activities such as card clubs, lodge, church groups, unions, community activities and the like? (CHECK ONLY ONE)

    9_____I take part in many activities
    0_____I take part in a few activities
    X_____I take part in practically no activities

5. Have most of your friends stopped working, or are most of your friends still working? (CHECK ONLY ONE)

    1_____I do not have any friends

    2_____Most of my friends have stopped working
    3_____Some of my friends have stopped, some of them are still working
    4_____Most of my friends are still working

6. About how many really close friends do you have here in town with whom you talk over personal matters? (CHECK ONLY ONE)

    6_____Many close friends
    7_____Some close friends
    8_____Few close friends
    9_____No close friends

7. Would you say you go around with a certain bunch of close friends who visit back and forth in each others homes? (CHECK ONLY ONE)

    0_____Yes
    X_____No

8. Do you prefer to have new things happening all the time, or do you prefer to have life go along at a steady pace? (CHECK ONLY ONE)

    0_____I prefer to have a lot of new things happening all the time
    X_____I prefer to have life go along at a steady pace

-12-

1. Do you have a hobby? (CHECK ONLY ONE)

   0_____No
   X_____Yes: What is it? _____

2. How much do you plan ahead the things that you will be doing next week
   or the week after? (CHECK ONLY ONE)

   1_____I make <u>many</u> plans
   2_____I make <u>few</u> plans
   3_____I make <u>almost</u> <u>no</u> plans

3. In general, how would you say you feel most of the time, in good spirits
   or in low spirits? (CHECK ONLY ONE)

   1_____I am usually in good spirits
   2_____I am in good spirits some of the time and in low spirits
         some of the time
   3_____I am usually in low spirits

4. Thinking back over your life, how easy would you say it has been for
   you to get used to the changes that have happened in your life? (CHECK
   ONLY ONE)

   1_____It has always been <u>very easy</u> for me to get used to changes
   2_____It has always been <u>fairly easy</u> for me to get used to changes
   3_____It has always been <u>fairly difficult</u>
   4_____It has always been <u>very difficult</u>

5. All in all, how much happiness would you say you find in life today?
   (CHECK ONLY ONE)

   1_____Almost none
   2_____Some, but not very much
   3_____A good deal

6. How do you think of yourself as far as age goes--do you think of yourself as: (CHECK ONLY ONE)

   1_____Elderly
   2_____Middle-aged
   3_____Late middle-aged
   4_____Old

7. On the whole, how satisfied would you say you are with your way of
   life today? (CHECK ONLY ONE)

   1_____Very satisfied
   2_____Fairly satisfied
   3_____Not very satisfied
   4_____Not satisfied at all

8. Some people say that most people can be trusted. Others say you can't
   be too careful in your dealings with people. How do you feel about it?
   (CHECK ONLY ONE)

   0_____Most people can be trusted
   X_____You can't be too careful in your dealings with people

9. Would you say that most people are more inclined to help others, or more
   inclined to look out for themselves? (CHECK ONLY ONE)

   0_____Most people are inclined to help others
   X_____Most people are inclined to look out for themselves

1. If you had your choice, which of the following would you <u>most</u> like to
    be? (CHECK ONLY ONE)

    1_____Independent
    2_____Successful
    3_____Well-liked

2. Is your standard of living better today or was it better during most
    of your lifetime? (CHECK ONLY ONE)

    1_____My standard of living is better today
    2_____My standard of living was better during most of my lifetime
    3_____My standard of living has not changed

3. Here are some statements that people answer in different ways. Read ea
    one carefully and decide whether you tend to agree or disagree with it
    If you tend to agree with the statement, check <u>YES</u>. If you tend to
    disagree, check <u>NO</u>. <u>Be sure to check something for each one</u>.

	If you Agree (1)	If you Disagree (2)	(3)
Older people should stop working and give younger people a chance	___YES	___NO	___UNDECID
Almost everything these days is a racket	___YES	___NO	___UNDECID
In my opinion, a person's job is what gives meaning to life	___YES	___NO	___UNDECID
Things just keep getting worse and worse for me as I get older	___YES	___NO	___UNDECID
If you don't watch yourself, people will take advantage of you	___YES	___NO	___UNDECID
These days I find myself giving up hope of trying to improve myself	___YES	___NO	___UNDECID
These days I get the feeling that my health is gradually getting worse	___YES	___NO	___UNDECID
I had a pretty good idea of what my life would be like in retirement even before I stopped working	___YES	___NO	___UNDECIDE
These days I get the feeling that I'm just not a part of things	___YES	___NO	___UNDECIDE
When you get right down to it, a job is just a way of making a living	___YES	___NO	___UNDECIDE
It gets harder and harder for me to keep up the pace as I get older	___YES	___NO	___UNDECIDE
If they can afford it, when people get older they ought to stop work and take things easy	___YES	___NO	___UNDECIDE

<u>BE SURE YOU CHECKED SOMETHING FOR EVERY ITEM</u>

-14-

1. What is your present living arrangement?   (CHECK ONLY ONE)

    1_____ I own my home
    2_____ I rent a house
    3_____ I rent an apartment
    4_____ I rent a room
    5_____ Some other living arrangement: What? _____

2. Do you consider your present income enough to meet your living expenses?
   (CHECK ONLY ONE)

    0_____ It is enough
    X_____ It is not enough

3. ON THIS QUESTION, CHECK AS MANY ANSWERS AS YOU THINK SHOULD BE INCLUDED.
   Who do you think should provide for the older person who has stopped
   working, if he needs help in taking care of his problem?

    1_____ The federal government
    2_____ Each state government
    3_____ The local government
    4_____ Community agencies
    5_____ The company he worked for
    6_____ His union
    7_____ His family

4. Where does your income go - that is, how much of your income is spent
   for the major expenditures of food, housing (including utilities), and
   medical care (medical, dental, drugs)? (CHECK ONLY ONE)

    1_____ Almost all of my income is used for food, housing and medical
           care
    2_____ About three-fourths of my income is used for food, housing
           and medical care
    3_____ About half of my income is used for food, housing and medical
           care
    4_____ Less than half of my income is used for food, housing and
           medical care

5. Which of the above items requires the largest part of your income?
   (CHECK ONLY ONE)

    6_____ Food
    7_____ Housing
    8_____ Health

6. How would you rate your health at the present time? (CHECK ONLY ONE)

    1_____ Excellent
    2_____ Good
    3_____ Fair
    4_____ Poor
    5_____ Very poor

7. Do you think that most retired people are able to take care of their
   medical expenses themselves? (CHECK ONLY ONE)

    0_____ Most retired people are able to take care of their own
           medical expenses
    X_____ Most retired people need help in taking care of their
           medical expenses

-15-

1. Do you have any particular physical or health problems at present? (CHECK ONLY ONE)

   0_____No
   X_____Yes: What? _____

2. ON THIS QUESTION, CHECK AS MANY ANSWERS AS YOU NEED TO. For what reaso have you been seen by a doctor during the past year?

   1_____I have not been seen by a doctor

   2_____For regular examination by the company doctor
   3_____For regular examination by my own doctor
   4_____For illness, seen only in doctor's office
   5_____For illness, seen at home
   6_____For first aid or an accident
   7_____Admitted to hospital

3. Who do you think should provide for the older person who has stopped working if he needs help in meeting his medical expenses? (ON THIS QUESTION, CHECK AS MANY ANSWERS AS YOU THINK SHOULD BE INCLUDED)

   1_____The federal government
   2_____Each state government
   3_____The local government
   4_____Community agencies
   5_____The company he worked for
   6_____His union
   7_____His family

4. If you were just starting out in your work which would you prefer: (CHECK ONLY ONE)

   0_____I would prefer a job which pays well although not so secure
   X_____I would prefer a job that is steady although not paying well

5. How often do you attend religious services? (CHECK ONLY ONE)

   1_____I attend often and regularly
   2_____I attend quite often but not regularly
   3_____Sometimes
   4_____Hardly ever
   5_____I never attend regular services

6. In what way have your feelings toward religion changed, if at all, during the last few years? (CHECK ONLY ONE)

   1_____I personally value religion more than I used to
   2_____I personally value religion less than I used to
   3_____My feelings toward religion have not changed

7. Would you say you are a religious person, or doesn't religion mean very much to you? (CHECK ONLY ONE)

   1_____I'd say I am a religious person
   2_____Religion doesn't mean very much to me
   3_____Undecided

1. Some people believe that satisfaction in life is the result of religious faith; others believe that satisfaction in life is the result of your own efforts.   Which do you most nearly agree with?   (CHECK ONLY ONE)

    0 _____ Satisfaction in life is the result of religious faith
    X _____ Satisfaction in life is the result of your own efforts

2. How many of your close friends are people who also worked at the place where you used to work?   (CHECK ONLY ONE)

    1 _____ All of my close friends are from my former place of work
    2 _____ Most of my close friends are from my former place of work
    3 _____ Some of my close friends are from my former place of work
    4 _____ None of my close friends are from my former place of work

3. On this question, just go down the list and check how often you do each of the following things: (PUT A CHECK IN FROMT OF EITHER "OFTEN" OR "SOMETIMES" OR "HARDLY EVER OR NEVER" FOR EVERY ITEM IN THE LIST)

HOW OFTEN DO YOU   (5)   (6)   (7)   (8)

Miss being with other people at work	___OFTEN	___SOMETIMES	___HARDLY EVER OR NEVER
Have times when you just don't know what to do to keep occupied	___OFTEN	___SOMETIMES	___HARDLY EVER OR NEVER
Miss the feeling of doing a good job	___OFTEN	___SOMETIMES	___HARDLY EVER OR NEVER
Feel lonely	___OFTEN	___SOMETIMES	___HARDLY EVER OR NEVER
Feel that you want to go back to work	___OFTEN	___SOMETIMES	___HARDLY EVER OR NEVER
Find yourself feeling "blue"	___OFTEN	___SOMETIMES	___HARDLY EVER OR NEVER
Worry about not having a job	___OFTEN	___SOMETIMES	___HARDLY EVER OR NEVER
Get the feeling that your life today is not very useful	___OFTEN	___SOMETIMES	___HARDLY EVER OR NEVER
Worry about money matters	___OFTEN	___SOMETIMES	___HARDLY EVER OR NEVER
Get upset by the things that happen in your day-to-day living	___OFTEN	___SOMETIMES	___HARDLY EVER OR NEVER
Wish you had a chance to live your life over	___OFTEN	___SOMETIMES	___HARDLY EVER OR NEVER
Find yourself wishing you were younger	___OFTEN	___SOMETIMES	___HARDLY EVER OR NEVER

BE SURE YOU CHECKED SOMETHING FOR EVERY ITEM

-17-

1. <u>Before you stopped working</u>, did you make any plans for anything you expected or hoped to do when you stopped working?   (CHECK ONLY ONE)

   1_____No, I did not make any plans for when I no longer would be working
   2_____Yes, I made plans: What? _____

2. Has it been possible for you to carry out the plans that you made befor₃ you stopped working? (CHECK ONLY ONE)

   1_____I did not make any plans for when I would no longer be working
   2_____It has not been possible for me to carry out my plans but I expect to do so
   3_____It has not been possible, and I do <u>not</u> expect to do so
   4_____Yes, it has been possible for me to carry out the plans that I made before stopping work

3. <u>Since you stopped working</u>, how much have you talked about your company' retirement program? (CHECK ONLY ONE)

   1_____I have talked about it a great deal
   2_____I have talked about it some but not very much
   3_____I have talked about it a little
   4_____I have not talked about it

4. All in all, how difficult have you found not working? (CHECK ONLY ONE)

   1_____I have found it <u>very difficult</u>
   2_____I have found it <u>fairly difficult</u>
   3_____I have <u>not</u> found <u>it difficult</u>

5. Do you think stopping work has made your health better or worse? (CHECK ONLY ONE)

   1_____Stopping work has made my health <u>better</u>
   2_____Stopping work has made my health <u>worse</u>
   3_____Stopping work has made <u>no difference</u> in my health

6. Do you think stopping work has made you less satisfied with your way of life today? (CHECK ONLY ONE)

   1_____Yes
   2_____No
   3_____Undecided

7. Do you think that stopping work has made you think of yourself as older or younger? (CHECK ONLY ONE)

   1_____Stopping work has made me think of myself as <u>older</u>
   2_____Stopping work has made me think of myself as <u>younger</u>
   3_____Stopping work has made <u>no difference</u>

8. Do you think that stopping work has given you the feeling that your life today is not very useful? (CHECK ONLY ONE)

   1_____Yes
   2_____No
   3_____Undecided

1. When you were still gainfully employed, how important was your job to you? (CHECK ONLY ONE)

    1 _____ The most important thing in my life
    2 _____ Very important, but no more importan than certain other things
    3 _____ Just so-so
    4 _____ Less important than many other things
    5 _____ Just a way to make a living

2. Before you stopped working, did you have an accurate idea of how much your retirement income would be? (CHECK ONLY ONE)

    1 _____ Yes, I knew what my income would be
    2 _____ No, I expected more than I am getting
    3 _____ No, I expected less than I am getting
    4 _____ No, I had no idea of what my retirement income would be

3. ON THIS QUESTION, CHECK ONLY ONE ANSWER. About how much does your total income from all sources amount to a MONTH?

    1 _____ Less than $50 a month
    2 _____ More than $50 but less than $100 a month
    3 _____ More than $100 but less than $150 a month
    4 _____ More than $150 but less than $200 a month
    5 _____ More than $200 but less than $250 a month
    6 _____ More than $250 but less than $300 a month
    7 _____ More than $300 a month
    0 _____ I don't know

4. ON THIS QUESTION, CHECK ONLY ONE ANSWER. Do your annuities, bonds, investments and savings amount to:

    1 _____ Less than $2,500
    2 _____ More than $2,500 but less than $10,000
    3 _____ More than $10,000 but less than $30,000
    4 _____ More than $30,000 but less than $50,000
    5 _____ More than $50,000

    6 _____ I do not have any annuities, bonds, investments or savings

5. Where does your income come from now? (ON THIS QUESTION, CHECK AS MANY ANSWERS AS YOU NEED TO)

    1 _____ Other members of my family
    2 _____ Social Security
    3 _____ Pension from my former employer
    4 _____ Old Age Assistance (Public or Private Welfare)
    5 _____ Savings
    6 _____ Bonds and investments
    7 _____ Income from property
    8 _____ Insurance annuities
    9 _____ Other: What? _____

1. ON THIS QUESTION, CHECK AS MANY ANSWERS AS YOU NEED TO TELL ALL THE THINGS THAT GIVE YOU THE GREATEST COMFORT AND SATISFACTION IN LIFE. Which ones give you the most comfort and satisfaction in life today?

   1_____ Just being with my family at home
   2_____ Working around the house, garden or yard
   3_____ Having relatives other than my children visit me
   4_____ Doing things I like to do by myself
   5_____ My religion or church work
   6_____ Spending time with close friends
   7_____ Just sitting and thinking about things
   8_____ Reading
   9_____ My recreation outside the home
   0_____ Getting out to visit relatives other than my children

2. ON THIS QUESTION, CHECK AS MANY ANSWERS AS APPLY TO YOU. What changes for the WORSE have taken place in your life since you filled out our previous questionnaire?

   Changes for the WORSE

   1_____ Change in my health
   2_____ Not working
   3_____ Change in residence
   4_____ Change in my family
   5_____ Change in income
   6_____ Death in my family: Who? _____
   7_____ Change in my outlook on life
   8_____ Other changes for the worse: What? _____

   9_____ No changes for the worse

3. Now, what changes for the BETTER have taken place in your life since you filled out our previous questionnaire? (CHECK AS MANY ANSWERS AS APPLY TO YOU)

   Changes for the BETTER

   1_____ Change in my health
   2_____ Not working
   3_____ Change in residence
   4_____ Change in my family
   5_____ Change in income
   6_____ Change in my outlook on life
   7_____ Other changes for the better: What? _____

   8_____ No changes for the better

4. When were you born? Month _____ Day _____ Year _____

5. Sex:

   0_____ Male
   X_____ Female

6. In what city and state were you born? _____
   (If not born in the United States, which country?)

                    HAVE YOU ANSWERED EVERY PAGE?
                    HAVE YOU CHECKED SOMETHING FOR EACH QUESTION?

                    BE SURE YOU HAVE ALSO COMPLETED THE ENCLOSED MEDICAL
                    QUESTIONNAIRE AND HAVE INCLUDED IT IN THE RETURN ENVELOPE!

Bibliography

Anderson, J. E. 1961. Comments on Max Kaplan's "Toward a Theory of Leisure for Social Gerontology." Pp. 428–432 in R. W. Kleemeier, ed., *Aging and Leisure*. New York: Oxford University Press.

Barron, M. L., G. F. Streib, and E. A. Suchman. 1952. "Research on the Social Disorganization of Retirement." *American Sociological Review* 17: 479–482.

Bates, F. L. 1956. "Position, Role, and Status: A Reformulation of Concepts." *Social Forces* 24: 313–321.

Berger, P. L. 1964. "Some General Observations on the Problem of Work." Pp. 211–241 in P. L. Berger, ed., *The Human Shape of Work*. New York: Macmillan.

Biddle, B. J., and E. J. Thomas. 1966. *Role Theory: Concepts and Research*. New York: John Wiley.

Blau, Z. S. 1956. "Changes in Status and Age Identification." *American Sociological Review* 21: 198–203.

Blumer, H. 1954. "What Is Wrong with Social Theory?" *American Sociological Review* 19: 3–11.

Bracey, H. E. 1966. *In Retirement*. Baton Rouge: Louisiana State University Press.

Burgess, E. W., ed. 1960. *Aging in Western Societies*. Chicago: University of Chicago Press.

Butler, R. N. 1968. "The Life Review: An Interpretation of Reminiscence in the Aged." Pp. 486–496 in B. Neugarten, ed., *Middle Age and Aging: A Reader in Social Psychology*. Chicago: University of Chicago Press.

Carp, F. M. 1968. "Some Components of Disengagement." *Journal of Gerontology* 23: 382–386.

Centers, Richard. 1949. *The Psychology of Social Classes.* Princeton, N.J.: Princeton University Press.

Cicourel, A. V. 1964. *Method and Measurement in Sociology.* New York: Free Press of Glencoe.

Clark, M., and B. Anderson. 1967. *Culture and Aging: An Anthropological Study of Older Americans.* Springfield, Ill.: Charles G. Thomas.

Cottrell, L. S., Jr. 1942. "The Adjustment of the Individual to His Age and Sex Roles." *American Sociological Review* 7: 617–620.

Cumming, E. 1963. "Further Thoughts on the Theory of Disengagement." *International Social Science Journal* 15: 377–393.

——, and W. E. Henry. 1961. *Growing Old: The Process of Disengagement.* New York: Basic Books.

Cumming, E., *et al.* 1960. "Disengagement: A Tentative Theory of Aging." *Sociometry* 23: 23–35.

Damianopoulos, E. 1961, "A Formal Statement of Disengagement Theory." Pp. 210–218 in E. Cumming and W. E. Henry, *Growing Old: The Process of Disengagement.* New York: Basic Books.

Deutsch, A., ed. 1963. *The Encyclopedia of Mental Health.* New York: Franklin Watts.

Donahue, W., H. L. Orbach, and O. Pollak. 1960. "Retirement: The Emerging Social Pattern." Pp. 330–406 in C. Tibbitts, ed., *Handbook of Social Gerontology.* Chicago: University of Chicago Press.

Dubin, R. 1956. "Industrial Workers' Worlds: A Study of the Central Life Interests of Industrial Workers." *Social Problems* 3: 131–142.

Dublin, L., A. Lotka, and M. Spiegelman. 1949. *Length of Life.* Rev. ed. New York: Ronald Press.

Epstein, L. A., and J. H. Murray. 1967. *The Aged Population of the United States.* Research Report No. 19, Office of Research and Statistics, Social Security Administration, U.S. Department of Health, Education, and Welfare. Washington, D. C.: Government Printing Office.

Feuer, L. 1963. "What Is Alienation? The Career of a Concept."

Pp. 127–147 in M. Stein and A. Vidich, eds., *Sociology on Trial.* Englewood Cliffs, N.J.: Prentice-Hall.

Friedmann, E. A., and R. J. Havighurst. 1954. *The Meaning of Work and Retirement.* Chicago: University of Chicago Press.

Glenn, N. D. 1969. "Aging, Disengagement, and Opinionation." *Public Opinion Quarterly* 33: 17–33.

Gordon, M. M., and C. H. Anderson. 1964. "The Blue-Collar Worker at Leisure." Pp. 407–416 in A. B. Shostak and W. Gomberg, eds., *Blue-Collar World.* Englewood Cliffs, N.J.: Prentice-Hall.

Gurin, G., J. Veroff, and S. Feld. 1960. *Americans View Their Mental Health.* New York: Basic Books.

Guttman, L. 1949. "The Problem of Attitude and Opinion Measurement" and "The Basis for Scalogram Analysis." Pp. 46–90 in S. A. Stouffer *et al., Measurement and Prediction,* Vol. IV: *Studies of Social Psychology in World War II.* Princeton: Princeton University Press.

Hamlin, R. M. 1967. "A Utility Theory of Old Age." *The Gerontologist* 7: 37–45.

Harlan, W. H. 1954. "The Meaning of Work and Retirement for Coalminers." Pp. 53–98 in E. A. Friedmann and R. J. Havighurst, eds., *The Meaning of Work and Retirement.* Chicago: University of Chicago Press.

Havighurst, R. J. 1950. "Problems of Sampling and Interviewing in Studies of Old People." *Journal of Gerontology* 5: 158–167.

——. 1952. "Social and Psychological Needs of the Aging." *Annals of the American Academy of Political and Social Sciences* 279: 11–17.

——. 1955. "Employment, Retirement, and Education in the Mature Years." Pp. 57–62 in I. L. Webber, ed., *Aging and Retirement.* Institute of Gerontology Series, Vol. 5. Gainesville: University of Florida Press.

——. 1961. "Successful Aging." *The Gerontologist* 1: 8–13.

——, B. L. Neugarten, and S. S. Tobin. 1968. "Disengagement and Patterns of Aging." Pp. 161–172 in B. L. Neugarten, ed., *Middle Age and Aging: A Reader in Social Psychology.* Chicago: University of Chicago Press.

Heiss, J. 1968. "An Introduction to the Elements of Role Theory." Pp. 3–27 in J. Heiss, ed., *Family Roles and Interaction: An Anthology.* Chicago: Rand McNally.

Hill, R., and D. A. Hansen. 1960. "The Identification of Conceptual Frameworks Utilized in Family Study." *Marriage and Family Living* 22: 299–311.

Hirschi, T., and H. C. Selvin. 1966. "False Criteria of Causality in Delinquency Research." *Social Problems* 13: 254–268.

Jeffers, F. G., C. Eisdorfer, and E. W. Busse. 1962. "Measurement of Age Identification: A Methodological Note." *Journal of Gerontology* 17: 437–439.

Kaplan, M. 1961. "Toward a Theory of Leisure for Social Gerontology." Pp. 389–412 in R. W. Kleemeier, ed., *Aging and Leisure.* New York: Oxford University Press.

Kleemeier, R. W. 1964. "Leisure and Disengagement in Retirement." *The Gerontologist* 4: 180–184.

Kuhlen, R. G. 1959. "Aging and Life-Adjustment." Pp. 852–897 in J. E. Birren, ed., *Handbook of Aging and the Individual.* Chicago: University of Chicago Press.

Kutner, B., *et al.* 1956. *Five Hundred over Sixty.* New York: Russell Sage Foundation.

Larson, O. F. 1966. "Rural Social Organization and Social Change." Pp. 25–48 in H. J. Schweitzer, ed., *Rural Sociology in a Changing Urbanized World.* Special Publication No. 11. Urbana: University of Illinois, College of Agriculture.

Lipset, S. M., M. Trow, and J. Coleman. 1962. *Union Democracy.* Garden City, N.Y.: Doubleday Anchor Books.

Maddox, G. L., Jr. 1964. "Disengagement Theory: A Critical Evaluation." *The Gerontologist* 4: 80–83.

Martin, J., and A. Doran. 1966. "Evidence Concerning the Relationship between Health and Retirement." *Sociological Review* n.s. 14: 329–343.

McMahan, C. A., and T. R. Ford. 1955. "Surviving the First Five Years of Retirement." *Journal of Gerontology* 10: 212–215.

Merton, R. K. 1957a. "The Role-Set: Problems in Sociological Theory." *British Journal of Sociology* 8: 106–120.

——. 1957b. *Social Theory and Social Structure.* Rev. ed. Glencoe, Ill.: Free Press.

——, and E. Barber. 1963. "Sociological Ambivalence." Pp. 91–

120 in E. A. Tiryakian, ed., *Sociological Theory, Values, and Sociocultural Change*. New York: Free Press of Glencoe.

Michelon, L. C.   1954. "The New Leisure Class." *American Journal of Sociology* 59: 371–378.

Moore, W. E.   1951. "The Aged in Industrial Societies." Pp. 519–537 in W. E. Moore, *Industrial Relations and The Social Order*. Rev. ed. New York: Macmillan.

——.   1969. "Social Structure and Behavior." Pp. 283–322 in G. Lindzey and E. Aronson, eds., *The Handbook of Social Psychology*, Vol. IV. 2d ed. Reading, Mass.: Addison-Wesley.

Morgan, J. N., Martin H. David, W. J. Cohen, and H. E. Brazer. 1962. *Income and Welfare in the United States*. New York: McGraw-Hill.

Morse, N., and R. Weiss.   1955. "The Function and Meaning of Work and the Job." *American Sociological Review* 20: 191–198.

Myers, R. J.   1954. "Factors in Interpreting Mortality after Retirement." *Journal of the American Statistical Association* 49: 499–507.

Neugarten, B., and R. J. Havighurst.   1969. "Disengagement Reconsidered in a Cross-National Context." Pp. 138–146 in R. J. Havighurst *et al.*, eds., *Adjustment to Retirement: A Cross-National Study*. Assen, The Netherlands: Van Gorcum.

Orbach, H. L.   1967. "Social and Institutional Aspects of Industrial Workers' Retirement." Pp. 533–560 in *Retirement and the Individual*. Hearings before the Subcommittee on Retirement and the Individual, U.S. Senate, Ninetieth Congress, First Session. Washington, D.C.: Government Printing Office, 1967.

Orr, D. W.   1963. "The Adult Male." Pp. 126–143 in A. Deutsch, ed., *The Encyclopedia of Mental Health*, Vol. I. New York: Franklin Watts.

Palmore, E. B.   1965. "Differences in the Retirement Patterns of Men and Women." *The Gerontologist* 5: 4–8.

Parsons, T.   1954. "Age and Sex in the Social Structure of the United States." Pp. 89–103 in T. Parsons, *Essays in Sociological Theory*. Glencoe, Ill.: Free Press.

Peck, R.   1956. "Psychological Developments in the Second Half of Life." Pp. 42–53 in J. E. Anderson, ed., *Psychological Aspects of Aging*. Washington, D.C.: American Psychological Association.

Phillips, B. S.   1957.   "A Role Theory Approach to Adjustment in Old Age." *American Sociological Review* 22: 212–217.

———. 1966. *Social Research: Strategy and Tactics.* New York: Macmillan.

President's Council on Aging.   1963.   *The Older American.* Washington, D.C.: Government Printing Office.

Riley, M. W., A. Foner, *et al.*   1968. *Aging in Society.* New York: Russell Sage Foundation.

Rose, A. M. 1954. *Theory and Methods in the Social Sciences.* Minneapolis: University of Minnesota Press.

———. 1962. "Preface," and "A Systematic Summary of Symbolic Interaction Theory." Pp. vii–xii and 3–19 in A. M. Rose, ed., *Human Behavior and Social Processes.* Boston: Houghton Mifflin.

———. 1964. "A Current Theoretical Issue in Social Gerontology." *The Gerontologist* 4: 46–50.

Rose, C. L.   1965.   "Representativeness of Volunteer Subjects in a Longitudinal Aging Study." *Human Development* 8: 152–156.

Rosow, I.   1967. *Social Integration of the Aged.* New York: Free Press.

———. 1968. "Socialization to Old Age." Mimeo. Cleveland, O.: Western Reserve University.

Saltz, R.   1968.   "Foster-Grandparents and Institutionalized Young Children." Mimeo. Detroit, Mich.: Merrill-Palmer Institute.

Sarbin, T. R., and V. L. Allen.   1968. "Role Theory." Pp. 488–567 in G. Lindzey and E. Aronson, eds., *The Handbook of Social Psychology,* Vol. I. 2d ed. Reading, Mass.: Addison-Wesley.

Schneider, C. J.   1964.   "Adjustment of Employed Women to Retirement." Ph.D. Dissertation, Cornell University.

Scott, F. G.   1957.   "Mail Questionnaire Used in a Study of Older Women." *Sociology and Social Research* 41: 281–284.

Seeman, M.   1959. "On the Meaning of Alienation." *American Sociological Review* 24: 783–791.

Shanas, E., *et al.*   1968. *Old People in Three Industrial Societies.* London: Routledge and Kegan Paul.

Simpson, I. H., *et al.*   1966. "Work and Retirement." Pp. 45–129 in I. H. Simpson and J. C. McKinney, eds., *Social Aspects of Aging.* Durham, N.C.: Duke University Press.

Slavick, F. 1966. *Compulsory and Flexible Retirement in the American Economy.* Ithaca, N.Y.: Cornell University, New York State School of Industrial and Labor Relations.

Steiner, P. O., and R. Dorfman. 1957. *The Economic Status of the Aged.* Berkeley and Los Angeles: University of California Press.

Stokes, R. G., and G. L. Maddox, Jr. 1967. "Some Social Factors on Retirement Adaptation." *Journal of Gerontology* 22: 329–333.

Streib, G. F. 1956. "Morale of the Retired." *Social Problems* 3: 270–276.

———. 1963. "Longitudinal Studies in Social Gerontology." Pp. 25–39 in R. H. Williams, C. Tibbitts, and W. Donahue, eds., *Processes of Aging: Social and Psychological Perspectives,* Vol. II. New York: Atherton Press.

———. 1966. "Participants and Drop-Outs in a Longitudinal Study." *Journal of Gerontology* 21: 200–209.

———. 1968. "Disengagement Theory in Socio-Cultural Perspective." *International Journal of Psychiatry* 6: 69–76.

Suchman, E. A., B. S. Phillips, and G. F. Streib. 1958. "An Analysis of the Validity of Health Questionnaires." *Social Forces* 36: 223–232.

Taietz. P., G. F. Streib, and M. L. Barron. 1956. *Adjustment to Retirement in Rural New York State.* Bulletin No. 919. Ithaca, N.Y.: Cornell University Agricultural Experiment Station.

Taves, M. J., and G. D. Hansen. 1963. "Seventeen Hundred Elderly Citizens." Pp. 73–181 in A. M. Rose, ed., *Aging in Minnesota.* Minneapolis: University of Minnesota Press.

Thompson, W. E. 1956. "The Impact of Retirement." Ph.D. Dissertation, Cornell University.

———. 1958. "Pre-Retirement Anticipation and Adjustment in Retirement." *Journal of Social Issues* 14: 35–45.

———, and G. F. Streib. 1958. "Situational Determinants: Health and Economic Deprivation in Retirement." *Journal of Social Issues* 14: 18–34.

Tibbitts, C. 1954. "Retirement Problems in American Society." *American Journal of Sociology* 59: 301–308.

———. 1960. "Origin, Scope and Fields of Social Gerontology." Pp. 3–26 in C. Tibbitts, ed., *Handbook of Social Gerontology.* Chicago: University of Chicago Press.

Tissue, T. 1970. "Downward Mobility in Old Age." *Social Problems* 18: 67–77.

Tuckman, J., and I. Lorge. 1954. "Classification of the Self as Young, Middle-Aged, or Old." *Geriatrics* 9: 534–536.

United States Bureau of the Census. 1953a. *Current Population Reports: Consumer Income.* Series P-60, No. 14. Washington, D.C.: Government Printing Office.

——. 1953b. *Census of Population, 1950.* Vol. II: *Characteristics of the Population,* Part 1. Washington, D.C.: Government Printing Office.

——. 1955. *Current Population Reports: Population Characteristics.* Series P-20, No. 60. Washington, D.C.: Government Printing Office.

Walkley, R.P., *et al.* 1965. *Retirement Housing in California.* Berkeley, Cal.: Diablo Press.

Wilensky, H. L. 1961. "Orderly Careers and Social Participation: The Impact of Work History on Social Integration in the Middle Mass." *American Sociological Review* 26: 521–539.

Williams, R. M., Jr. 1960. *American Society.* 2d ed. New York: Alfred A. Knopf.

Wray, R. P. 1969. "Projects in Gerontology: Training, Teaching Research, and Community Action." Pp. 255–261 in R. R. Boyd and C. G. Oakes, eds., *Foundations of Practical Gerontology.* Columbia: University of South Carolina Press.

Wrong, D. H. 1961. "The Oversocialized Conception of Man in Modern Sociology." *American Sociological Review* 26: 183–193.

Youmans, E. G. 1967. "Family Disengagement among Older Urban and Rural Women." *Journal of Gerontology* 22: 209–211.

Zola, I. K. 1962. "Feelings about Age among Older People." *Journal of Gerontology* 17: 65–68.

Name Index

Subject Index

Retirement in American Society

Designed by R. E. Rosenbaum.
Composed by Vail-Ballou Press, Inc.
in 11 point linotype Baskerville, 2 points leaded,
with display lines in monotype Bulmer.
Printed letterpress and offset by Vail-Ballou Press
on Warren's 1854 text, 60 pound basis,
with the Cornell University Press watermark.
Bound by Vail-Ballou Press
in Interlaken ALP book cloth
and stamped in All Purpose foil.